The Origins of Neoliberalism

The Origins of Neoliberalism

Modeling the Economy from Jesus to Foucault

DOTAN LESHEM

Columbia

University

Press

New York

Columbia University Press
Publishers Since 1893
New York   Chichester, West Sussex
cup.columbia.edu

Copyright © 2016 Columbia University Press
Paperback edition, 2017

Library of Congress Cataloging-in-Publication Data
Names: Leshem, Dotan, author.
Title: The origins of neoliberalism: modeling the economy from Jesus to
    Foucault / Dotan Leshem.
Description: New York: Columbia University Press, 2016. | Includes
    bibliographical references and index.
Identifiers: LCCN 2015039848 | ISBN 978-0-231-17776-4 (cloth: alk. paper) |
    ISBN 978-0-231-17777-1 (pbk. : alk. paper) | ISBN 978-0-231-54174-9
    (e-book)
Subjects: LCSH: Economics—Religious aspects—Christianity. |
    Neoliberalism—Religious aspects—Christianity. | Economics—History.
Classification: LCC BR115.E3 L39 2016 | DDC 330.01—dc23
LC record available at http://lccn.loc.gov/2015039848

Columbia University Press books are printed on permanent and
durable acid-free paper.
Printed in the United States of America

COVER IMAGE (DETAIL): Pierre Hubert Subleyras, *The Mass of Saint Basil*,
1746. Oil on canvas, 54 × 31 1/8 in. © The Metropolitan Museum of Art /
Art Resource, NY.

Contents

Acknowledgments

The road to publishing this book began nearly a decade ago as a dissertation that was written in Hebrew at the Hermeneutics and Cultural Studies Program at Bar-Ilan University under the supervision of Ariella Azoulay and Yuval Yonay. I thank Ariella for her mentorship in critical reading and Yuval for curbing the excesses of my writing. At that time I was blessed with the scholarly friendship of my fellow Ph.D. students Tamar Sharon and Doron Nachum, and of my fellow scholars at the Van Leer Jerusalem Institute, Arik Sherman, Yossi Yonah, and Yehuda Shenhav. A special thanks goes to Fr. Michael Azkoul for his kind yet strict guidance in orthodox reading of the Church Fathers, to Olivier Thomas Venard for an enchanting discussion that made so many things crystal clear for the first time, and Avital Wohlman for her masterful review of the dissertation.

I wish to thank the Minerva Humanities Center at Tel Aviv University and the Dan David Prize for granting me a postdoctoral fellowship at the Political Lexicon Group, headed by Adi Ophir. They granted me the precious time and space needed to complete the research for this book, as well as for writing a first draft in English that I was able to send to non-Hebrew readers. I was fortunate to receive comments on it from John Milbank, David Burrell, Michel Callon, and Bruno Latour. I am grateful for their insight and encouragement.

I thank the Fulbright Foundation for granting me a postdoctoral scholarship that enabled me to spend a year at the Department of Religion at Princeton University, which proved to be immensely fruitful. I wish to thank my host, Jeffrey Stout, for his inspiring guidance. At Princeton I had the scholarly joy of becoming friends with On Barak, Alexis Torrance, Nicholas Marinides, and Mihai Grigore. I thank Peter Brown, Helmut Reimitz, William Jordan, Daniel Heller Roazen, Angelos Chaniotis, and Eric Gregory for their comments on drafts of the manuscript (or parts of it).

I wish to thank Stathis Gourgouris, head of the Institute for Comparative Literature and Society at Columbia University, for hosting me as a visiting scholar. I was truly privileged to enjoy the benevolent guidance in the form of comments on the manuscript by Etienne Balibar and Gil Anidjar, which improved it greatly. I also wish to thank participants in the "Foucault on Economics" seminar for exuberant discussions, which found their way into the concluding chapter, as well as Issam Aburaiya for many friendly discussions and helpful suggestions. Many thanks to the Department of Government and Political Theory at Haifa University for granting me an institutional postdoctoral scholarship that enabled me to bring this project to a close.

I want to thank Wendy Lochner, Susan Pensak, Christine Dunbar, and Alexander Davis at Columbia University Press for their vital help in bringing this book to press. Heartfelt appreciation goes to Riccardo Lufrani for his fraternal love, David Moatty for his jazzy friendship, and Oz Gore for his challenging camaraderie.

Above all, I thank Navit for her enduring and loving support, which made all this possible and Yul for making each day a little brighter.

Parts of the introduction appeared as "Oikonomia in the Age of Empires," in *History of the Human Sciences* 26 (1): 29–51. Chapter 5 and sections of of chapter 6 appeared as "Embedding Agamben's Critique of Foucault: The Pastoral and Theological Origins of Governmentally," in *Theory, Culture and Society* 32 (3): 93–113. Parts of chapter 6 appeared as "Aristotle Economizes the Market," *Boundary 2* 40 (3): 39–57.

When possible, I referred to the best available English translation of the Greek sources. At times I made some minor changes in the translation. The most common of them was translating *oikonomia,* a word for which translators tend to use too many other words, to "economy" instead. All mistranslations are mine.

Abbreviations

AC	*Against Celsus*
AH	*Against Heresy*
AP	*Against Praxeas*
Eth.Nic.	*Nicomachean Ethics*
G2G	*From Glory to Glory*
HC	*Human Condition*
LM	*Life of Moses*
PG	*patrologia graeca*
Pol.	*Politics*
Xen.Ec.	Xenophon's *Economics*

The Origins of
Neoliberalism

Introduction

Economy Before Christ

The Three-Dimensional Human

Since its inception in Greek antiquity, the West imagined human life as evolving in a three-dimensional space: the economic, the political, and the philosophical, distinguished by boundaries set by law. Underlying the happy and self-sufficient Greek polis was the economy. Preconditioning philosophical life, unbound by this mortal coil, and glorified, if only momentarily, by the light of the eternal, was the economy, embedded in existential necessity. Unlike most authors who view the history of thought from the perspective of either the political or the philosophical dimension, this book attempts to retell the history of the three-dimensional human being from the less-traveled dimension of the economy. In particular, it reinserts into this history the most glorious and at the same time most ignored chapter of the human trinity of economy, politics, and philosophy in the Christianity of Late Antiquity. For it was in the era between the Councils of Nicea (325) and Chalcedon (451) that the one-dimensional *zoon oikonomikon* came to reign supreme in the human trinity. Save for a few exceptions (albeit revealing only a partial and at times misinformed story), this chapter has been relegated from our history as told by modern historians of economic, political, and philosophical thought. *The Origins of Neoliberalism* argues that without revealing the origins of our modernity in Late Antiquity our self-knowledge as modern creatures is misleading and partial, and failure to do so results in falling short of both reforming the modern human condition and/or radically transforming it. This may be seen from the many failed attempts so far.

Philological History of *Oikonomia*

The history of the economy conducted in the book is different from the usual economic histories. It is a philological history that traces the meanings attached to the notion of *oikonomia* since its original use as management and dispensation (*nemein*) of the *oikos* in Archaic Greek until today. Although not excluding concepts that traveled through Latin, such as prudence and law, it is essentially a history of the "West that speaks Greek," focusing on the transposition of its key concepts *oikonomia, politikeh, philosophia,* and *nomos.* It tells a nominalist history, that is, it begins by asking which successive semantic values have been attributed to the word *oikonomia* by different authors and discourses instead of asking how specific terms are used to describe a content that is supposedly known. Such a philological inquiry deconstructs the "retrospective" method generally used in economic history, histories of ideas or science that project the contemporary meaning attached to key concepts back into history. In the case of the economy, these retrospective histories commonly count for either 1. a history of the economy as a distinct sphere of existence whose meaning is unaltered throughout history, usually understood as encompassing the relations of production, consumption, and distribution; 2. history of "economy" as a rational disposition, based on the assumption that agents of history act "economically" and that the definition of the economic mode of conduct and of the agent remain unaltered throughout history. This sense gained currency in economics and history departments over the last half-century with the rise of "new economic history"; 3. finally, history of "economic thought," which occupies itself with reading texts by past writers about "the economy." The last presupposes (based on state-of-the-art economic theories) what the field and objects of "economics" are in themselves and then looks to the past only to identify cases of partial recognition, or misrecognition, of this sphere and its objects.

Conversely, this inquiry is based on the premise that one has to begin with tracing the meanings and applications of the word *oikonomia* that have prevailed at different moments in the history of the West. Attempting to think of the economy supposing that universals don't exist, such an inquiry abstains from taking for granted and simply describing the historical transformations of "economic institutions," "economic practices," such as the market economy, capitalism, etc. The reason being that any such description presupposes a stable understanding of the word *economy* or at least a tacit decision on why it is precisely this word that "names" what it names for us today. As a result of this choice, the book tells a history of the *economy* that is different than the one taught in departments of economics or the one presented in general historiographical works. Instead, it is a history of the meaning attributed to the word *oikonomia* and its applications that signal out the Christianity of Late Antiquity as *the* transformative moment of its meaning and consequently of the ordering of the human trinity.

Although word choices, whether innocent, contingent, or deliberate, can have little to no influence on the nature of what it names, this is not the case with oikonomia. As the latter history unfolds in the book, it becomes evident that, upon migrating from the institution of the ancient *oikos* to the Christian *ecclesia* and later to the liberal *market*, the economization of these institutions was framed within the limits of an invariant question *because* of its seemingly different previous meaning and not *in spite* of it. Reinserting the relegated Christian chapter into the history of the economy provides the essential hermeneutical key for the explication of its core invariant meaning, one that is simultaneously open to broad variations and compelling. A comparative account of the economy of the oikos, ecclesia and market based on such a philological history suggests a typology of four criteria according to which a model of human action is called an economy: 1. it involve the acquisition of a theoretical and practical disposition of prudence; 2. which faces the human condition of excess that transcends human rationality; 3. this rational engagement with excess generates surplus; finally, 4. this action takes place in a distinct "economic" sphere alongside other spheres such as the political and the philosophical. This fourfold typology of economy also establishes the Christian moment as *the* missing link, which, nevertheless, functions as the turning point in the use history of the economy between the ancient oikos where excess was despised, the economic sphere kept to minimum, and the neoliberal marketized economy where excess is desired, the economy infinitely growing.

The Archives of Genealogical Inquiry Into the Marketized Economy: Arendt, Foucault, Agamben

The philological history of oikonomia set the stage for a genealogical inquiry into the rise of the economic at the expense of the political and philosophical is framed by Hannah Arendt's and Michel Foucault's genealogies. Doing so, the book aligns itself with the path taken by Giorgio Agamben, who laid a genealogical critique of the modern economy by bringing together and getting behind the thought of these two great minds (Agamben 1998:120), reintroducing Greek patristic theological economy as the embryonic point of modern governmentality.[1]

HANNAH ARENDT

In her genealogy of the modern human condition, Arendt systematically documented the history of the communal dimensions of human life. She died before she finished charting the whereabouts of *The Life of the Mind* within itself, let alone the marks it left on the economic and political dimensions. In her work the role played by the legal framework is only described in passing. Arendt points out two crucial moments in the history of communal life. Her story begins with the rise of the political sphere as distinct from the economic one in classical Athens and ends in modernity with the rise of the economy, "its activities, problems, and organizational devices—from the shadowy interior of the household into the public sphere,"[2] in the bounds of what she calls "the social," against which "the private and intimate, on the one hand, and the political (in the narrower sense of the word), on the other, have proved incapable of defending themselves."[3]

Of the two, Arendt chose to reconstruct the political side of the story, a choice that may account for her sketchy narration of the economic one. Her mistreatment can be traced both in her scornful and inaccurate description of classical Greek oikonomia (see Leshem 2013a) and in her lack of awareness of what is entailed by the subordination of politics to the society of believers in Christ's economy. But the gravest consequence of her focus on the political side, further blurred by her thorough knowledge of Augustine, was her ignorance of Greek contemporaries of the bishop of Hippo.[4]

MICHEL FOUCAULT

It is exactly here that Michel Foucault's longstanding engagement with the economy in nearly all of the crucial moments in the history of Western thought, beginning with classical Athens, via patristic, mercantile, liberal, and neoliberal thought, becomes essential when recapping the economic side of the story.[5] The most crucial among his multivalent contributions to the history of the economy was the insertion of patristic economic art into the story, linking what he called, in an atypical anachronism, pastorate or pastoral power and governmentality instead of ecclesiastical economy and political economy respectively:

> Pastorate does not coincide with politics, pedagogy, or rhetoric. It is something entirely different. It is an art of "governing men," and I think this is where we should look for the origin, the point of formation, of crystallization, the embryonic point of the governmentality whose entry into politics, at the end of the sixteenth and in the seventeenth and eighteenth centuries, marks the threshold of the modern state. The modern state is born, I think, when governmentality became a calculated and reflected practice. The Christian pastorate seems to me to be the background of this process.
>
> (Foucault 2007:165)

Foucault explained his abstention from using the term *economy* to refer to patristic economy by saying that "'economy' (économie) is evidently not the French word best suited to translate *oikonomia psuchon*" (192). The same can be said considering his use of governmentality instead of political economy: "The word 'economy' designated a form of government in the sixteenth century; in the eighteenth century, through a series of complex processes that are absolutely crucial for our history, it will designate a level of reality and a field of intervention for government. So, there you have what is governing and being governed" (95).[6]

As rightly observed by Agamben, Foucault did not fully establish patristic oikonomia as the place where the formation of our late modern economy and government is crystallized, as he had only begun the excavation of the patristic chapter in the archeology of the human trinity. Attempting to bring Foucault's work to completion, this book addresses four main gaps in his genealogy of economy: 1. The gap between pastoral power, conducted on the microlevel of the economy of salvation, and governmentality enacted on the macrolevel of political economy; 2. the gap between philosophical life, which forms the object of inquiry of *The Hermeneutics of the Subject*, and the conduct of communal life by "pastoral power" described in *Security, Territory, Population*; 3. the gap between imperial politics and the ecclesiastical economy, a relationship reshaped in the patristic age, which remained enigmatic for Foucault (Foucault 2007:154–55); 4. Foucault does not allude to the (theological) knowledge of divine economy that informs the art and theory of pastoral power.

GIORGIO AGAMBEN

The last objection is raised by Giorgio Agamben's thorough critique of Foucault's genealogy of the economy in *The Kingdom and the Glory* (2011). In it he argues that Foucault fails to notice that oikonomia was first displaced onto Trinitarian theology, only later to be translated into the art of (economic) pastorship. Thus, claims Agamben, in order to be able to argue that one can recover the meaning of economy and government in pastorate, one has to identify how it belongs to a divine oikonomia (110). Moreover, Agamben argues that this error casts a shadow onto the whole of Foucault's genealogy of economy and government because one should conduct a genealogy of economic theory (which he terms economic theology) rather than economic art, aiming for a "Theological Genealogy of Economy and Government." Although this book was not written with the intention of refuting Agamben's thesis (if anything, my book performs a displacement of the Christian origins of the neoliberal economy), it can be read as one.

The first two chapters ground the main displacement of Agamben's genealogy. This is done by showing that the key moment in the genealogy of the neoliberal marketized economy is not the early elaboration of Trinitarian theology in the second century CE, but rather the formulation of the

Christian creed of the Trinity and of the incarnation in the fourth and fifth centuries. This seemingly secondary rectification has far-reaching consequences. First, it allows a Foucauldian rejoinder to his critique in chapter 5. Second, it enables me to argue, in chapter 6, that it is the principle of growth that is crucial for the notion of economy and government and not, as argued by Agamben, "providential" administration.

A result of displacing the focal point to fourth-century orthodoxy is that yet another distinction arises, this time between the divine economy for humans and providential care for the world. Here, as elsewhere, Agamben's focus on pre-Nicean Christian theology (in this case-Clement of Alexandria; see Agamben 2011:47–48) rather than on the more sophisticated conceptual language of the later Fathers seems to be the cause of Agamben's confusion. Equating economy and providence not only pronounces a view that was identified with the Arian heterodoxy of the fourth century but also misidentifies (Agamben 2011:283–84) the original denotation of providential care that appears in Smith's liberal market economy as the secularization of orthodox Christianity rather than of a stoic/Arian concept.

Moreover, displacing the point of formation of contemporary economy and government to the era between the Councils of Nicea and Chalcedon brings into question Agamben's notion of economic theology. The reason being that from that time onward economy and theology could no longer function as interchangeable notions and instead designated the operation of two distinct spheres: the internal organization of the triune Godhead in the case of theology and the worldly manifestation of God in that of the economy. Another crucial point of divergence between Agamben's elaboration of Christian oikonomia and my own is his unorthodox elucidation of Trinitarian theology and his insistence on the anarchic nature of the Son.[7] As with the distinction between oikonomia, theology, and providence, setting the original denotation of economy and government in fourth-century orthodoxy has far-reaching consequences for a genealogical inquiry into contemporary economy and government. In this case, staying loyal to the orthodox formulation of the Father-Son relationship renders Agamben's genealogy meaningless and at the same time accounts for the apparatus that dispenses economic growth.

Agamben's rushed treatment of the pre-Christian history of oikonomia seems to cause him to misidentify other aspects of the concept that are crucial for any attempt at an accurate critique of the neoliberal marketized economy. The first of these has to do with the pre-Christian economic form of knowledge. Contrary to Agamben's limitation of economic knowledge to nonepistemic practical knowledge (Agamben 2011:19), economics (*oikonomikeh*) was seen by most schools of pre-Christian thought as "consisting of a theoretical and a practical disposition" (Stobaeus 1884–1912:II, 7:11d),[8] meaning that philosophical reflections on oikonomia were carried out in the context of either a theoretical discourse or a technical one. In both cases the ethical disposition one has to acquire when dealing with economic matters was kept in mind. The articulation of economic knowledge with reference to the theory-art-ethics triad lends support to Foucault's genealogical inquiries into pastorate and later into ascetic practices of truth telling in his lectures, *On the Government of the Living* (2014a) and *Wrong Doing-Truth Telling* (2014b). Further more, as discussed throughout these chapters, a comparative study of ancient, Christian, and contemporary economic knowledge within the bounds of the triangle of theory-art-ethics is indispensible for a critique of neoliberal marketized economy.

Last, Agamben's downplaying of the ethical dimension of economic knowledge—this time vis-à-vis utilitarian considerations—carries devastating consequences for any attempt to rethink anew the human trinity. The exposure of the primacy of the ethical dimension of the economy and the inability of unmasking the moral persona disqualifies Agamben's assertion that "bare life" is what is revealed in the "particular condition of life that is the camp,"[9] establishing as such a starting point for a new political philosophy (see Leshem 2014c).[10]

Toward a New Political Philosophy: An Ethical Economy

In an attempt to establish both a historical and theoretical displacement of the origins of the neoliberal economy, the book concentrates on a detailed reconstruction of the Christian creed as it was elaborated between Nicea and Chalcedon. Following the role oikonomia played in the formation of Christian orthodoxy by drawing on exegetical and apologetic tracts, homilies and eulogies, manuals and correspondence, as well as Church canons and creeds, the book charts how Christianity brought about both a unique formation of the human trinity and distinctive ethico-political horizons.

Recounting the introduction of Christ's economy, growth, progressive history, political subjectivity, and pastoral authority into Greek-speaking Late Antiquity sets the background for a critical discussion of how these techno-theoretical apparatuses of governing self and others were appropriated by the moderns before trying to think of avenues toward a new political philosophy. Such a modification also introduces a new periodization into the Arendtian genealogy of modernity, which consists of five moments in the history of the human trinity: the classical formation, the imperial formation, the Christian formation, the liberal formation, and the neoliberal formation. The reintroduction of the Christian moment into the history of the economy and of the human trinity backdates to the fourth century CE several new phenomena typically associated with the modern one. On top of the emergence of a (Christian) society whose main concern is the growth of the economy, the book discusses the emergence of a distinction between economy and theology, the subjugation of politics to the economy, the migration of freedom from the realm of politics to that of the economy, the designation of politics as the sphere entrusted with a monopoly over the means of legal violence, the economization of philosophical life, and the positioning of the law as acting in the service of the economy and as demarcating the outer boundaries that the economy may sometimes overstep.

The book not only explores philological, historical, and genealogical projects but also an ontological project of rethinking the contemporary ordering of the human trinity of economy, politics, and philosophy as interpreted by Arendt in her *Human Condition*. Grounded on a redefinition of the economic human condition as excess, the book rectifies Arendt's formation of the human trinity. Based on this ontological modification, the book sets the ground for the *ethical project* of imagining an alternative political philosophy to that of the contemporary neoliberal marketized economy.

Plan of the Book

Setting the stage for a discussion of oikonomia in the Christianity of Late Antiquity, the rest of this introduction recounts the history of oikonomia and its relation to politics, philosophy, and the market in classical antiquity, followed by a short history of fundamental changes undergone by the human trinity in the imperial era.

Chapter 1, "From Oikos to Ecclesia," reviews the history of the concept of oikonomia in Christian thought from the Pauline letters and up to the third century CE. It begins with a review of the meanings attributed to oikonomia in the Pauline letters, followed by a survey of the new meanings attached to the concept in apostolic and early apologetic literature. Toward the turn of the second century, oikonomia was consolidated into a key concept: Clement of Alexandria developed the pedagogical model for conducting the economy; Tertullian used the concept to describe the inner organization of the Trinity; and Irenaeus of Lyons revolutionized economic theory and set the stage for a radical change in the conceptualization of time, history, and space. The chapter concludes with the aftermath of these changes.

Chapter 2, "Modeling the Economy," reformulates the Christian doctrine into three "economic models" and a transcription principle that enables their concatenation. These models are used in the subsequent three chapters that describe how Christianity remodeled the economy's relation with philosophy, politics, and the legal framework. The first model portrays the inner organization of the Trinity. The second economic model describes the hypostatic union that takes place in the economy of the incarnation. The third economic model encapsulates a description of that which takes place in the economic *perichoresis*—that is, in the all-inclusive/all-penetrative communion between God and human in the economy of the incarnation. The principle of transcription is the mechanism that connects these models, creates a hierarchy among them, and additionally enables the economy's unlimited growth. The afterword unfolds a trial balance of the economy in the classical, imperial, and Christian eras. Based on the results of the trial balance, the chapter concludes with a definition of the scope and method of Christian oikonomia.

Chapter 3, "Economy and Philosophy," addresses philosophy as a way of Christian life via a critique of Foucault's *Hermeneutics of the Subject*. Conducting a genealogy of philosophical life that runs from Plato through the third-century Christian philosopher Origen and then to Gregory of Nyssa reveals three misconceptions in Foucault's account of Christian philosophical life: as, first, a parting with philosophical tradition; second, depicting the Christian technologies of the self as self-alienating; and, last, ignoring the communal aspect of Christian philosophical life. Accounting for these misconceptions by a close reading of Gregory of Nyssa reveals that he was the first in Western history to formulate a theory of economic growth. In so doing, he presented to humanity as a whole and to each and every human subject a choice between two economies: an ever-growing economy in which they may practice their freedom or a circular economy in which everything that grows is doomed to decay and perish.

Chapter 4, "Economy and Politics," reintroduces a much-ignored chapter of patristic political theory into the history of political thought and political theology. A short history of the first three hundred years of patristic exegesis of Philippians 3:20–21, Mathew 22:21, Romans 13:1–7, and 1 Timothy 2:1–2, as well as the way these verses interplay in homilies, recaptures patristic political thought as coherent and systematic, based on three principles: 1. regarding political sovereignty as embedded in an economic context; 2. keeping the political and the economic institutions distinct; and 3. assuming a disposition of a limited self-subjection to political authorities. The main body of the chapter is dedicated to an excavation of the political thought of John Chrysostom, who adapts and develops these principles to the post-Constantinian empire. Among his numerous contributions to the formation of Christian political thought discussed in the chapter, Chrysostom transformed the relation between economy and politics by subjecting the latter to the service of the former. Before concluding, the chapter demonstrates how the economic models are transcribed into imperial law and security mechanisms, thereby answering Foucault's enigma concerning the relation between imperial and ecclesiastical power formations in the Christian East.

Chapter 5, "Economy and the Legal Framework," returns to Agamben's genealogy of economy discussed in the introduction. In particular, it refutes his critique of Foucault's genealogy of pastoral power. It does so, first, by setting the theoretical framework that situates the exercise of pastoral power in the state of exception as an imitation of divine economy and, second, by conducting a genealogy of the formulation of such use in the first canon of Basil the Great, the letters of Cyril of Alexandria, and in a manual written by Eulogius. The chapter then discusses the resemblances and differences between pastoral economy and political sovereignty as revealed in the state of exception.

Chapter 6, "From Ecclesiastical to Market Economy," opens with a short summary of the historical findings of the book and how they modify Foucault's genealogy of philosophy and economy. The second section revises

Arendt's genealogy of politics by backdating the rise of the social to the fourth century CE and by redefining the economic human condition as excess. Next, it demonstrates how predating the discovery of economic growth to the Late Antiquity pastoral economy changes our understanding of the neoliberal marketized economy. Based on this new understanding, the chapter then suggests that modern economists embrace an anarchic pantheism rather than simply secularizing economic growth theory. This is followed by a presentation of a balance sheet of the neoliberal, classical, and Christian definitions of the economy and its relations to politics, philosophy, as well as a discussion of two of the main ethical consequences of this account for a critical understanding of the present.

A Brief History of Pre-Christian Economy
CLASSICAL ECONOMY

Neither the mistreatment of the economic dimension of human life nor the prejudice toward it by historians of thought begins with their neglect of the Christian economy of salvation. This neglect may be traced back to the economy's first denotation as management and dispensation of the oikos, as it has been all but ignored that Aristotle claimed that humans were the only *economic* (and not political) creatures (zoon oikonomikon), who, as possessors of logos, have "perception of good and bad, right and wrong and the other moral qualities" (*Pol.* 1253a). It is for that reason he commences his discourse on politics stating that "we must begin with speaking of the economy" (*Pol.* 1253B).

This modern neglect reflects the pre-Christian general prejudice against the economy, accompanying it ever since its first appearance in a poem by Phocylides (sixth century BC), where the poet compares women to "four breeds [of animals]: bee, bitch, and savage-looking sow, and mare." He advises his friends to marry a bee, which is the best of the lot, because she is a "good oikonomos who knows how to work." Missing from modern accounts of ancient economy such as Arendt's is the ancient idea that demonstrating a high level of economic know-how was considered virtuous. Such demonstration was a woman's only way to excel, live a virtuous life, and perpetuate herself, as females were denied access to the nobler forms of life of politics and philosophy.

The histories of the human trinity of economy, politics, and philosophy are interwoven. This is testified by the fact that the word *oikonomia* hardly appears in texts composed before the rise of the polis and the birth of Socrates, *the* philosopher. Its absence from archaic texts is not caused by a lack of reflection on the activity of oikos management; it is dealt with in great detail in Hesiod's *Work and Days* without the word *oikonomia* appearing in it even once. One may assume that for the economy to be demarcated, it took a rising awareness of the political sphere as distinct from the economic one and the emergence of a distinct philosophy of the human. Philosophers such as Plato wished to eradicate the distinction between economy and politics. Aristotle, who dedicated his second book of *Politics* to reframing the distinction between them by law, did so in an attempt to establish the polis as the sole community in which man is able to live a happy communal life to its fullest degree. He presented three criteria for a happy communal life: the level of self-sufficiency achieved by the community, the degree of multiplicity that appears in it, and the extent to which its principle of action is guided by virtue.[11] While Aristotle succeeded in his mission of establishing the polis as a multiple, self-sufficient, and virtuous community, he nevertheless describes the economic community as consisting of the same qualities, even if to a lesser degree, a fact that is ignored by Arendt.

Aristotle also elicited the received view of the composition of the human trinity of economy, politics, and philosophy among pre-Christian Greek philosophers.[12] According to this view, economic activity dealt with the satisfaction of the bare necessities of life and with the generation of surplus leisure time that was meant to allow the master of the household, the *oikodespotes*, to conduct a leisurely life, whether a philosophical or a political one. This could be done in two ways: "either increasing his [the master's] revenues through free means of procurement or by cutting down on expenses."[13] Xenophon already brought together the philosophical (Socratic) and the political (sophist) arts of generating surplus in the *Oikonomikos*.[14] In it, the classical conception of wealth as a means to a higher end is personified in three interlocutors: Socrates, Critobulus, who seeks Socrates' theoretical guidance in the first dialogue of the *Oikonomikos*, and Ischomachus, who instructs Socrates in the art of economics in the second dialogue. While Critobulus is submerged in economic activity without being able to generate surplus, Socrates and Ischomachus are both praised for their skill at generating it.[15] Socrates, the philosopher, does so by moderating his needs,[16] while Ischomachus, the model citizen (*polites*), is praised as one of "those who are able not only to govern their own oikos but also to accumulate a surplus so that they can adorn the polis and support their friends well; such men must certainly be considered men of strength and abundance."[17]

As already discussed, economics (oikonomikeh) was seen by most schools of pre-Christian thought as "consisting of a theoretical and a practical disposition" (Stobaeus 1884–1912:II, 7:11d),[18] meaning that philosophical reflections on the economy were meant to be carried out in the context of either a theoretical discourse or a technical one. In both cases the ethical disposition one has to acquire when dealing with economic matters needs to be kept in mind.

As part of his theoretical discussion in the *Oikonomikos*, Xenophon offers a definition of oikonomia: "The name of a branch of theoretical knowledge, and this knowledge appeared to be that by which men can increase oikos, and an oikos appeared to be identical with the total of one's property, and we said that property is that which is useful for life, and useful things turned out to be all those things that one knows how to use" (*Xen.Ec.* 6:4). Xenophon's definition is composed of four sub-definitions: 1. oikonomia as a branch of theoretical knowledge; 2. the *oikos* as the totality of one's property; 3. property as that which is useful for life; and 4. oikonomia as the knowledge by which men increase that which is useful for life. Most philosophical schools in Greek-speaking antiquity (with the exception of the Cynics) defined the economic sphere as one in which man, when faced with excessive means, acquires a theoretical and practical prudent disposition in order to comply with his needs and generate surplus that appears outside its boundaries. This definition is extracted in Leshem 2013a by showing how the following concepts operated in these texts: the origin of the excess that appears in the economic domain, the essence of wealth and its end, and oikonomia's form of knowledge. A close reading of the vast discussions about the essence of wealth and its end shows that the writers held a subjective measure of wealth. As they saw it, wealth could not be measured by such "objective" criteria as monetary value, but instead was defined as anything that satisfies the wants of man and participates in the generation of surplus external to the economic domain. Oikonomia as a form of practical life presupposes a disposition of prudence translated into both practical and theoretical knowledge. Excess was seen by ancient Greek writers as a human condition that forms part of the ontology of abundance capable of satisfying all of man's needs and beyond. Excess itself was thought to be found in nature, both human and cosmological, while man was seen as capable of harnessing this excess to generate a human-made surplus that is to be found outside the boundaries of the economic domain. The surplus generated by the economy was destined to allow the *oikodespotes* to participate in politics and engage in philosophy, demonstrating benevolence toward his friends, allowing them leisure time that would enable them to participate in politics and engage in philosophy and to sustain by liturgies the institutions and activities peculiar to the political community.

When dealing with the *Art of Economics* (Leshem 2014a), Bryson the neo-Pythagorean is no exception in dividing: "the economy is complete in four things: A. property B. slaves and servants. C. the wife. D. the children" (Bryson 1928:145).[19] The *economy of things* draws very little attention from the ancient philosophers, in contrast with modern economic discourse. When they did discuss it, they focused on defining the proper limits to wealth (both generation and accumulation), while the question of how things should be prudently economized, once the proper limit has been set, is rarely mentioned. And when discussed, it does not go beyond lay banalities such as "the oikonomos must . . . have the faculty of acquiring, and . . . that of preserving what he has acquired; otherwise there is no more benefit in acquiring than in baling with a colander, or in the proverbial wine-jar with a hole in the bottom" (Pseudo-Aristotle 1910:1344b). Philodemus, who was the most sophisticated on the subject, goes so far as to suggest a critique of the received view that one should maintain a fixed level of expenditure and spread one's investment in order to minimize risk (see Tsouna 2007:174, 183). The discussion of the *economy of slaves* is more elaborate and can be divided into two broad categories: the work of Aristotle, who described the slave's unique position as a human-thing, and that of all other authors, who dedicated their treatises to the "science of using slaves" (*Pol.* 1255b). This art included multiple technologies of classification, management, and supervision that were to guide the master and the wife in their "use" of slaves.

Above all, the oikos was perceived as a partnership between the *matron* and the master (*Xen.Ec.* 7:12), which "aims not merely at existence, but at a happy existence" (Pseudo-Aristotle 1910:1343b), and the economy of the former by the latter occupied much of the ancient philosophers' attention. The matron, surprisingly missing from most modern accounts of the ancient economy, is of the greatest significance for any genealogy of the economy, as we are each, as a modern *homo economicus*, her descendant. The matron was the first person in our Western history to live a one-dimensional economic life as a freeborn person, and the first to experience happiness and demonstrate virtue restricted from a political or philosophical life. Contrary to the master, who in the political mode of government can become a ruler without being ruled, the matron, even when governing the interior of the house, is always already mastered by her husband. She partakes in government only within the confines of the *economy* and does so as one governed, subjected to the rule of her master. She is expected to do so by demonstrating soundness of mind, in which she is superior even to the master (Phyntis in Waithe 1987:27), or she is at least capable of excelling just as much (*Xen.Ec.* 7:42). What is missing from the "feminine" version of the economic art is the thing that lies at the heart of the "masculine" texts dealing with the essence of wealth and its end: namely, that one has to set a limit to wealth getting so as to allow him to pursue the ideal mode of life by practicing politics and/or engaging in philosophy. The "feminine" version of the economy's end is not contradictory to the "masculine" one; rather, it works in its service. The economic harmony between the sexes is a result of the singular position that the matron occupies in the oikos and the mode by which she demonstrates the virtue of soundness of mind in it. The matron, as the one entrusted with the management of preservation, use, and consumption, contributes to wealth generation by efficient inventory management, by prudent use, and by temperate consumption. At the same time, she is capable of contributing to the generation of extra-economic surplus for her master. Prudent preservation, use, and consumption may, undoubtedly, free the master, who is entrusted with the task of supplying use objects and consumption items, to engage in leisurely occupations.

The partnership between master and matron (unlike government over children and slaves) does not coincide with any of the public forms of government discussed by Aristotle: it is located somewhere between an aristocratic and a political form of rule.[20] It is a genuine economic government that has no equivalent in the political sphere. Moreover, "justice between master and matron is Economic Justice in the real sense, though this too is different from Political Justice" (*Eth.Nic.* 1134b).

THE IMPERIAL FORMATION OF THE HUMAN TRINITY

With the rise of the Hellenistic and the Roman empires, the equilibrium between philosophy, politics, and the economy has changed. Of the three dimensions, politics was the one that exceeded the walls of the polis and began to be conducted on an imperial scale. Law was the first to change in the service of politics: instead of protecting politics by framing it, just like the walls of the polis, it became politics' main vehicle of expansion.[21] As a result of this expansion across what was considered the civilized world, politics was in great need of a new form of oikonomia to serve it in times of peace. At the same time, philosophical life too underwent a major transformation. Stoic thought, which was far less zealous in maintaining a clear-cut distinction between the political and economic communities, first became the philosophy of the Hellenic world, later the "ideology" of the Roman Empire.[22]

The zeitgeist of the expansion and breaking down of walls did not pass over oikonomia and has changed it almost beyond recognition. Just as politics exceeded the walls of the polis, so did oikonomia exceed the boundaries of the oikos, even if it took another path. An economic colonization of the arts and sciences, as well as of various spheres of existence, took place. Whatever people did, wherever they turned, they were bound to economize. In the sphere of the relations between humans and themselves, both body and ethical conduct were seen as economized, that is, prudently managed; in the political sphere, both nongovernmental organizations and governmental ones were economized; the cosmos itself was conceived as economized by God/Nature. The arts and sciences suffered the same fate, and the term *oikonomia* appeared in almost every one of them.

Among all the spheres, the arts and sciences that were economized, the story of oikonomia in the field of rhetoric is of fundamental importance. Within it a crucial episode in the story of the human trinity of economy, politics, and philosophy unfolds. In order to retell the episode, one must return to the moment when politics and philosophy were distinguished from oikonomia. At that time, mastery of oikonomia was seen as a prerequisite for conducting a leisurely life, whether theoretical or political. The question whether a theoretical or a political life was more virtuous stood at the heart of a harsh controversy between two factions: the philosophers and the rhetoricians. One can find traces of this debate in two of Plato's Socratic dialogues, where the word *rhetoric* appears for the first time in his writings.[23]

In *Gorgias* and in most of *Phaedrus*, Plato dismisses rhetoric altogether as ridiculous, as nonscience (ἄτεχνον),[24] as habitude (ἐμπειρία), and as flattery. The relation between rhetoric and the true political art is compared to the relation between cookery and medicine—the first in the pairing of the analogy being the arts/empirical know-how devoted to the soul, the second those devoted to the body (1967:462–66). Despite this insult, toward the end of *Phaedrus* Plato acknowledges a way in which rhetoric can be "saved" and turned into a science. According to Plato: "The method of the art of healing is much the same as that of rhetoric. . . . In both cases you must analyze a nature, in one that of the body and in the other that of the soul, if you are to proceed in a scientific manner, not merely by practice and routine, to impart health and strength to the body by prescribing medicine and diet, or by proper discourses and training to give to the soul the desired belief and virtue" (270b). In true Platonic spirit, saving rhetoric was to be accomplished by enslaving political speech to philosophical truth. Subordinating rhetoric to dialectic resembles Plato's idea that the political sphere should be governed by a philosopher king (266b–d, 269b–70). After all, if one wants to address the multitude and persuade them, one must use some sort of public speech. So that rhetoric may be set straight, Plato shifts its attention from speech itself to the interlocutors, namely to the speaker and listeners. Plato asserts that the speaker should convey a message of truth, instead of articulating what is probable (272–73), and to aim at making his listeners more virtuous, rather than winning their approval (271–72). In doing so, Plato shifts the focus of rhetoric from the public sphere, where speech itself appears, to what happens in the mind of the speaker and the soul of the listeners.

Later in the dialogue, as was customary at the time, Plato divides the art of rhetoric into content and form.[25] The content of rhetorical activity is pregiven, while its form is "what . . . remains of rhetoric."[26] In contrast, the philosophical search for truthful content takes place in private and is thus invisible to the public eye,[27] being an inner dialogue between a person and the self. In other words, the search for truth must become dialectical. Not only must the content, the idea, be sought in a philosophical manner;

more important, the object of the search must be the philosophical Object par excellence, namely, Truth as revealed in the good and in the beautiful.

The second, visible aspect of form is left for rhetoric proper. Rhetoric could become a science rather than habitude if, and only if, it becomes subordinate to dialectics. Regarding the visible side of the equation—the public one—Plato is much more modest in his demands. After all, rhetoric as the art of persuasion carries its own sphere of application—the souls of the multitude. Therefore, all that Plato requires from rhetoric proper is to take its job seriously. Just as the physician is required to map the various maladies that might inflict the human body and to the remedies corresponding to them, so the orator is required to map maladies that might inflict the human soul and to the forms of speech that correspond to them. Based on this mapping, the orator must diagnose which form of speech is most effective for improving the spiritual condition of the particular audience he is facing and then apply it.[28] Plato, then, acknowledges the need for a science of persuasion, but insists that its only merit is to serve as a vehicle of philosophical truth. In order to uphold this role for rhetoric, he divides it into two branches—one dealing with the visible and the other with the invisible. While the visible sphere is where rhetoric proper is applied, the invisible sphere should remain utterly philosophical in method as well as in content.

Here as elsewhere, Plato was followed by Aristotle, who dedicated a treatise to the subject of rhetoric. As in many other cases, Aristotle found a middle way, arguing for the existence of the two arts side by side:

> Rhetoric is a counterpart of Dialectic; for both have to do with matters that are in a manner within the cognizance of all men and not confined to any special science. Hence all men in a manner have a share of both; for all, up to a certain point, endeavor to criticize or uphold an argument, to defend themselves or to accuse. Now, the majority of people do this either at random or with a familiarity arising from habit. But since both these ways are possible, it is clear that matters can be reduced to a system.[29]

While not yet employing the notion of oikonomia, Aristotle breaks down the Platonic form into two: *taxis* (τάξις) and *lexis* (λέξις),[30] organization and style, which are added to what he calls invention (εὕρεσις)—a term that corresponds more or less to the Platonic notion of content. Later rhetorical

theories added the element of delivery and sometimes also that of memo-
rizing the speech. Sometimes rhetoric was divided into four branches, not
including memorization.[31]

As the anonymous composer of the *Rhetorica ad herennium* argues:

> The speaker, then, should possess the faculties of Invention, Arrange-
> ment, Style, Memory, and Delivery. Invention is the devising of matter,
> true or plausible, that would make the case convincing. Arrangement
> [*dispositio*][32] is the ordering and distribution of the matter, making clear
> the place to which each thing is to be assigned. Style is the adaptation of
> suitable words and sentences to the matter devised. Memory is the firm
> retention in the mind of the matter, words, and arrangement. Delivery is
> the graceful regulation of voice, countenance, and gesture.[33]

In the centuries to follow, the scholars of rhetoric would further develop
the internal division of each of the major components of rhetoric. What we
witness there is not just the development of the technologies of public
speech. More important for our inquiry is the fact that Aristotle recognized arrangement as a distinct branch of rhetoric. In order to persuade
the multitude, two kinds of "form" must be distinguished: the arrangement of thought and its appearance in public. The introduction of arrangement and the further subdivision of rhetoric set the stage for the appearance of oikonomia in rhetoric. This is due to the fact that, as shown earlier,
oikonomia had become synonymous with prudent arrangement in most
arts and sciences.

Although he recognized the importance of arranging thought out of
public sight, Aristotle did not use the term *oikonomia* to denote this activity. A possible explanation for why he refrained from doing so can be found
in the only occurrence of the term in his *Rhetoric*, where Aristotle criticizes
Alcidamas for using the term in the context of political speech. Illustrating
why Alcidamas's style "appears frigid, for he uses epithets not as a season-
ing but as a regular dish,"[34] Aristotle mentions that Alcidamas had used the
phrase "oikonomos of his listeners' pleasure" (οἰκονόμος τῆς τῶν
ἀκουόντων ἡδονῆς).[35] Since Aristotle uses the noun *oikonomos* in his *Poetics*,[36] one can assume that his reason for objecting to the use of the term in
public speech was his wish to observe a clear demarcation line between
the political and the economic spheres. This is the very same line of

demarcation that Alcidamas pointedly does not observe, because of his eagerness to overstylize political speech.

THE OIKONOMIA OF THOUGHT

The first to introduce the concept oikonomia into rhetorical theory was Hermagoras of Temnos of the second century BC. Hermagoras, who led the revival of rhetoric in an atmosphere that was full of Platonic hostility toward the art of persuasion, was "the most important Greek rhetorician" and "the most famous professional teacher of rhetoric in the Hellenistic period."[37] His detailed, and apparently "dry as dust" six or seven books on rhetoric were the most influential of the Roman age.[38] Although most of his writings did not survive, their scheme can be reconstructed from the works of ancient writers who relied on his work,[39] most notably Romans such as Cicero and Quintilian. Although contemporary scholars consider his greatest contribution to be his thorough examination of invention and his development of the notion of *statis* (identifying and reaching an agreement on the subject under discussion);[40] he was also the first to introduce the concept of oikonomia into rhetoric. As a theorist of rhetorical writing in a hostile philosophical environment, Hermagoras pointed out what might be described as the greatest disadvantage of philosophical thought: it is essentially a private affair,[41] and, as such, it is conditioned just like any other private affair. For philosophy to appear in public, it needs to be economized. Considering that, ever since its first appearance in a poem by Phocylides, any activity that was to be economized was despised and thought of as a means to a higher end—namely to the life of leisure—it is hard to think of a greater insult to philosophy. We can virtually hear Hermagoras explaining to his opponents that, after all, philosophy is like any other economic activity. It is part of man's interaction with the cosmos, and like any such activity it must be subordinate to politics and not vice versa. Even if belated, a rejoinder to the Platonic insult was found.

According to Hermagoras, oikonomia was composed of four branches: judgment, division, order (*taxis*), and style (*lexis*).[42] Grouping these different matters, most notably style, under oikonomia was unusual and was not adopted by later rhetoricians.[43] This does not mean that oikonomia was lost to ancient rhetoric,[44] but rather that until its baptism into Christianity it was again restricted to the invisible sphere. Allowing oikonomia to appear in the political sphere did not make sense in a world that observed the distinction between private and public—between, on the one hand, economic activity, which now included the organization of the products of thought, and, on the other hand, political speech and action. This, I believe, is the reason why later writers did not follow in the footsteps of Hermagoras and did not include style as part of oikonomia. By excluding style from oikonomia, they reestablished the distinction between private and public and returned oikonomia to its former prepolitical domain.

The retreat of oikonomia from the visible, public sphere into the invisible one can be found in Dionysius of Halicarnassus.[45] Oikonomia, according to Dionysius, is the organization of content before it is rendered into speech.[46] The foregoing citation teaches us a great deal about oikonomia's trajectory since its inception: in this striking piece, Dionysius informs us that as long as rhetoric is involved, *economizing* thought is more important than thought itself. According to Dionysius, oikonomia "relate[s] to the more technical side of his subject-matter, what is called oikonomikeh of the discourse, something that is desirable in all kind of writing, whether one choose philosophical or rhetorical subjects. The matter in question has to do with the division [*diairesis*], order [*taxis*] and development [*exergasia*]."[47]

In other words, any thought, be it the philosophical Truth or the rhetorical Probable, must be economized before it is rendered in speech. The tendency to distance the thought process from the public sphere and to stress the importance of its oikonomia will be strengthened by later developments in rhetorical theory. In various manuscripts from the second century CE onward a new distinction arises: this time between oikonomia and *taxis/ordo*. Oikonomia in these texts means the human-made order of thought that is set forth in order to persuade the multitude. This artificial order is contrasted to the natural order of occurrences. By contrasting oikonomia and taxis the rhetoricians were yet again distancing the thought process from the public eye. As an anonymous writer put it: "Taxis differs from oikonomia because taxis, on the one hand, is characterized by a following of the chief points and by knowing how to use them in accordance with their natural order (*kata taxis*), which one first, or which second. But oikonomia, on the other hand, is characterized by expediency; for very often we overthrow the natural order on account of expediency, and

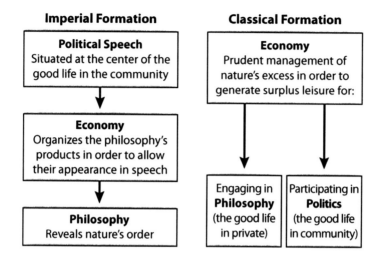

FIGURE 0.1. THE HUMAN TRINITY IN ITS CLASSICAL AND IMPERIAL FORMATIONS

use the first event, if it is expedient, second. It occurs also when we leave out some one of the main event."[48] Distinguishing between oikonomia and the natural order once again widens the gap between the thought process and the political sphere. The products of thought, the representations of the natural order, are the raw material to be economized so that it will be suitable for public appearance.

1

From Oikos to Ecclesia

Oikonomia in Scripture

The word *oikonomia* (ὀικονομία) appears twice in the Septuagint, both in Isaiah 22.[1] *Oikonomos* (ὀικονόμος) appears twelve times, most of these being translations of the Hebrew the one who's (in charge) on the house אשר על הבית. These rare appearances, combined with *oikonomos* being transliterated in Jewish texts from the same period,[2] and with Hellenic Jewish texts borrowing the common Stoic use of the term as government of the cosmos, led John Reumann (1992:16, 1967:151–53, 156–57) to determine that the Christian use of the concept came from the Greek-speaking world (and not the Hebrew one), a view shared by Gerhard Richter (Richter 2005:91–92).

Oikonomia was not a key concept in the New Testament, where it is found nine times, *oikonomos* ten times, and the verb *oikonomeo* only once. The origin of its meaning,[3] as "dispensation of revealed divine mystery," is found in Paul's letter to the Ephesians.[4]

> He made known to us the mystery of His will, according to His kind intention which He purposed in Him; with a view to an economy of the fullness of ages to recapitulate all in Christ, things in the heavens and thing on the earth.
>
> (Ephesians 1:9–10)

To enlighten all what is the economy of the mystery which from eternity
has been hid in God who created all things.

(Ephesians 3:9)

Reumann, Richter, and Agamben all (Reumann 1967:166; Richter 2005:90;
Agamben 2011:21–25) argue against the received view that Paul used the
word to signify God's salvific plan that reveals itself in history, suggesting
that oikonomia in Paul need to be understood as management of God's
mysteries (μυστήρια), a word that is found next to most of *oikonomia/
oikonomos* appearances in Paul. Even if we were to accept the view that
oikonomia does not mean the fulfillment of a neatly ordered divine plan in
Paul's mind, at the very least it means the inner-worldly management of
the divine mystery in accordance with God's intention (Reumann
1967:166). So, even in the minimalist version, at least some of the attributes of economy as God's salvific plan, which subsists in him before creation, along with the modes by which it unfolds in worldly time and space,
can be traced back to Paul.[5]

The boundaries of economic space are defined in Paul's *via negativa*
by setting an absolute boundary and one relative to it. The absolute
boundary is equated with the created world, as oikonomia, so long as it
is the fulfillment of the divine plan (let alone if it is "nothing more" than
the management of the revealed divine mystery), which takes place in
the bounds of the created world and cannot exceed cosmological space
back into divinity in itself. Oikonomia's relative boundary is revealed
when taking into account that as long as it means the revelation of the
divine plan since the creation of the world up to the end of times (the
economy of the incarnation to be situated at the center of this drama),
then history of salvation does not coincide with the history of the cosmos, but takes place within it bounds.[6] By saying that the economy will
be fulfilled when both the celestial and the earthly will be recapitulated
in Christ, Paul rendered Stoic distinctions between the intimate, the
economic, the political, and the cosmopolitical inoperative,[7] the reason
for this being that the same economy will, in the fullness of the age, appear in all of them and annihilate both spheres and the distinctions between them. By saying so, he also implied a need for a new spatial distinction in the age that lies between the revelation of the "new
economy" in Christ and the fullness of the ages, one that will distinguish

between what is part of the new economy and what has not been included in it yet.

THE ECONOMISTS OF SALVATION

Paul, too, is the origin of the use of *oikonomos* to describe the role of bishops in the realization of the plan and the revelation of the mysteries (see Tooley 1966:82, 84): "Whereof I am made a minister [of the Church], according to the economy of God which is given to me for you, to fulfill the word of God" (Colossians 1:25).[8] His use of *oikonomos* to describe the role of the bishop marks a change in the economic literature of antiquity. For one, he was the first to proudly self-identify as an oikonomos and to address his fellow economists in his letters, whereas neither the classical economist nor the imperial one focused attention on the economic literature of their time, and they did not author the advisory economic literature that was addressed to their masters. If at all, economists were referred to in this literature as part of "the master's science[, which] is the science of employing slaves" (*Pol.* 1252.b), those who need to be classified, managed, and supervised (see Leshem 2014a).

Paul describes the Christian oikonomos as Christ's servant who is entrusted with the duty of interpreting and teaching the divine plan, namely that, as the oikonomia is fulfilled when the mysteries are revealed, its recapitulation in the fullness of the ages is dependent on him enlightening all. Paul also establishes a model for future economists (beside, of course, offering himself as a model) as well as a set of disciplinary measures. He describes the devotion demanded from the economists as follows: "Let a man regard us in this manner, as servants of Christ and economists of the mysteries of God; In this case, moreover, it is required of economists that one be found trustworthy" (1 Corinthians 4:1–2). The economists do their job without a reward: "For if I do this voluntarily, I have a reward; but if against my will, I have an economy entrusted to me" (1 Corinthians 9:17). Moreover, the job description given by Paul includes the required qualities of character:

> For the bishop must be above reproach as God's steward, not self-willed, not quick-tempered, not addicted to wine, not pugnacious, not fond of sordid gain; Rather hospitable, loving what is good, sensible, just, devout, self-controlled.[9]

> (Titus 1:7–8)

Not to teach strange doctrines; nor to devote themselves to myths and endless genealogies, which promote speculations rather than the economy from God that is by faith.

(1 Timothy 1:3–4)

Paul's positioning of the bishop as an oikonomos who is entrusted with the execution of a plan dictated by a higher authority, being notified to a certain extent as to its essence and goals, does not exceed the "job description" of the oikonomos position in the ancient oikos. The difference between the Christian economists and their predecessors lies in the radical change of the nature of the economic activity they are entrusted with and the master they serve, so that instead of being charged with the management of the earthliest of all things in the service of their *despotes*, the Christian economist is entrusted with the management of divine matters and with the mission of divinization for the sake of their subordinates. Another crucial difference between the two is that the Christian economist labors to include all spheres of life in the economy instead of generating political and philosophical spheres that are "economicless."

The Apostolic Fathers and the Early Apologists: Justin Martyr, Tatian, Ignatius, Athenagoras, Theophilus of Antioch

Some rather limited expansion of the meanings attached to oikonomia can be traced to Christian texts composed in the second half of the first century and the first half of the second.[10]

Economy as God's salvific plan, actuated in the Christ event, is found in Ignatius of Antioch, the only Apostolic Father who used oikonomia (Letter to the Ephesians 18:2, 20.1). Ignatius does so with reference to God's plan incarnated, beginning with the Son's conception in Mary's womb, through his suffering on the cross, and up until his resurrection. Other appearances of oikonomia as incarnation (the most common meaning in Christian literature prior to Irenaeus, according to Markus 1958:92) can be found in the "Apology" of Aristides (2004:15.2), in Athenagoras's *Plea for the Christians* (2004: 22.4), and in six out of ten times in Justin Martyr's *Dialog with Trypho* (2002c: 30.3, 31.1, 45.4, 77.5, 103.3, 120.1).[11]

Economy referring to the bishop position can be found in Ignatius's "Epistle to the Ephesians" (2002b:6.1) and in Justin Martyr (2002c). Ignatius's demand from the Ephesians "to receive every one whom the despot of the oikos sends on his oikonomia . . . [and to] look upon the bishop even as we would upon the Lord Himself" marks another development in the reverence of the oikonomos as bishop, who now must be treated as if he were the master himself.

While oikonomia as God's salvific plan incarnated in Christ and oikonomos as the position of bishop can be found in Paul, the economy as a divine intervention in created world in other historical events, economy as morally questionable behavior and the economy of transcription were all added by early apologists.

Economy as divine intervention in created world is organized along a synchronic axis and a diachronic one. The former can be described as bringing together the Stoic conception of economy as a divine oversight (πρόνοια/ providence) over the cosmos and the Jewish one of creation ex nihilo.[12] Economy bearing this meaning appears in Theophilus of Antioch's *Ad Autolycum* (Theophilus 1970:73) where it refers to the plan of the hexameron (six days of creation).[13] The economy of oversight can be found in Tatian's "Address to the Greeks" where it means the organization of matter (in the world: ὕλης οἰκονομία) of both human body and cosmos (Tatian 2004:12.2–3). Diachronic economy is found in Justin Martyr (2002c), who uses oikonomia to describes divine intervention in the history of salvation, such as God not sparing Nineveh (107), Jesus being circumcised and observing other Jewish legal ceremonies (67), Jacob's bigamy (134), and David's mischief in the "matter of Urriah's wife" (141).

ECONOMY AS A MORALLY QUESTIONABLE BEHAVIOR

In the last four events mentioned a shady moral conduct, preformed either by God or his delegates, triggered Justin to enlighten all as to the nature of the economy that led them to do so. The explanation given by Martyr was that diversion from the righteous course of action was done in the service of a greater cause—the salvation of the world.

As discussed elsewhere,[14] using the term *oikonomia* in order to justify shady behavior was not a Christian innovation. As it were, a tension between the intended goals and the justness of the measures taken—between

utility and justice—accompanied the economy from the moment the political sphere was distinguished from it. In classical texts, dedicated to
economy as oikos management, this tension was settled by governing the
economy with soundness of mind that was aided by the formation of several modes of extralegal (and, as such, apolitical) forms of justice that
were set in order to normalize the economy (see Leshem 2013c). But nor-
malizing the oikos did not settle the question once and for all; this tension, inherent to the economy, reappeared whenever the economy exceeded its boundaries into a new sphere. The problematic relations
between economy and truth telling became explicit well before Christianity, when the term *oikonomia* migrated into the field of rhetoric where it
was used to denote the subjection of the organization of verities to serve
the argument. As described in the introduction, it begun with Plato accus-
ing the rhetoricians that their speech was not committed to the mission
of conveying a true message and that they did not attempt to make the
interlocutor's soul a more virtuous one. Instead of doing so, Plato argued,
the rhetorician used flattery to win the multitude's consent, resulting in
rhetoric becoming a science only if it imitated the model of the physician.
The Church Fathers, who used the mode of conduct of the physician (as
well as the pedagogue) as exemplary fairly often, demonstrate that the
subjection of rhetoric in the service of divine truth does not solve rhetoric's problematic relations (or the economy's, for that matter) with truth
telling in public speech. This is because, the moment rhetoric serves the
economy of truth, revelations of only partial verities, keeping silence at
the price of letting interlocutors assume false propositions to be true, and
uttering complete lies intentionally are all licensed. Paradoxically, instead of solving the problem of lying in rhetoric, its subjection in the service of truth qualifies lying.[15]

The problem the person conveying a message in the service of divine
truth incarnated in the economy has to tackle is to discern the distance
that verities can be economized in order to secure the salvation of the
souls of those under his care. He is forced to deal with questions: When
does economizing truth become a lie? Is lying part of the economy? And,
ultimately, what are the boundaries of the economy? As if things were not
complicated enough, these questions undergo yet another sophistication
as a consequence of two processes taking place simultaneously: 1. the subjection of rhetoric in the service of the economy of salvation (Mondzain

2005:13); 2. Subjecting economy itself to a higher truth laying outside its bounds, which licenses the oikonomos to suspend the laws that bind public speech in a political sphere (i.e., one that is governed by law) so that, as argued in an extremely popular manual written by the Christian master of rhetoric John Chrysostom, "it is possible then to make use of deceit for a good purpose, or rather that in such a case it ought not to be called deceit, but a kind of oikonomia worthy of all admiration" (John Chrysostom 2004b:II.1). Chrysostom does so relying on the model of the physician who lies occasionally to his patient as a necessary part of healing (I.8) by presenting the priest as someone who cure the soul by Word (IV.3), using the platonic metaphor to license the exact opposite of Plato.

The pedagogical model justifies revealing partial truth when Christ qua pedagogue serves as the model. Origen (1998:18.6) makes an analogy between "the divine oikonomia for human matters," which includes accommodation for the intellectual level, language, and customs of the addressees, to the way adults address a toddler, arguing that a partial concealment of truth is mostly needed when approaching people who are like "children" that did not mature in their faith (referring to those who are not yet members of the society of believers in Christ's economy or the ones who are new to it). The economy of truth adopted by the economist-pedagogue begins with an examination of the believer/interlocutor's soul. Given his estimation of it, the economist accommodates truth to fit the exact prescription befiting the believer's spiritual level. The latter is conceived as a student who progresses slowly toward encountering unconcealed truth, when the economist/pedagogue reveals it in accordance with the stage he reached on his road to enlightenment.

Both the physician model, to qualify lying, and the pedagogic one that qualifies truth accommodation rely on an authoritative relation that is used to license the economy of speech. Common to both physician and pedagogue is that their authority is derived from the excessive knowledge they posses, which persuades the student/patient to trust their judgment in guiding his psychic/somatic life. What has changed following their chrismation by the economists, who assert authority and excess knowledge, is that these authoritative relations are now taking place in the ecclesia, until Christianity *the political* of all spaces and, as such, denied of any institutionalized authoritative relations. As the ecclesiastical economy was in dire need of other models to replace despotic rule over slaves, in addition to the master's rule over the matron as it exceeded the oikos boundaries into the public sphere, it made use of the two other nonpublic modes of conduct (pedagogue/student, physician/patient) at hand.

Keeping silence at the price of letting interlocutors assume false propositions to be true is the third kind of speech economy used by the Church Fathers. *The* model to follow was Basil the Great's abstention from publicly declaring the full divinity of the Holy Spirit. Both Athanasius (2004d:letters 62, 63), and Basil's intimate friend Gregory of Nazianzus (letter 58 in Daily 2006a, 2003:oration 63) justified his deception on the grounds of oikonomia. Letter 58, addressed to Basil himself, demonstrates the difficulties raised by Basil's economy of keeping silence. Gregory tells Basil of a party attended by distinguished members of their social milieu when all of a sudden a "so called philosopher" questioned the orthodoxy of Basil decision to refrain from publicly declaring the full divinity of the Holy Spirit. Gregory rushed to defend his friend against such outrageous allegations, arguing that Basil, as a public figure, had to economize truth in order to defend orthodoxy at times when the emperor was leaning toward heterodoxy. Alas, the guests were not convinced and replied that Basil is economizing fear instead of doctrine and that his silent economy is nothing but "a vapid way of playing with words" (letter 58, translated in Daley 2006:180). One may suspect that Gregory himself was not fully convinced, as toward the end of the letter he asks Basil to delineate how far the economy of speech can go. Which is another reincarnation of the age-old question that arises whenever the economy exceeds its boundaries into a new sphere and/or art.

ECONOMY'S PRINCIPLE OF MOVEMENT

Tatian was the first to use oikonomia to describe God the Father begetting His Son:

> Him (the Logos) we know to be the beginning of the world. But He came into being by participation, not by abscission; for what is cut off is separated from the original substance, but that which comes by participation, making its economy, does not render him deficient from whom it is taken. For just as from one torch many fires are lighted, but the light of the first torch is not lessened by the kindling of many torches, so the Logos,

coming forth from the Logos-power of the Father, has not divested of the Logos-power Him who begat Him. I myself, for instance, talk, and you hear; yet, certainly, I who converse do not become destitute of speech [logos] by the transmission of speech, but by the utterance of my voice I endeavour to reduce to order the unarranged matter in your minds. And as the Logos, begotten in the beginning, begat in turn our world, having first created for Himself the necessary matter, so also I, in imitation of the Logos, being begotten again, and having become possessed of the truth, am trying to reduce to order the confused matter which is kindred with myself. For matter is not, like God, without beginning, nor, as having no beginning, is of equal power with God; it is begotten, and not produced by any other being, but brought into existence by the Framer of all things alone.

(Tatian 2004:5.1–5.3)

As noted by various translators, this passage, and the word *oikonomia* in particular, is extremely hard to translate (see for example Grant 1958:126). In the translation given here *oikonomia* is translated as "choice of function," but Whitaker translated it to "distinctive function" (Tatian 1982:11), Grant to "arrangement" (1958:126), Richter to "like the household" (2005:113), and Prestige to "economy" (1964:102–3). In the quotation Tatian presents two different modes to relating things: the first mode, which displays great affinities to Agamben's description of the political relation, is by exclusion and dissociation. The second, which he calls oikonomia, is division by inclusion. In the "narrow" Christian context, oikonomia is used to demonstrate, first, that by begetting the Son the Father does not lose anything of his power nor his prudence (see Grant 1958:126–28); second, it signifies that the economy of the Son allows more than merely safeguarding excess in the Godhead but also enables the generation of a surplus world created through the Son (the logos). This can take place because the generation of the world as surplus existing outside the economy does not subtract anything from the Son, nor from the Father, and has no effect on the ongoing excessive nature of the relation between the Father and His Son, so, on the one hand, they are fully distinguished from each other and, on the other hand, they share the same nature and essence.

Reading Tatian's definition as a general reflection on the concept of oikonomia suggests that it is the clearest expression of economy's "metaphysical" principle of movement, one that is found in all of the re-incarnations of economy throughout history. As such, it states that the inner organization of the economy allows employing the excess imma-nent to it such that its internal division, as part of its prudent organiza-tion for the purpose of generating surplus, is not achieved by abscission from the origin of excess, but rather by including all into it. According to this definition of the economic way of relating things, excess generates surplus by inclusive distinction in a distinguished sphere so that the common is not lost in distinction.

Tatian's definition is not only the clearest expression of economy's metaphysical principle of movement. It also plays an important role in the development of Christian dogma, as it is the first attempt to use economy's principle of movement to describe the inner organization of the Godhead, later developed by Hippolitus and Tertullian, who both used the term for that purpose. And although the word *oikonomia*, and the necessary excess attached to it,[16] were later excluded from the Godhead and restricted to divine operations within the bounds of the created world, its principle of movement will remain the one that describes the relation between the three persons of the Godhead in itself, outside the created world.

Later Apologists: Irenaeus, Tertullian, Clement of Alexandria

Oikonomia gained currency and became a key concept in Irenaeus of Lyons (115–202), who used economy to explore the Christian conception of his-tory; Tertullian (c. 160–c. 220), who further elaborated Tatian's use of economy in order to structure interdivine relations; and Clement of Alex-andria (c. 150–c. 215),[17] who economized philosophy as a way of life by bringing together exegesis as theoretical praxis and pedagogy as a model for managing Christianity as a philosophical school.

IRENAEUS: ECONOMY AS WORLDLY TIME

Irenaeus made oikonomia a key concept (Markus 1958:92) in Christianity and was the first to offer a full description of God's economy as unified and fundamental concept in Christian thought (Minns 1994:56–57; Behr

2000:33).[18] Much like his predecessors, Irenaeus's use of oikonomia is derived from Ephesians 1:9–10 (Clifford and Anatolios 2005:748), which he interpreted as "the mysterious plan to recapitulate all in the fullness of ages." Irenaeus's effort to enlighten all as to what the economy is about is performed by positing recapitulation (ἀνακεφαλαιώσασθαι),[19] fullness (πλήρωμα), and age (αἰών) as the concepts that form the building blocks of the economy.

Eric Osborn presents the role played by the concept of economy in Irenaeus's thought in the following way:

> In Irenaeus, oikonomia becomes central, unifying creation and recapitulation. In the singular it refers chiefly to the incarnation and in the plural to the old testament manifestations of the word. . . . Too large for exact definition, oikonomia can be taken as the ruling metaphor which holds Irenaeus' theology together. . . . The economy is the history of humanity. . . . The economy is the history of salvation, a succession of times or seasons where man participates in God.
>
> (Osborn 2001:78–79)

> Everything that God does is part of his economy and every part of his economy is in relation to its recapitulation.
>
> (Osborn 2000:12)

> The first purpose of the economy was to accustom man to God and to accustom God to man. . . . The coordinates of the economy are vertical (descent and ascent of God's son to redeem the earth) and horizontal (the unbroken line of God's saving activity from the beginning to the end of time).
>
> (Osborn 2001:80, 87)

Much as in Paul's case, Irenaeus's use of economy is a consequence of its central role in Greek-speaking culture, this time in its use by Gnosticism (Widmen quoted in Behr 2000:33). Beside that, their texts are markedly different, since Paul's letters form part of the apostolic literature, intended to "spread the Word" of revealed gospel, while Irenaeus's style is polemical, as testified by the title of his major work, "Against Heresies." Large parts of this treatise are dedicated to refute the Valentinian set of beliefs. As part of this effort, in a gesture customary among the apologists, Irenaeus baptizes his opponents' concepts into Christianity by altering their meaning. Economy is one of the key concepts Irenaeus (re)baptized, if not *the* concept (Behr 2000:33; Grant 1997). It appears 120 times in Irenaeus, 33 of them relating to the Valentinian economy (D'ales 1919:1–9), all of them referring to God's economy while avoiding its use in different contexts, as do many of the other Fathers.

THE VALENTINIAN ECONOMY

The Gnostic (such as the Valentinians) use of *economy* is borrowed from Stoicism, which used the term to describe the way the cosmos is dispensed by divine oversight (Markus 1958:94). Oikonomia is grasped in the Valentinian version as the economy of fullness (οἰκονομία τοῦ πληρώματος; Markus 1954:212) and is used to describe the drama of creation (cosmogony) and the relation between God and, afterward, the created world. The Valentinian ontology, described in great details by Irenaeus in the first out of five books of *Against Heresies*, was an eclectic mix of Hellenic, Christian, and Jewish concepts. As the Valentinian story goes, in the beginning there was one self-sufficient God who was a mixture of male and female. At a certain stage this God limited himself and created a space called *pleroma* (fullness), which is inhabited by thirty spiritual entities (named *aeons*) that emanated from the one God in the same manner that branches come out of a tree (*AH* II.17.6) and a ray of light emanate from the sun (II.13.5, II.17.7). These eternal and immutable entities are ordered in the pleroma according to their proximity to God, which also determines their ability to know him, as God is known only to the entity named Nous who mediates this knowledge to the rest of them (I.1.1, I.2.5). At some point Sophia, the youngest entity, which is situated at the bottom of the scale of proximity, has sinned in attempting to know God by herself. As a result, she was expelled from the pleroma. In response to her supplications to return to the pleroma, which met with the support of the other entities, Sophia was cut in half, the upper part returned to the pleroma, while the bottom (named "unborn idea") was expelled. As part of her "repentance," Sophia generated, through the biblical God, also called Demiurge, the created world. The latter is to be saved by Christ, who descended from the pleroma to redeem the world. This complex ensemble, which describes the relation between God and world, summarized abruptly in the foregoing, is termed oikonomia. Put differently, the Valentinian economy is the hierarchical chain of relation between God, who fills to the exact amount each one of the spiritual entities according to its grade on the scale (Markus 1954:213), so that the "economy of fullness (pleroma)" is a hierarchic organization of the cosmos dependent on God the Father, the One who is everything and contain everything and who (ful)fills each according to his location in the scale of proximity. Indicating the apparent "fallacies" of the Valentinian conception served Irenaeus in formulating how the economy appears in his (orthodox) eyes by focusing on 1. the materialization of the economy; 2. economic anthropology; 3. narrowing the distance between God and human; and 4. the economy unfolding in time rather than space.[20]

The Christian economy materializes for the first time in the writing of Irenaeus when he turns the Valentinian "economy of fullness" on its head and talks about "the fullness of the economy."[21] As a result of this dramatic turnaround, the economy—the fullness of mysteries—becomes the object of the philosophical gaze. It is described by Irenaeus as the history of the divine plan conducted in the bounds of the world that begins with creation, at its epicenter the incarnation of the Son of God in the son of Adam, and culminates with recapitulation at the fullness of the ages, which from this time forward will become the favored object of Christian theoretical life.

As on past occasions when the economy exceeded its boundaries, the first problem Pauline economists had to tackle was setting new boundaries. Dealing with this problem, Irenaeus followed Paul and positioned an eschatological boundary to the economy by setting its recapitulation in the fullness of the ages. Also in the spirit of Paul, he positioned a double spatial boundary so that its absolute one coincides with the limits of time and space and its relative boundary is limited by the human capacity to contain the appearances in time and space of someone who exceeds it, a God whose nature is unknowable.

Unlike the Stoic (and Valentinian) use of oikonomia, which rendered it synonymous with (divine) providential oversight over the whole of creation, Irenaeus deploys the concept by attempting "to describe in details the oikonomia of God which is for the sake of man's becoming" (AH I:10.3).[22]

Irenaeus is decisive on this point, arguing that God created the world for the sake of humans and not the other way around (see *AH* V.29.1), as the Son incarnated for humans and not for any other creature (*AH* V.14.2), when in each of God's historical economies human is revealed to God and God to human (*AH* IV.20.7). Nothing more expresses the importance of humans in the economy as the crucial role Irenaeus ascribes to man's becoming vicious in sin. Although he shares with the Valentinians the claim that the story begins with an original sin, he proclaimed that this is a human sin and not the will to know of a divine entity, and "it was for this end [salvation of humans] that the Word of God was made man, and He who was the Son of God became the Son of man, that man, having been taken into the Word, and receiving the adoption, might become the son of God. For by no other means could we have attained to incorruptibility and immorality, unless we had been united to incorruptibility and immorality" (*AH* III.19.1).

Irenaeus held that Valentinian positioning the pleroma as a mediator between God and humans generates an intolerable distance between the two. Even worse, "Gnosticism keeps oikonomia within the divine pleroma and allows it to be reflected in the lower world" (Osborn 2001:78), an action that results in the economy being a strictly divine enterprise, keeping the human outside its boundaries. Trying to close the Gnostic gap between God and humans, Irenaeus insists that through the economy God is attached to the world in a direct and nonmediated way (Behr 2000:19), as well as denying the existence of two God the Fathers (the original one from which the pleroma emanated and the Demiurge who created the world). On yet another crucial point, Irenaeus makes sure to distinguish himself from the Valentinian conception of the Son as a created being, insisting on him being fully divine and, as such, existing before the dawn of creation. Irenaeus also disagreed with the Valentinians on the matter of the depth of the descending, i.e., to what extent did the Son resume human nature. Against the Valentinian claim that Christ is solely a spiritual entity, Irenaeus is firm in his belief that the Son incarnated in the flesh.[23] Moreover, the bishop of Lyons situated the economy of the incarnation at the heart of God's economy and regarded it as the most important event to have happened in the history of the economy, a notion that was reflected in later texts in which *oikonomia* usually refers to the incarnation (see Prestige 1964:105).

Irenaeus was the first to transpose the economy from a spatial axis to a temporal one, supplementing it with a once-in-lifetime promise of the revelation of a glorious mystery. Interpreting the economy as the (hi) story of the divine plan to recapitulate all in Christ in the fullness of the ages as occurring in time revolutionized the context of the appearance of the self, the human communities, and the communion between God and human. Presenting the economy as a story that unfolds in time is expressed in Irenaeus's critique of the Valentinian economy as drawing the relation between God and world as spatial (and deterministic), in which, at the end of the day, when order will be restored, each component will return to its natural setting. As described by John Behr, disputing the spatial conception of God-world relations, Irenaeus argued that the "divine economy thus begins in the glory which the Word had with the Father before the Creation of the world, and culminates in the glorification of the Incarnate Son by the Father, a glory in which the disciples, by beholding, participate. . . . The second important feature of this divine economy is that it is historical: it unfolds in time . . . the aim of the whole economy is twofold: first, the perfection of man by, second, the realization of and manifestation of the economies of God" (Behr 2000:37, 40, 46). The allure that Irenaeus cast over his readership must have skyrocketed when taking into account that the alternative was to put on the same outworn personae (masks) and to partake in a hackneyed play that repeats itself over and over again like a serpent biting its own tail in the cosmological oeuvre. For the latter was the story told in the histories of Polybius, who "was just the first, coming from the outside, to see certain things that the Romans didn't see because they took them for granted" (Arendt in Arendt and Jaspers 1992:667); for before Irenaeus it was taken for granted that the political community, which is the product of the prudent effort to harness the excess found in the economy of nature for the purpose of generating surplus that exceeds its boundaries, cannot in the long run exceed the circular economy of nature (φύσεως οικονομία; Polybius 1889:6.9.10–13). It is nothing more than another failed attempt to transcend the economic condition that humans are subjected to, as their recurring failure to establish a political community that will be distinguished from the economy is used by fortune (τύχη) to demonstrate its economy (see Polybius 1889:1.4.6).[24] This is achieved by making present the fact that even the most human of all deeds is, in the final account, part of the cosmological economy of growth and decay and as such incarcerated in a circular movement so that the political sphere is only seemingly stable, but in fact trapped in a never-ending circular movement; just as it grew into existence, it will decay and be replaced by yet another political sphere, and so on and so forth.

Compared with the despair and boredom that the subjection of the political community to the eternal circular economy of nature brings about, Irenaeus offers a progressive narrative that never repeats itself. He does so by distinguishing between four different economies, each referring to different ages or "modes of revelations" of the divine plan, arguing that in each God "signed" a covenant—the first with Adam, then with Noah, Moses, and finally the economy of the incarnation (*AH* III:11.8). As if that alone was not enough to capture his readers' hearts, Irenaeus spices the story with suspense, narrating a historical "thriller" in which we join the story at a moment just before midnight, a moment before the story will reach its *eschaton*, as the crucial moment of the story already occurred in broad daylight when the Son of God returned from the dead to beat Satan once and for all! And, as described in the following chapters, the Church Fathers concluded that at this very moment people are invited to participate in the story and put on the virgin personae if they wish to be granted the opportunity to take part in the happy ending.

TERTULLIAN

Tertullian and Hippolitus,[25] on whom Agamben relies in his explorations into theological economy,[26] further developed Tatian's use of oikonomia to describe the inner relations of the Godhead by adding the persona of the Holy Spirit to that of God the Father and God the Son. Tertullian does so in an attempt to persuade the lay believer (to which he referred explicitly in *AP* III) that God's unity and plurality are reconcilable, as "monarchy and economy must go together . . . the economy distributes unity into trinity so the three are one in quality, substance and power (status, subsantia, Potestas) but distinct in sequence, aspect and manifestation (Gradus, forma, species)" (Osborn 2003:121).[27]

The coexistence of unity and plurality is presented by Tertullian as the "economy of the mystery" (*oiknomiae sacramentum*), where the use of economy is meant to solve the mystery of this coexistence. This is done by situating the origin of the economy in God's monarchy (literally one origin), which dispenses plurality. In the same manner, Tertullian's attempt to redefine the concept of the monarchy by arguing that "the sole rule of the Father is itself Trinitarian in character, in the sense that the Son and Spirit carry out the Father's intention in the manner of dutifully commissioned agents" (McCruden 2002:328–29), establishes itself on the meaning attached to economy as oikos management ever since Xenophon's *oiko-nomikos*; The unity and continuity of the master rulership over his oikos did not suffer any harm when, as part of its distribution/organization, he delegated power to his matron and to his stewards.

In spite of its evident advantages in solving the mystery of the coexistence of unity and plurality in God, the use of oikonomia to describe the relations between the three persons of the Godhead was not pursued (Prestige 1964:111; Markus 1958:91), at least not for millennia. Contrary to Agamben's accusation leveled against modern theologians (2011:51–52) for introducing a caesura between oikonomia in the Trinity and its use as divine manifestations inside the world, beginning in the fourth century the use of oikonomia was restricted to the latter. At that time, theology was distinguished from economy, the former dealing with the Godhead in and of itself and the latter referring to any divine manifestation, as clearly demonstrated by Basil the Great's exegesis of Philippians 3:21: "It is universally known to anyone who has put his mind to the meaning of the text of the Apostle that he is not setting forth to us the mode of *Theologia* but he has given us that which pertains to *oikonomia*" (*Against Eunomius* II:3, cited in LaCugna 1993:40). According to Markus, economy was excluded from the Godhead because the Christians needed to distinguish themselves from the Valentinians who used economy to describe the activity that is taking place in the pleroma (Markus 1958:97). If Markus is correct, then the Valentinian use of the term has a twofold influence on economy's career in Christianity,[28] as Irenaeus used it to describe the conduct of God's salvific plan in the world against the Valentinian use restricting it the bounds of the pleroma. However, Tertullian's economization of the Trinity carried great influence on later generations, as economy's expulsion from the Godhead did not change the mode by which the relations between the three personae of the Godhead were described by Hippolitus and Tertullian, that is to say, even though the principal of movement of the Godhead wasn't called economy, it continued to be used as a vehicle be which the Godhead was mediated.

CLEMENT OF ALEXANDRIA

Clement constituted the economy of salvation as an intellectual-pedagogical journey,[29] as if he interprets Ephesians 3:9 in the following manner: "the economy of the incarnation enlightens all to know the mysteries hid from eternity in God who created all things," when enlightenment is to be understood as a philosophical one. Clement presents two economic progressions that are taking place simultaneously on humanity's way to recapitulation in the fullness of the ages: a historical "macroeconomic" process that is meant to educate and train humanity as a whole and a "microeconomic" process of training and educating the human subject. At the heart of both is the logos, which appears as pedagogue of the whole of humanity,[30] while the economy of the incarnation serves as the "hermeneutical key" to a true exegesis of divine revelations in the Old Testament and in (profane) Greek philosophy.

As put by Judith Kovacs, "Clement sometimes uses οἰκονομίᾳ to refer specifically to the incarnation. But it can also . . . refer more broadly to the all-embracing pedagogy by which the Logos seeks to lift all people up to God" (Kovacs 2001:7). Clement holds that the logos, who enables humans to decipher the mysteries of the economy on his way to salvation, revealed himself fully for the first time in the economy of the incarnation. As a result, the latter stands at the beginning of a new historical era that will end in the fullness of the ages. Moreover, the economy of the incarnation marks the endpoint of the two economies that existed prior to it: the Jewish and the Greek one, as he believed that, much like Jewish prophecy, the Greek philosophers caught a glimpse of the manifestation of the divine by their theoretical gaze.[31] By proposing that the mysteries of the economy are revealed in Greek philosophy, even if only to a certain extent, Clement allowed philosophy's appropriation by Christianity. However, he is quick to set a limit to it, arguing that, just like the Jewish economy, the Greek one also ended its role with the economy of the incarnation (Clement, 2004b: VI.17) and that Christian gnosis unites the best of Jewish revelation and Greek philosophy by using Greek theory in the exegesis of Scripture. Moreover, Clement argues that the full revelation of the logos in the economy of the incarnation allows reading anew Jewish Scripture and Greek philosophy as documentations of partial revelations of the logos throughout history. As discussed by Meijering (1989), literary criticism of the first centuries CE was preoccupied with exposing the economy used by the author of the literary text. Clement uses this obsession saying that Christian interpretation seeks the economy of the One who is surely the greatest author of them all, to which Origen adds, God's greatest work: the cosmos (Benjamins 1994:138–211).[32] Placing the Christian sage as an interpreter implies that he is expected to read divine revelations in the economy "intertextually," combining Scripture and nature, as it is only an intertextual reading of the works in which the divine economy is inscribed that will enable him to decipher God's mysterious plan. As can be seen, God appears in the writings of Origen as superauthor, since the economy of his work is as perfect as it gets. Given this perfect economy, the oikonomos mission is to enlighten all by revealing the mysteries of the economy through an intertextual readings of his works. Clement's and Origen's appropriation of literary criticism is yet another demonstration of how oikonomia, which was only a branch of arts and theories, turned to include them so that, in this instance, textual analysis becomes an economic art.

Besides being *the* hermeneutical key, the economy of the incarnation also acts as the point of convergence between the macro and the microeconomy, where the macroeconomic events are turned into a microeconomic practice, as "the saviour's economy teaches us to conduct ourselves so that we may resemble god, and to accept the economy as the guiding principle of all our education [παιδείας]" (Clement, *Stromata* I:11, translated in Hadot 1995:128). The pedagogical progress one has to go through as part of the economy appears in a nutshell when Clement writes at the beginning of *The Instructor* that "eagerly desiring, then, to perfect us by a gradation conducive to salvation, suited for efficacious discipline, a beautiful economy is observed by the all-benignant Word, who first exhorts, then trains, and finally teaches" (Clement 2004a:I.1).

The central place Clement ascribed to the threefold microeconomy of salvation that each person has to go through is exemplified in three treatises (*Protrepticus, Paedagogus, Stromata*) that are dedicated to each stage. The first preaches to non-Christians in the hope of converting them; the second is meant to train those being baptized; the third is directed to advanced believers (Behr 2000:135, 215).[33] Moreover, the economy of the logos also serves as the model for the conduct to be used by the oikonomos, just "as the [Christian] Gnostic imitates the virtue of the Logos and his contemplation of the Father, so he also mimics his pedagogical methods" (Kovacs 2001:17). The oikonomos "adapts his teaching to different types of students. He organizes the curriculum in an orderly way, so as to facilitate the upward progress of his students. He understands his pedagogical task as care for souls, a training that is not limited to intellectual matters but is concerned about the purification and reorientation of the whole person . . . [and] the use of concealment" (Kovacs 2001:17).

Economy Changes the Conception of Time, Space, and the Concept of History

The "Ireanean revolution" set the ground for a radical change in the conception of time, space, and God-world relations that Orthodox Christianity stirred in Greek thought, as described by Panagiōtēs Tzamalikos: "With Christianity the problem of world in time becomes of main priority. To be sure, some pagan schools of thought did quest for the purpose of history. . . . What was entirely new, though, was the question of an overall *meaning* of human history—a purpose originated in the ὸικονομία, the dispensation of God within the world since its creation" (Tzamalikos 2007:1).

EXCEEDING THE CIRCULAR ECONOMY OF TIME

All schools of thought in antiquity shared the concept of the human (and, for that matter, the whole cosmos) as subjected to a circular economy of time. Plato, for example, held that "even that which we have named time" is "an eternal image, moving according to number" (1925d, *Timaeus* 37d) where time and eternity belong to a completely different order of things, so that eternity was not understood as time that is stretched forever and ever. The circularity in which time moves was conceived by the ancient Greeks as a shady image belonging to the order of becoming that was time's way to become the moving image of eternity, itself seen as belonging to the order of being that exists outside time. Because the world is subjected to a constant change, circular cosmological (literally, "ordered") time set by divinity/nature is the ingenious way of making change resemble constant eternity.[34] In other words, the circularity of time enables a world subjected to constant change to overcome that change and not to "truly" change, as every change—any new thing that comes into life—is predestined to decay and disappear from the face of the earth so that, at the end of the day, nothing really changes. Therefore the change the world is subjected to is purposeless, it has no telos and is nothing but a moving image of eternity in which nothing really changes (see Azkoul 1968a:57–58; Cullmann 1964:54).

Human desire for self-perpetuation aims at overcoming the circular economy of nature, as the latter may well secure the existence of the human race, but, at the same time, it decrees oblivion for individual person. The desire and the means for self-perpetuation are discussed in Plato's *Symposium* in the section in which Diotima instructs Socrates on matters of eroticism. In her questions Diotima teaches Socrates that Eros, the son of Resource [πόρος] and Poverty (πενία; Plato 1925c, *Symposium* 203b–c), embodies the eagerness and straining of "begetting on a beautiful thing by means of both the body and the soul" (*Symposium* 206b) by which humans perpetuate themselves.

The pre-Christian concept of history is to be understood against the background of the circular economy of time and the desire for self-perpetuation. As presented by Arendt, "The subject matter of [classical] history is these interruptions—the extraordinary, in other words" (Arendt 1977:43). It originated in archaic literature where the hero underwent deification (ἀποθέωσις) in many cases (Lenz 2007:47–67). History was then an extraordinary account of every transgression of the circular economy of time, in which (mortal) humans perpetuated themselves by making the human condition of mortality present. The latter was understood as the capacity "to move along a rectilinear line in a universe where everything, if it moves at all, moves in a cyclical order . . . the human capacity to achieve this was remembrance, Mnemosyne, who therefore was regarded as the mother of all the other muses" (Arendt 1977:42–43). In other words, the subject matter of classical history was the perpetuation of the human condition, which dictates that each human life, as a single person, is rectilinear in contrast to the life of the human species, which is conditioned by the circular economy of time, so that by perpetuating themselves as singular beings in the memory of others humans transcend the circular economy of cosmological time.

In classical thought the transgression (as the telos) is discernible in the spatial (not temporal) contrast between the eternal world of ideas and the becoming world that exists in time (Cullmann 1964:37–38, 51–52, 61).[35] These time/space relations find their expression in classical texts dedicated to the economy of the oikos in which the economic sphere was prudently managed in order to generate surplus time for the master/ citizen who, time on his hands to be spent as he wills, could participate in the political community by appearing in the public sphere and/or engage in philosophy and gaze at the eternal. In both cases the exception is spatial. The revolution in history that Irenaeus steered had begun by transposing economy from the spatial axis to the temporal one.

THE FUTURE AGE TO COME IN THE ECONOMY

Unlike the Hellenistic conception of history as containing everything that exceeds the circular economy, Christian history is the story of the economy of salvation. According to Christian historiography, both time and history begin with creation (on the beginning of time, see Basil the Great 1963: I:6). Time is conceived as a dimension in which God reveals himself to humans. Introducing the concepts of age (αἰών) and crucial moment (καιρός), historical time is constituted as moving along a rectilinear line, as described by Cullmann:

> The characteristic thing about Kairos is that it has to do with a definite point of time which has a fixed content, while aion designates a duration of time, a defined or undefined extent of time. . . . It is not human deliberation but a divine decision that makes this or that date a kairos, a point of time that has a special place in the execution of God's plan of salvation. Because the realization of the divine plan of salvation is bound to such time points or kairoi chosen by God, therefore it is a redemptive history. Not all fragments of ongoing time constitute redemptive history in the narrower sense, but rather these specific points, these kairoi, singled out from time as a whole.
>
> (Cullmann 1964:39–40)

As a result, economy as history of salvation is thought to be the sum total of the crucial moments that are "religiously decisive time, ordained of God, wherein judgment and salvation are realized in and through human choice" (Minear 1944:81) and the economy is manifested as god's salvific plan, the crucial moment being the incarnation of God the Son in the economy. Those crucial moments share two evident qualities: first, the recapitulation of the economy in the fullness of the ages was hidden in God before the creation of the world, that is, before historical time itself began; second, in these moments the future age to come—the *eschaton* (ἔσχατον) as the moment when a new age will begin at the fullness of the ages—is made present. Put differently, these moments do not only bring salvation according to a plan that was conceived before the creation of time, but at the very same time they bring about the temporality that will consist in the post-salvation era.

Christian historical time can be divided into three "periods." The first period is the one to exist before the beginning of time (in a strict sense it is not a period because it lays totally outside of time).[36] The second period is composed of several ages, in most cases seven (Azkoul 1968a:65).[37] This period includes the present age that begins with the economy of the incarnation and will end at the fullness of the ages.[38] The third period is the future age to come, the "eighth day" (Daniélou 1956:262–86). It shares with the ages of the second period the quality of temporality (Cullmann 1964:63). Unlike the current ages, the future age to come has a beginning, but no end, and it brings forth time of a different order, which I will term "eternality." The latter is distinguished from classical eternity by its belonging to the order of time and, by that, that it is not conceived as an origin situated in the beginning of worldly time, but at its end, following the *eschaton* in the future age to come. The exact nature of the future age to come is yet another economic mystery, one that both Basil the Great and John of Damascus described as an age in which the sun never sets.[39]

That each age is distinguished by its singular storyline, as the economy of the Adamic age is not the same as the Mosaic one, manifests the rectilinear quality of Christian time in the ordering of the ages along a timeline that begins with creation and ends at the fullness of the ages. The circular economy of time's incompatibility in acting as a framework for Christian history is not restricted to its inability to offer a way in which the ages can be ordered. The same is true for the conception of the crucial moments. Each of these moments is a singular one that will never reoccur. Unlike the imperial circular economy of time that obliterates the meaning of any singular moment, Christ economy describes *The Crucial Moment* to have ever occurred—the incarnation of God the Son.

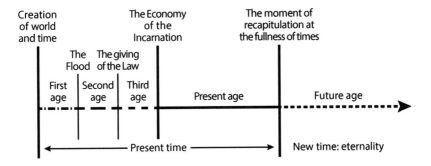

FIGURE 1.1. CHRISTIAN ECONOMY OF TIME

HISTORIES OF EXCEPTION

While both Hellenic (classical and imperial) and Christian thought concep-tualize history as composed of exceptional moments, they differ in their conception of the character and content of the exceptional. In Christian thought the exception is no longer of a spatial order; it is an exception that takes place in time that became rectilinear. What appears in the crucial moments that constitute Christian history is an exception from the "monochronic" linearity of time in which the future age to come is made present. It is, first and foremost, a "breach" or a "transgression" of the temporal, not the spatial, order of things. While in classical thought histo-ry contains the moments where the circular economy of time is exceeded, the thing to appear in these moments being another space, in Christian thought the economy itself is exceptional, the thing to reveal itself in it be-ing the time of the future age to come.

Platonic melancholic archaism that desires to return to eternity, which is conceived as the origin of time, is replaced by the desire to participate in the *eschaton* in the fullness of the ages, at the exact moment when all will be recapitulated in Christ and a new age of eternity will open. This escha-tological desire is expressed in two modes: 1. the economy as a whole is di-rected toward its recapitulation in the *eschaton*; 2. the *eschaton* itself is made present in the Christian economy at the heart of liturgy at the mys-tery (sacrament) of the Eucharist (Daniélou 1956:262–86). Christian history understood as an economy of salvation is the sum total of the moments in which the linearity of time is breached and the future age to come is made present. In other words, the Christian exception is distinguished by mak-ing present the future age to come and the new time of eternality.

The Christian concept of history is distinguished from the classical one by yet another important quality, as Christian history is composed of crucial moments that are connected and ordered along a line that begins with creation and ends in an endless eternity. The history of the Christian economy is constituted by crucial moments while many other moments, which do not bear the mark of eternality, are not perpetuated by it. Read together, the crucial moments convey a story of a progress, of a movement toward a telos that is situated in time, so that the concept of human history as a story of progress that is constituted of crucial moments makes its debut in Westernized history. The conceptualization of history as the story of human progress is accompanied by an acknowledgment that the moments that take crucial part in the story are not equally crucial for its development and, consequently, for the progress of the human race. *An example* of that is the economy of the incarnation, which stands at the epicenter of history. Such moments as the economy of the incarnation are constitutive moments. In these constitutive moments a new covenant is signed, a new age begins, and the economy is redispensed and adjusted to the new circumstances.

THE ALTERATION OF SPACE

The revolution that Christian theory steered in Greek thought brings more that "just" transposing the exception from the spatial axis to the temporal one, as it changed the time-space sequence and the way that human spheres of life are ordered. In the classical moment, economic space was managed for the purpose of supplying the master/citizen with leisure time so as to enjoy the good life, whether by participating in the political life that takes place in the public sphere or by engaging in philosophy by yearning to gaze and beget in the world of ideas. The Christian mode of conduct is markedly different. In that mode of conduct humans cannot exceed time; the desire to perpetuate oneself by exceeding is transformed into the economic desire to experience a different kind of time instead of a different kind of space. However, moving towards the different kind of time takes place in space. Transgressive desire is fulfilled by generating a space where the divine, which resides out of time and space, reveals itself in both. A new space of appearance—the society of believers in Christ economy—is constituted for the sole purpose of recapitulating all into it by dispensing the exceptional time of the future age to come. The new so-ciety is conducted in a new sphere that transgresses the ancient distinc-tion of space as a private sphere where the earthly economic partnership is conducted and as the public sphere where the political community is at home. It is neither private nor public, strictly speaking, and has changed almost beyond recognition the nature of both oikos and polis. The political community, taken as example, is conceived for the first time in history as a means to a higher end that lies outside its boundaries—the economy of salvation that is conducted in the society of believers. The *rise of the social* that took place in the fourth century is accompanied by another distinc-tion that is constituted in divinity between God in himself, which is the subject matter of theology, and God as he reveals himself to humans in the economy. The similitude that the ancients evoked between God and world accompanied by a mediator, such as the soul or the logos, was replaced in fourth-century Christianity by the comprehension that there is an un-bridgeable gap between the creating God and created world (Zizioulas 1985:29–54; Louth 1981:75–77).

ECONOMY AND THEOLOGY

As with so many other concepts appropriated by the Christians, theology (θεολογία, "literally discourse about God"), was commonly used at least since the classical age. Classical philosophers used it when relating to ar-chaic myths concerning the gods in their attempt to account for the gen-eration and conduct of the cosmos,[40] and in Aristotle's sixth book of *Meta-physics* theology is described as the most esteemed branch of theoretical philosophy (over mathematics and physics), itself the most esteemed of all forms of knowledge. Situating theology as superior to all other philosophi-cal endeavors, above physics and ethics this time, is "attested to Platonism at least since the time of Plutarch" (Hadot 1995:137). According to Brian Daley, the Christian use of the term was restricted in the beginning to the description of heresies and non-Christian theories. Origen was the first to use the term in order to describe Christian discourse concerning God (Daley 2006b:42) baptizing the threefold construct of ethics, physics, and theology to Christianity.[41] The Christian use of the term as describing the third stage in the quest to know God and commune with him is radically changed at the beginning of the fourth century when the Jewish conception of creation ex nihilo was matched with the Neoplatonic conception of God in himself as unknowable to humans. This conceptualization formed a new "archeological layer" of knowledge that was shared by orthodoxy and heterodoxy alike, as demonstrated in the Christological debate that took place at the first half of that century. Both factions agreed that one should not deduce from the inability to know God in himself the denial of a possibility of a positive knowledge (*kataphatic*) of God from his operations; for, as Hellenized as it may have been, Christianity remained a religion of divine revelation. So, in order to accommodate the contradicting conception (revelation of God who is unknown), a clear-cut distinction was made between the discourse of God in himself—theology in its strict sense—and economy that includes the discourse concerning God as revealed in his operations in created world. While theology was restricted to an *apothatic* discourse (i.e., negative theology) of God in himself, who subsists outside time and space, economy came to include any *kataphatic* discourse whose object is the revealed operations of the divine in time and space, such as Christology, eschatology, ecclesiology, and soteriology (Azkoul 1995:72) and every other Christian science except theology. Calling Church Fathers, such as Justin Martyr, who excelled in economic theory, "the Philosopher," and each of the three who dealt with theology in its strict sense "the theologian" (Azkoul 1995:40) testifies to the inclusion of anything given to the philosopher's gaze within the bounds of the economy.

The first clear distinction between economy and theology can be traced back to Eusebius of Caesarea's *Ecclesiastical History* (Richter 2005:235); in the opening section where he laid out the plan of the book he wrote: "My work will begin, as I have said, with the economy [οἰκονομίας] of the Saviour Christ—which is loftier and greater than human conception—and with a discussion of his divinity [θεολογίας]. For it is necessary, inasmuch as we derive even our name from Christ, for one who proposes to write a history of the Christ to begin with the very origin of Christ, an economy [οἰκονομίας] more divine than many think" (Eusebius 2002:1:8–9). The distinction between economy and theology can also be found several times in Athanasius, who was the salient spokesperson on behalf of orthodoxy in the first half of the fourth century,[42] and it was completed by the Cappadocian Fathers in the second half of the century. According to this distinction, which can be found in Theodoret of Cyrus,[43] Maximus the Confessor,[44] John of Damascus,[45] and Theodore the Studite,[46]

Theology The Godhead out of time and space		
The society of believers in **Christ's Economy** (the communion between divinity as revealed in the world and humans)		
The Profane World Partnership in all that is human and outside the economy, including:		
Household	**Polis**	**Cosmopolitical Empire**

FIGURE 1.2. ECONOMY IN SPACE

any divine revelation necessarily takes place in the economy and as such is given over to theoretical discourse and technical know-how. As a consequence of the inclusion of the divine as it is reveals itself, the object revealed to the most esteemed theoretical gaze is included in the economy. On the other hand, theology endorses a mystical gaze in search of God (which is distinguished from the kataphatic theoretical gaze in search of him in the economy) so that the strict sense of theology becomes the discourse engaging in the thing that is (not) revealed in the mystical experience. As presented in a short letter written by Basil the Great in response to the inquiries of Amphilochius: "I do know that He exists; what His essence is, I look at as beyond intelligence. How then am I saved? Through faith. It is faith sufficient to know that God exists, without knowing what He is; and He is a rewarder of them that seek Him. So knowledge of the divine essence involves perception of His incomprehensibility, and the object of our worship is not that of which we comprehend the essence, but of which we comprehend that the essence exists" (Basil the Great 2003b: letter 234). The distinction between theology and economy introduced two far-reaching ramifications of space. The first was the distinction between the Godhead that subsists out of space and everything that exists in the world. The second was a distinction in the world between things that form part of the economy, i.e., are included in the space of appearance of the divine in the world, and profane matters, whether public or private.

As a result, human space is divided into three. The first is divinity as subsisting outside time and space, the second is occupied by the economy in which God and man both participate, while the third is a partnership in everything human that is not a part of the economy, such as the classical partnerships of the oikos and polis as well as the imperial *cosmopolis*.

COSMOLOGY AND ANTHROPOLOGY

The constitution of a human-divine economy is formed while keeping intact the Stoic providential relation between God and cosmos.[47] Many of the Church Fathers maintained the Stoic use of *oikonomia* to describe the mode in which the world is conducted and ordered by divine providence/nature (which entails an ontology of abundance—in contrast to the modern economic ontology of scarcity) and is subjected to the circular economy of cosmological time. Two early example of this use are the anonymous author of the *Epistle to Diognetus* (2002:IV:5), who described the changing of the seasons as God's economy, and the author of the apostolic constitution who writes that "the economy of the universe always continues, the stars do not cease for even an instant in their regular movements produced by the ordinance of God" (translation in Daniélou 1956:232).

Alongside the conservation of the cosmological sphere as created sphere in which God reveal himself, the Church Fathers erected a distinct sphere reserved for the human-divine economy, as expressed by Maximus the Confessor: "In breadth He is glorified by us, because of His most wise providence, which binds all things together, and His economy for our sake, which is passing marvelous and transcendently ineffable" (Maximus the Confessor, difficulty 10, translated in Louth 1996:121). The relations between God and cosmos were most often named oversight (see Azkoul 1968b:72–81). Even when called oikonomia the Fathers kept the distinction between the anthropological and the cosmological economies intact,[48] so that the human-divine economy, which Prestige terms "the special economy" (1964:xxi), appears against the background of a world existing by the grace of God. As argued by George Williams, the distinction between cosmological and anthropological economies was one of the points that separated the orthodox camp, which emphasized the word incarnated as part of the special relations between God and humans, and the Arian heterodoxy of the fourth century, which emphasized the word as the creator of the cosmos (Williams 1951a:12).[49]

2

Modeling the Economy

Economic Models

One of the consequences of Christianity's emergence in the fourth century as an imperial religion was that the meanings attached to *oikonomia* in the Christian mind became commonly sensed by the inhabitants of the empire. The shift in the prevailing meaning of the economy was accompanied by changes in its relations with philosophical life, the legal framework, and politics. These changes are the focus of the subsequent three chapters: chapter 3 traces the ways in which philosophical life was contained in the economy, chapter 4 presents the ways in which the relations between economy and politics were modeled in patristic theory and in church-state relations in the Eastern Christian Empire, and chapter 5 describes how pastoral economy operates in the state of exception. All the changes in relations of the economy to philosophy, as well as politics and the legal framework, were initiated by the redesign of the economic models discussed in this chapter.

The *first model* portrays the inner organization of the relationship that I term the Ontological Communion between the three personae of the Godhead: God the Father, God the Son, and the Holy Spirit.[1] The Ontological Communion subsists outside time and space and exceeds human reason, being depicted as *the* Self-sufficient (αὐτάρκης) community ever-to-subsist: a community that, against human reason, is the most unified of all possible communities and the one that manifests the greatest level of plurality. The Ontological Communion is perceived as an all-inclusive partnership, as a full communion of everything, including the partners' natures and their essences, each of the personae participating in it is wholly penetrated by his fellows and contains them to the fullest (a dynamic known as *perichoresis*). According to the Church Fathers, it is the full communion of interpenetration and mutual inclusion that subsists as the condition of appearance of the singular mode of being (*hypostasis*) of each of the Godhead's personae. So, for example, the singular mode of being of the Father is revealed in the way he penetrated the Son and the Holy Spirit and is contained by them. As I will show in chapter 3, the Ontological Communion will ultimately function as the model according to which the society of believers in Christ's economy (i.e., the Church) is designed.

The *second economic model* describes the hypostatic union that takes place in the economy of the incarnation. This model was formulated as follows by participants of the Fourth Ecumenical Council in the Chalcedonian Creed: in the economy of the incarnation, human nature and divine nature are united unconfusedly, immutably, indivisibly, inseparably in one persona and one hypostasis (ἀσυγχύτως, ἀτρέπτως, ἀδιαιρέτως, ἀχωρίστως. . . . εἰς ἓν πρόσωπον καὶ μίαν ὑπόστασιν). Much as in the first model, this one attempts to definine a *self-sufficient excess* that inherently exceeds human rationality. As discussed in chapter 4, the hypostatic union models the relationship between the society of believers in Christ's economy and the political community in the Eastern Christian Empire.

The *third economic model* encapsulates a description of that which takes place in perichoresis, that is, in the all-inclusive/all-penetrative communion between God and man in the economy of the incarnation. As my analysis shows, the boundaries of perichoresis are "undefined by definition": human sin and divine nature (this nature is the essence of the Ontological Communion, shared by the three personae of the Godhead) must remain outside its boundaries; within them are clearly located those operations of the persona of God the Son and sin-free man that unfold in the economy of the incarnation. These operations include erotic desire for God, self-askesis, accommodation (συγκατάβασις) to human nature, and love of humans (φιλανθρωπία) in accordance with their nature. As I demonstrate in chapter 5, this model informed the bishops' art of pastoral economy.

A number of reasons justify the anachronistic naming of these *prototypes* "models," a truly modern concept. The first implies the close linkage that can be found between them and the contemporary notion of economy, as both theorized with models and artfully conducted through models. Second, the concept of a "model," at least in its present-day usage, captures two dimensions that are lost when using the concept of prototype, now overloaded with no small number of (psychological) meanings. The first dimension is the dynamic quality of the thing being modeled. In both Late Antique Christianity and contemporary economics, the economic model describes activity operating in balance, a state of affairs that contemporary economists call equilibrium.[2] In both instances, the model describes a dynamic mode of conduct of similitudes. The second dimension captured by the concept of model is its twofold function as something that describes the world *and* also functions as an ideal to be sought after, serving for the active reshaping of the world in the hands of the economists, guided by their enlightening *theoria* (whether they be economists of salvation or contemporary ones of the market).[3] Differently put, the economic model describes the mysterious principle that actuates reality and is a paragon to be imitated, a mimesis by which the economy's proper conduct and growth are secured.

The principle of transcription is the mechanism that connects these models, establishes a hierarchy among them, and in addition enables economy's unlimited growth. It made its debut in Tatian's *Address to the Greeks*, where it is called economy and appears in the Godhead itself. It originates in the Ontological Communion, in the relationship between God the Father and God the Son; in this relationship the Father is the absolute monarch (literally, singular origin) and the Son is his perfect image transcribed. What singles out these original image relations is that nothing gets lost in transcription; the Son is the image of the Father, but he is also of the same essence and wholly contains and fully penetrates him. The transcription exceeds the Godhead into created world through the economy of the incarnation when the persona of God the Son is transcribed into created world in the sole persona of Christ, who in turn subsists as the inner-worldly transcript of the Godhead without anything of its nature being lost in the process. Freely acting from this crucial moment of inception onward, the inner-worldly transcription, economized in the Holy Spirit (the third persona of the Godhead), is concatenated. By means of

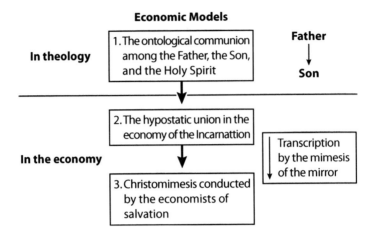

FIGURE 2.1. TRANSCRIPTION OF THE ECONOMIC MODELS

this concatenation, the economy grows, and new spheres are purified from human sin. These new, now purified, spheres are qualified in their turn to act as a transcript of the economy incarnated and concatenate it further. Through this principle of inclusive purification, the economy, incarnated in the flesh of one man, will be able to expand and encompass the whole of humanity. The principle of transcription is described as a relation of similitude that I term "the mimesis of the mirror."

In order to fully appreciate how the mimesis of the mirror functions, we should bear in mind that the ancient theory of optics was quite different from the modern one. As recounted by Plato (1925d, *Timaeus* 46, 1925b, *Sophist* 266), when gazing at a mirror, the ray of light emerging from the eye meets a ray proceeding from the perceived object, and the image that appears in the mirror is formed by a mixture of both. According to these optics, the image perceived in the mirror has real existence on its surface.[4] The Christian mirror is a miraculous one to be distinguished from the earthly mirror. The persona appearing in it is made up of the two rays united "unconfusedly, immutably, indivisibly and inseparably." The second economic model describes the persona of God the Son (that appears in the *mirror of being* that is described by the first model) as he participated in the economy of the incarnation, that is, in the *mirror of becoming*.[5] In the third model, which perpetuates the third link in the transcription chain, a mimesis of that which is held in common between God and humans is conducted in the persona that appears in the mirror of becoming (i.e., in the economy of the incarnation).

The First Economic Model

In the ontology held by the Church Fathers, the Godhead is a community (the Ontological Communion) in which the economy of mystery is always already present. The Ontological Communion, according to this conception, existed before time was created and before the first human partnership was established. Its internal organization was formulated in the "Cappadocian settlement" as "one essence—three modes of being" (μία ουσία—τρείς υποστάσεις). Basil the Great, his close friend Gregory of Nazianzus, and his younger brother Gregory of Nyssa, all natives of the region of Cappadocia (hence the Cappadocian Fathers), formulated this settlement as an answer to "the great problem of the fourth century[, which] was to express at once divine unity and diversity, the coincidence in God of the monad and the triad" (Lossky 1978:40).

The approach taken by the Cappadocian Fathers, encapsulated in the aforementioned formula, is twofold: on the one hand it produces a distinction, and on the other hand an identity. A distinction is made between the common nature/essence and the singular mode of being; an identity is made between the persona and the singular mode of being.

1. The Cappadocian Fathers distinguished between two, somewhat technical terms, which were practically synonymous in theoretical texts, Greek and Christian alike, up to that time: *ousia* and *hypostasis*.[6] A distinction between the two, if one existed, was observable in everyday language, where *hypostasis* was rendered as "subsistence," and apparently "among certain stoics, it had assumed the sense of distinct substance, of the individual" (Lossky 1978:41). According to the Cappadocian Fathers, who charged the concepts with a new and distinct meaning, God the Father, God the Son, and the Holy Spirit are distinguished by their mode of being, but undistinguished in their common essence (Basil the Great 2003a:59), a unity that originates in the communion (*koinonia*) of the Godhead (Basil the Great 2003a:45).[7] A common essence is shared by the self-sustained communion of the Godhead, this essence being the communion itself. As described by

Theodoret of Cyrus: "For profane wisdom there is no difference between ousia and hypostases. For ousia means that which is, and hypostases that which subsists. But according to the teaching of the Fathers, there is between ousia and hypostasis the same difference as between common and particular" (Lossky 1976:51).

2. Alongside the distinction between the common essence and the singular mode of being, the Cappadocian Fathers paired the latter with persona.[8] By doing so they equated internal essence with the mask it puts on when appearing in front of others, rendering them identical. According to Zizioulas "By calling the Person a 'mode of being' . . . the Cappadocians introduced a revolution into Greek ontology, since they said for the first time in the history of philosophy 1. that a *prosopon* is not secondary to being, but its hypostasis; and 2. that a hypostasis, that is, an ontological category, is relational in its very nature, it is *prosopon*" (Zizioulas 2006:186). Vladimir Lossky 1978:41–42 summarized this two-fold course in the following manner:

> Ousia and hypostasis were, at the outset, practically synonyms, both being concerned with the sphere of being. The Fathers, by specializing their meaning, came to be able, without external hindrance, to root personhood in being, and to personalize ontology. Ousia, in the Trinity, is not an abstract idea of divinity, a rational essence binding three divine individuals. . . . As for hypostasis—and it is here, under the influence of Christianity, that a true advancement of thought emerges—it no longer contains anything individual. . . . The hypostases, on the other hand, are infinitely united and infinitely different: they are the divine nature, but none possesses it, none breaks it to its own exclusivity. It is precisely because they share it without restriction, that the latter is not divided. And this indivisible nature gives every hypostasis its depth, confirms its uniqueness, reveals itself in the unity of the unique, in this communion in which every person, without confusion, shares integrally in all the others: the more they are one the more they are diverse, since nothing of the communal nature escapes them; and the more they are diverse the more they are one, since their unity is not impersonal unity, but a fertile tension of irreducible diversity an abundance of "circumincession [perichoresis] without mixture or confusion" (St. John of Damascus).

Despite their resemblance, there is one crucial difference between the mode of being's appearance in the persona and the mode in which the self reveals itself in public within the political community.[9] The political community of the classical moment is a limited partnership, one that necessitates the existence of spaces and things kept beyond its boundaries in order for it to subsist (see *HC* 50–54). It was for this reason that Aristotle limited the political community to a copartnership in place (τόπος), rulership, and law. Matters are quite different in the Ontological Communion. Within it, each mode of being is revealed in the persona by full communion in the essence itself and nothing is left out of communion.[10] The worldly distinction between t he limited partnership of politics—in which the self reveals itself through the persona—and the economic partnership in everything between master and matron does not exist in the Ontological Communion. Here, miraculously, plurality appears in unity that appears in plurality; it is *the* truly self-sufficient community precisely because it is the most unified of all possible communities *and* the one that manifests the greatest level of plurality. It lacks the primordial necessity of economic unity as a condition for the appearance of the persona in political plurality. The distinction between the two communities (political and economic), like the existential presence of necessity, is conceived as a by-product of the human condition.[11] The communion is seen as a *full communion* in everything, notwithstanding the nature and essence of its participants: the Ontological Communion is an all-penetrating communion in which the persona is identical to the mode of being. Put differently, full communion is "the condition of appearance" of the singular mode of being in the persona: the fuller the communion, the brighter the appearance of the persona in the mirror of being. That which is held in common by the three personae of the Godhead is precisely this all-penetrative/all-inclusive partnership.[12] The level of sharing in it exceeds by far that of the economic partnership between the master and the matron of the earthly oikos, the kind that Plato suggested ought to be conducted in the polis (a proposition so outrageous that Aristotle devoted the entire second book of his *Politics* to refuting it).

Thus, the Cappadocian settlement can be represented as follows: in order to attain the goal in service of which the distinction between the economic and the political communities was established, namely, to perpetuate the singular mode of being of each and everyone in his or her persona, what needs to be done is to radicalize the platonic community into a community that includes the self and penetrates it fully. Such a community, which does not submit to the human condition of distinction between (communities of) unity and (community of) plurality, is transcribed into the society of believers in Christ's economy. This conception is expressed in great clarity in Letter 38,[13] which is attributed to Basil the Great, and was apparently composed by his younger brother Gregory of Nyssa:[14]

> And with respect to the nature of each individual Person, no distinction is perceived between one and the next; but within the community [koinonia] of the ousia the individual characteristics of each one shine forth. . . . For all the attributes of the Father are beheld in the Son, and all the attributes of the Son are in the Father, inasmuch as the Son wholly abides in the Father and, in turn, has the Father wholly in Himself. Thus the hypostasis of the Son is, as it were, the form and character of the knowledge of the Father; and the hypostasis of the Father is made known in the form of the Son, their observed individuality remaining among them as a clear distinction between their hypostases.
>
> (Basil the Great 2003b, Letter 38)[15]

The Cappadocian concept of the persona, upon whose genuinely innovative nature both Lossky and Zizioulas insist,[16] is accompanied by the appearance of a new model for conducting the conduct of the society of believers.

Perichoresis in the Ontological Communion

The Cappadocian author of Letter 38 describes what would a few centuries later be called by John of Damascus, in his summary of orthodox dogma, perichoresis.[17] This concept, originating most likely from the Stoic concept of mixture, "means a complete mutual interpenetration of two substances that preserves the identity and properties of each intact" (Harrison 1991:54); it is "the mutual coextension . . . of two things into one another at all points" (Wolfson 1956:420). The concept of perichoresis is used to describe the partnership of the Ontological Communion as a mutual interpenetration/inclusion. Each of the partakers in the divine nature is penetrated by his partners and includes them to the fullest. As described by John of Damascus:

The abiding and resting of the Persons in one another is not in such a manner that they coalesce or become confused, but, rather, so that they adhere to one another, for they are without interval between them and inseparable and their mutual indwelling (περιχώρησιν) is without confusion. For the Son is in the Father and the Spirit, and the Spirit is in the Father and the Son, and the Father is in the Son and the Spirit, and there is no merging or blending or confusion.... It is impossible for this to be found in any created nature.

(John of Damascus 1958:I, 14)

And elsewhere:

In the Divinity we confess one nature, while we hold three really existing Persons. And we hold everything belonging to the nature and the essence to be simple, while we recognize the difference of the Persons as residing only in the three properties of being uncaused and Father, of being caused and Son, and of being caused and proceeding. And we understand them to be inseparable and without interval between them, and united to one another and mutually immanent (περιχωρούσας) without confusion. And we understand them, while being separated without interval, to be united without confusion, for they are three, even though they are united. For, although each is subsistent in itself, that is to say, is a perfect Person and has its own property or distinct manner of existence, they are united in their essence.

(John of Damascus 1958:III, 5)

In the Ontological Communion the persona is fully revealed in an all-penetrative/all-inclusive partnership. The metaphor of the mirror might help clarify things, so that we may grasp what the persona is and how the singular mode of being is reflected in it. Thus, for instance, the singular mode of being of God the Son is the mode in which the personae of the Father and the Holy Spirit are reflected in the mirror of being that he is. What distinguishes each of the personae in communion is the singular mode by which he is penetrated by, and includes to the fullest the other two personae; the deeper the inclusion/penetration the brighter the appearance of the persona in the mirror. In this ontology the singular persona, the "truth of the subject," can only reveal itself in full communion, in the mode in which the images of the others are reflected and participate in the persona *qua* mirror. This is *the economic model of the Ontological Communion.*

It should be noted that the transcription of the first economic model into human society has won some popularity among contemporary theologians. These theories, which came to be known as the "social Trinity," argue that "the church reflects the divine life," as Lossky (1978:40) puts it. The notion of the social Trinity can be found in writers affiliated with churches Orthodox, Catholic, and Protestant: its most prolific representatives in the Orthodox Church are Lossky and Zizioulas. In the Lutheran Church the idea came to be associated with Jorgen Moltmann, who advances what might be termed a theological republicanism. This program calls for the transcription of its idea of freedom into human society and for a redefinition of history as a struggle to create a community, in which the freedom of one does not come on the expense of another (thus replacing the concept of history as a struggle between individuals over power; Moltmann 1981). In the Catholic Church the idea was promoted by Catharine Mowry LaCugna (1993:243–317), who proposes an ontology of being-in-relation based upon the meaning of persona; LaCugna suggests understanding human existence as "a persona in relation." The social Trinity appears in the writing of feminist theologians such as Patricia Wilson-Kastner (1983:131–33), who promotes a feminist ethics of inclusion, community, and freedom, as well as in "liberation theologians" such as Leonardo Boff (1988:54), who invoke it in order to promote a material partnership.[18]

The Archaic Transcription: The Transcript Is of the Same Nature as the Origin

Alongside the full communion, implying full equality between God's three modes of being, differences exist in the character of the thing that distinguishes each of the personae. While the mode of revelation of the personae in the mirror is similar, the person that appears is not. The identity of the mode of revelation is accompanied by a hierarchy formed between the modes of being of the personae who share the divine nature. The persona of God the Father appears in his Son and in the Holy Spirit as a definite origin from which the Son is begotten and from which the Holy Spirit proceeds (Harrison 1993:190–91): "Now, the name of that which has no beginning is the Father, and of the Beginning the Son, and of that which is with the Beginning, the Holy Ghost, and the three have one Nature—God. And the union is the Father from Whom and to Whom the order of Persons runs its course, not so as to be confounded, but so as to be possessed, without distinction of time, of will, or of power" (Gregory of Nazianzus's Oration 42:15). "The doctrine of the monarchy had begun by basing the unity of God on the single person of God the Father" (Prestige 1964:254). God the Father, by virtue of his sheer Fatherhood, is the origin, while God the Son, being the Son, is the transcript. The uniqueness of the origin-transcript relationship unfolding in the Ontological Communion is that nothing gets lost in transcription.[19] The *principle of transcription* is described, yet again, with great clarity in Letter 38:

> We shall take up other expressions of the apostle, in which he says "the image of the invisible God" and again "the image of His goodness," not in order to divide the image from the archetype with respect to the principles of invisibility and goodness, but in order that it may be shown that that [the image] is the same as the prototype, even as it is different. For the principle of the image would not be preserved unless in all respects it retained a manifest and unalterable [likeness]. Accordingly, he who has conceived of the beauty of the image is also aware of the archetype. And he who receives into his mind the form, as it were, of the Son, forms an image also of the figure of the hypostasis of the Father, seeing the latter through the former—not seeing the unbegottenness of the Father in the copy (for then [the Son] would be in every way the same [as the Father] and not different), but discerning the unbegotten beauty in the begotten. For just as one, having perceived the reflection of the shape of the thing that is reflected in a bright mirror, has a vivid knowledge of the face represented [there] , thus he who recognizes the Son, through his knowledge of the Son, receives into his heart the figure of the Father's hypostasis.
>
> (Basil the Great 2003b:Letter 38)

The Son is indeed the image of the persona of the Father, yet at the same time is identical to him in essence and contains and penetrates him fully. We are presented here with a different set of relations between origin and transcribed image from those usually described as obtaining in Greek thought up until that point. As discussed in the first chapter, the ancient Greeks held that the origin and the image were distinguished by the order of which they formed a part: the original was of the order of being, while the image was of the order of becoming. Time was thought to move in a circle, since that was its way of reflecting eternity, to the greatest degree possible, in a world given to constant change. One consequence of this unbridgeable gap was that any image was considered, by necessity, a "pale shadow" of its origin to the same degree that circular time was a pale shadow of eternity. Situating both origin *and* transcribed image as equal members in the order of being introduced a radical change to be conceived in relations of transcription. This can be discerned in the way that the relation between the origin (God the Father) and the image (God the Son) is reflected and participates in the persona of the transcribed image, in the mirror of the being of the Son. The persona of the transcribed image that appears in the mirror contains the thing reflected in it in fullness without affecting its nature, allowing both modes of being (i.e., Father and Son/origin and copy) to be "unconfused and immutable." We encountered this principle of transcription for the first time in Tatian's claim that nothing of the origin is lost in the transcription of the Son. The second half of the equation is formulated in Letter 38: the Son is a perfect transcript of the Father, of a nature and essence identical to the Father's. The perichoresis that occurs in the Ontological Communion ensures that it will be so, since, on the one hand, there is nothing left in the Father that does not penetrate the Son while, on the other hand, there is no place in the Son where the Father is not present. Otherwise stated, nothing of the Father's mode of being is lost when it appears in the Son. This is the how Basil the Great describes the principle of transcription in his tractate *On the Holy Spirit*:

> So that according to the distinction of Persons, both are one and one, and according to the community of Nature, one. How, then, if one and one, are there not two Gods? Because we speak of a king, and of the king's image, and not of two kings. The majesty is not cloven in two, nor the glory divided. The sovereignty and authority over us is one, and so the doxology ascribed by us is not plural but one; because the honour paid to the image passes on to the prototype. Now what in the one case the image is by reason of imitation, that in the other case the Son is by nature; and as in works of art the likeness is dependent on the form, so in the case of the

divine and uncompounded nature the union consists in the communion of the Godhead.

(Basil the Great 2003a, De Spiritu Sancto 18:45)

The divine potency to fully penetrate a thing lying outside itself and transcribe itself into it without anything being lost either in the origin or in the transcribed image is not compromised when divinity participates and is reflected in the mirror of *becoming*. The outcome is that nothing gets lost in the transcript of the transcript; in its transcription there is a total lack of amortization. This divine potency would play a crucial role when divinity began to operate in created world in the economy of the incarnation at *the* crucial moment when the invisible revealed itself in the mirror of the visible, without losing anything of its nature. The principle of participation/reflection in the mirror allows an endless concatenation of divinity in the created world, which in turn allows the unlimited growth of the economy by inclusive purification of everything lying outside it; at the moment the divine appeared in the transcribed mirror, the mirror itself became fully capable of projecting the persona participating in it to yet another mirror. This is accomplished without the essence of the persona reflected being compromised along the way. See, for example, the way Gregory of Nyssa describes how the divine reflection in the human mind is reflected in his members:

For since the most beautiful and supreme good of all is the Divinity Itself, to which incline all things that have a tendency towards what is beautiful and good, we therefore say that the mind, as being in the image of the most beautiful, itself also remains in beauty and goodness so long as it partakes as far as is possible in its likeness to the archetype; but if it were at all to depart from this it is deprived of that beauty in which it was. And as we said that the mind was adorned by the likeness of the archetypal beauty, being formed as though it were a mirror to receive the figure of that which it expresses, we consider that the nature which is governed by it is attached to the mind in the same relation, and that it too is adorned by the beauty that the mind gives, being, so to say, a mirror of the mirror; and that by it is swayed and sustained the material element of that existence in which the nature is contemplated. Thus so long as one keeps in touch with the other, the communication of the

true beauty extends proportionally through the whole series, beautify-
ing by the superior nature that which comes next to it.

(Gregory of Nyssa 2004a, *On the Making of Man* 9–10)

This is that which reveals itself in the economy of the incarnation: God the
Son, the transcribed image of God the Father, appears in the (human) flesh
without losing anything of His divine nature. In other words, that which
appears in the mirror of becoming of the economy, in the appearance of
the mode of being of the Son (to be followed after Pentecost by the Holy
Spirit's appearance) is the reflection of the one divine essence held in common by the three personae of the Godhead. These three personae participate and are reflected in the persona that appeared in the world in the
"Christ event": that which is reflected and participates in the economy of
the incarnation are the personae who share divine essence, as they are reflected and participate in the mirror of God the Son and in the mirror of
the Holy Spirit, in the Ontological Communion.

The Second Economic Model: The Hypostatic Union in the Economy of the Incarnation

For human society to become a mirror in which the Godhead participates
and in which it is reflected, yet another mechanism is needed alongside
the principle of transcription that incarnates in the economy. This addi-
tional mechanism is the hypostatic union. The economy is what transpires
when a human freely chooses to gaze at and participate in the divine persona that reveals itself in the economy, whether of Christ's body, the
Church, the martyr's flesh, a human's own soul, and in the eyes of his fellow members in the society of believers. The hypostatic union that occurs
in the economy is described concisely in the declaration of faith composed
by the participants of the Fourth Ecumenical Council convened at Chalcedon in 451 CE:

> We all with one voice teach the confession of one and the same Son,
> our Lord Jesus Christ: the same perfect in divinity and perfect in hu-
> manity, the same truly God and truly man, of a rational soul and a
> body; consubstantial with the Father as regards his divinity, and the

In the hypostatic union, the human and divine natures unite

indivisibly, inseparably   unconfusedly, immutably

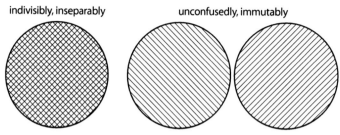

FIGURE 2.2. THE SECOND ECONOMIC MODEL

same consubstantial with us as regards his humanity; like us in all respects except for sin; begotten before the ages from the Father as regards his divinity, and in the last days the same for us and for our salvation from Mary, the virgin God-bearer as regards his humanity; one and the same Christ, Son, Lord, only-begotten, acknowledged in two natures which undergo no confusion, no change, no division, no separation; at no point was the difference between the natures taken away through the union, but rather the property of both natures is preserved and comes together into a single person and a single hypostases; he is not parted or divided into two persons, but is one and the same only-begotten Son, God, Word, Lord Jesus Christ.

(The Definition of Faith of the Council of Chalcedon)

The participants of the council declare that the hypostatic union is that which occurs in the economy. The incarnation is designated as such three times in the first, less frequently cited, part of the declaration that is dedicated to refuting a number of the heresies concerning the God Bearer (Θεοτόκος) Mary and the natures of Christ.[20] The authors of the Chalcedonian Creed declare that in the sole persona and mode of being of Christ the divine and human nature are united "unconfusedly, immutably, indivisibly, inseparably," thus in created world a self-sufficient excess that transcends human reason and logic appears,[21] since it can acknowledge either full union or full intersection, but cannot comprehend both occurring at once.

In the economy of the incarnation humans witness a perichoresis between a divine nature and a human nature.[22] In the divine-human perichoresis described by the second economic model, we encounter the mode through which the economy grows when transcription is accompanied by a perichoresis that sets in motion a process of purification by inclusion; the inclusive purification that took place in the hypostatic union when God the Son took upon himself (i.e., encompassed) human nature in its fullness. By doing so, he purified it from the sin that was transcribed in it ever since Adam sinned.

The perichoresis that takes place in the economy is an inner-worldly transcription of that which occurs in the Ontological Communion as summarized by John of Damascus.[23] "Now, just as the three Persons of the Holy Trinity are united without confusion and are distinct without separation and have number without the number causing division, or separation, or estrangement, or severance among them . . . so in the same way the natures of Christ, although united, are united without confusion, and, although mutually immanent (περιχωροῦσιν), do not suffer any change or transformation of one into the other" (John of Damascus 1958, The Orthodox Faith:III:5).[24] And, with direct reference to the mimesis, "although we say that the natures of the Lord are mutually immanent (περιχώρησις), we know that this immanence (perichoresis) comes from the divine nature" (III:7). The boundaries of the economic perichoresis appear in patristic thought as "undefined by definition." Not all of man partakes in the economy—only his purified nature. As for the divinity who partakes in the economy, the nature and essence of the Ontological Communion are kept outside the perichoresis. This absolute boundary is described by Basil the Great.[25] "We know our God from His principles of action [ἐνεργειῶν],[26] but do not undertake to approach near to His essence. His operations come down to us, but His essence remains beyond our reach" (Basil the Great 2003b, Letter 234:1). The economy's relative boundary is set by the principle of action of the Godhead revealing itself in the mirror of becoming through the persona of the Holy Spirit in the persona of the Son. On the human side of the economy, the boundary is set by human vice (the latter can be exceeded by the human economist when he imitates the divine mode of conduct that unfolds in the economy of the incarnation). One result of this double, absolute-relative boundary is that even when the economy exceeds the boundaries set by law, and its principle of action is revealed, man can never exceed the economy, and, as far as the human mind goes, nothing can exceed the boundaries of the economy.

We can now begin to evaluate the operation of the models that constitute the economy in patristic thought. The economy begins with the actuation of the principle of transcription when the persona of God the Son reveals itself in the mirror of becoming without anything being lost in transcription. At that instance the mirror in which the Son of God is reflected and participates is fully purified by the hypostatic union, in which "that which He has not assumed He has not healed; but that which is united to His Godhead is also saved" (Gregory of Nazianzus 1893b, Letter 101). The human that participates in the economy of the incarnation retains its distinctive nature, but this nature has already been purified; although human, he partakes of a divine persona, meaning that God is reflected and participates in him without God's losing anything of his nature manifested in the persona of the economy. This purification, in turn, allows the appearance of the Holy Spirit in the "economic body" after the Son's return to his Father. The persona in which the hypostatic union between the divine and the human occurs is by now ready to continue the concatenation and to reveal itself in yet another mirror, to purify it, and so forth, until the fullness of the ages. The mode of conduct that allows the growth of the economy by inclusive purification is described in chapter 4, where relations between economy and politics are discussed.

The Third Economic Model: Christomimesis

The third economic model captures that which occurs in the perichoresis of the persona of the economy in which a hypostatic union between God and man takes place. This model is of crucial importance since it guides the conduct of the human economist, who imitates it when conducting the conduct of others. The model describes that which is held in common between the divine nature that appears in the persona of the Son and sin-free human nature. This common thing is held to be a mystery; a mystery that occurs in the "economy suitable to the fullness of the ages, that is, the recapitulation of all things in Christ, things in the heavens and thing on the earth" (Ephesians 1:10), "the economy of the mystery which from eternity has been hid in God " (Ephesians 3:9). This is the same economy whose mysteries are explored in the vast majority of the patristic texts from the second half of the second century, in conformity with Paul's categorical

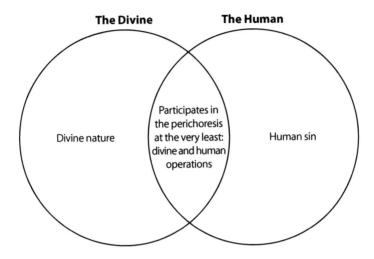

The Divine   **The Human**

Divine nature

Participates in
the perichoresis
at the very least:
divine and human
operations

Human sin

FIGURE 2.3. THE BOUNDARIES OF THE PERICHORESIS

imperative "to enlighten all [people] regarding the economy of the mystery" (Ephesians 3:9).[27]

Any attempt to define that which God shares with a human in the perichoresis occurring in the economy is bound to encounter obstacles. It is, after all, *the* mystery that lies at the kernel of the economy. I believe the fact that it is a mystery is the crux of the debate in contemporary literature that attempts to tackle the puzzle. It seems that the patristic mind is utterly certain that two things are left out of the communion between God and man: human sin and divine nature/essence. In no way does this communion involve the nature common to the three personae of the Godhead, an essence that by its nature "in and of itself transcends all conceptual comprehension, being inaccessible and unapproachable to speculative thoughts" (Gregory of Nyssa 2000:Homilies on the Beatitudes, Homily VI). On the other hand, it is a communion in something that is "like us in respects other than sin" as declared by the Chalcedonian Creed, so that which unfolds in the perichoresis, that which is held in communion between God and man, is their operations in the economy and in no way includes divine nature or human sin; man's operations include erotic desire for God, and God's include self-askesis, accommodation (συγκατάβασις) to human nature, and love of humans (φιλανθρωπία) in accordance with their nature.[28]

PRAXIS OF VIRGINITY: EROTICISM AND SELF-ASKESIS

In response to Diotima's questions, Socrates acknowledges that what appears in man when he approaches the self-sufficient in itself is the desire to beget in the beautiful, and among all men he is the one to

> look upon essential beauty entire, pure and unalloyed . . . [the one who] could behold the divine beauty itself, in its unique form. . . . Looking that way, observing that vision by the proper means, and having it ever with him. . . . He sees the beautiful through that which makes it visible, to breed not illusions but true examples of virtue, since his contact is not with illusion but with truth. So when he has begotten a true virtue and has reared it up. . . . And if another man is to be immortal so does he.
>
> (Plato 1925c, *Symposium*, 211–12)

The human persona who serves as the model of erotic desire to beget in the good and the beautiful is the one who achieved this in the economy of the incarnation: the Virgin Mary.[29] The begetting of God the Son by his Father is incarnated in a virgin named Mary who, longing for God with a nonsaturated desire, begot God in the flesh. The Virgin Mary, the sole human persona to participate in the economy of the incarnation, is called "the God bearer, for this name embraces the whole mystery of the economy" (John of Damascus 1958, *The Orthodox Faith* III:12). She exemplifies the erotic model for the economist, who, it scarcely deserves mention, is a man. The practice of virginity is modeled after the transcription of the Father in the Son, which is both reflected in and participates in the flesh of the Virgin Mary; "In the fifth century, this parallel between the Father and the Virgin officially entered the Church's dogma through its inclusion in the Chalcedonian Definition. . . . Her parenthood is the most exact human icon of the divine fatherhood" (Harrison 1993:206–10).[30] A clear expression of the economic model that is transcribed in the Virgin Mary appears at the beginning of a tractate named *On Virginity*:

> And here at the outset is a paradox, viz. that virginity is found in Him, Who has a Son and yet without passion has begotten Him. It is included too in the nature of this Only-begotten God, Who struck the first note of all this moral innocence; it shines forth equally in His pure and passionless generation.

Again a paradox; that the Son should be known to us by virginity. . . . It is the property of spiritual existence and of such singular excellence, yet by the love of God it has been bestowed on those who have received their life from the will of the flesh and from blood; . . . What happened in the stainless Mary when the fullness of the Godhead which was in Christ shone out through her, that happens in every soul that leads by rule the virgin life. No longer indeed does the Master come with bodily presence; we know Christ no longer according to the flesh; but, spiritually, He dwells in us and brings His Father with Him, as the Gospel somewhere tells.[31]

(Gregory of Nyssa 2004f, *On Virginity* 2)

Gregory of Nyssa, apparently echoing the conversation between Socrates and Diotima, writes that the desire for God is man's way of begetting himself in the spirit.[32] Moreover, according to Gregory, the desire for God nourishes itself, generating an excessive desire that is economized by a theoretical and practical disposition of prudence that in turn generates surplus. The surplus generated, which remains immanent to the economy (rather than being externalized), is the outgrowth of an unsaturated desire that feeds upon itself. The eroticism that incarnates in the persona of the Mother of God who begot "in the economy" is rendered into a desire to beget *in the Spirit, through the Son, to the Father* by cleansing the soul so that it becomes a stainless mirror in which the glory of God is reflected in the eyes of the other members in the society of believers. In a eulogy written by Gregory of Nazianzus in loving memory of his friend Basil, he describes the erotic practice of virginity as reflected in his eyes, when gazing at his friend's persona:

Who then paid more honour to virginity, or had more control of the flesh, not only by his personal example, but in those under his care? Whose are the convents, and the written regulations, by which he subdued every sense, and regulated every member, and won to the real practice of virginity, turning inward the view of beauty, from the visible to the invisible; and by wasting away the external, and withdrawing fuel from the flame, and revealing the secrets of the heart to God, Who is the only bridegroom of pure souls, and takes in with himself the watchful souls, if they go to meet him with lamps burning and a plentiful supply of oil?

(Gregory of Nazianzus 1983a:Oration 43:62)

The disposition of virginity is composed of theoretical and practical modes of conduct.[33] The theoretical mode includes turning one's gaze inward (in-sight, *en-optika*), toward the beauty that appears in the soul by revealing the secrets of the heart to God,[34] the groom from the Song of Songs, for whom the virgin soul longs. Gregory's reference to the Parable of the Ten Virgins elucidates the prudent mode of conduct in the economy,[35] i.e., the practical philosophy of askesis, which enables a theoretical desire for God. So that the door not be shut before the prudent virgin soul (Matthew 25:10–12), it must withdraw its "erotic energy" from the body ("withdrawing fuel from the flame"), keeping it available to beget in the Spirit by erotically desiring God. In order to do so, the virgin soul must reflect Basil's persona and allow him to participate in the mirror of her soul, "subduing every sense, regulating every member." It can be seen how the three forms of philosophical life enumerated by Foucault (in-sight, eroticism, askesis) are reflected in the persona of Basil the Great.[36] To these one must add a fourth, described by Foucault in *Security, Territory, Population* and in his 1980 lectures *On the Government of the Living*: the *philanthropia* Basil the Great exercised toward the souls whose economy was under his care. As Gregory insisted on pointing out, Basil economized virginity not only through his personal example. He did so by founding convents and writing manuals of regulations dedicated to the practice of virginity:

> Moreover he reconciled most excellently and united the solitary and the community life. These had been in many respects at variance and dissension, while neither of them was in absolute and unalloyed possession of good or evil: the one being more calm and settled, tending to union with God, yet not free from pride, inasmuch as its virtue lies beyond the means of testing or comparison; the other, which is of more practical service, being not free from the tendency to turbulence. He founded cells for ascetics and hermits, but at no great distance from his cenobitic communities, and, instead of distinguishing and separating the one from the other, as if by some intervening wall, he brought them together and united them, in order that the contemplative spirit might not be cut off from society, nor the active life be uninfluenced by the contemplative.

(Gregory of Nazianzus 2003a, Oration 43:62)

THE DIVINE OPERATION IN THE ECONOMY: INCLUSIVE PHILANTHROPY BY ACCOMMODATION

The philanthropy[37] demonstrated toward those whom the economist (who is situated at the heart of the society of believers as a transcribed image of God)[38] is called upon to economize, is defined by Nicholas Mystikos an "an imitation of divine philanthropy" in the form of "salvatory accommodation [οἰκονομία ... ἔστ σωτηριώδης συγκατάβασις]" (Nicholas Mystikos 1973, Letter 32).

Nicholas renders the economy as a mimesis of the philanthropy manifested by God the Son. Such a mimesis is conducted at the "microeconomic" level by accommodation to the souls whose economy is subject to the economist's supervision. These souls are the links concatenated from the economist in the "chain of purification" through his assumption of their sins (see Foucault 2007:170–72). At the "macroeconomic" level, this mimesis is set in motion when the "principle of economy" is enacted, conducted in relation to those *outside the economy and yet belonging*, as described in some detail in chapter 5.

Afterword: Trial Balance of Oikonomia in the Three Moments of Greek Antiquity

The formalization of the economic models enables accounting for a trial balance of the transformations and modifications of the definition of *economy* since it was first formulated in Socrates' dialogue with Critobulus. The definition of *economy* in the classical moment, which I extracted from pre-Christian texts,[39] was that, *faced with the human condition of excess, one must acquire a theoretical and practical disposition of prudence in order to fulfill the economy and generate surplus that is alien to it and appears outside its boundaries. This surplus, in turn, enables (but does not necessitate) the existence of a political community.*

In the Christian moment the economy is no longer the sphere where the multitudes are enslaved by the one so that he can appear in the public sphere. Instead, it has become a sphere where the multitudes willingly choose to partake in the One who is multiple. Given the essential difference between the classical and the Christian economies, it is surprising that the definition of the economy has hardly changed; all that is needed for it to suit the Orthodox definition is to replace one word—*outside* with *inside*—and erase four other words: *enable,"but does not.* The rest of the definition remains intact: *faced with the human condition of excess, one must acquire a theoretical and practical disposition of prudence in order to fulfill the economy and generate surplus that is alien to it and appears inside its boundaries. This surplus, in turn, necessitates the existence of a political community.* Four constitutive elements that take part in the alteration of that which is being defined immediately come to mind: 1. the origin of excess; 2. the act of alienation; 3. man's enterprise of perpetuating himself; 4. the political context (which is dealt with in chapter 4).

1. *The origin of excess* and the human condition that accompanies it have changed almost beyond recognition. Notwithstanding the differences between the answers offered by various schools of thought, most of the ancients identified the circularity of nature as the origin of excess that appears in the economy. In the Christian formation its origin is considered to be the Ontological Communion between the three personae of the Godhead.

2. In the *classical formation* the political community alienates itself from the economy. In the *imperial formation* we witness how man strains to avoid alienation and to become at home in the world. In the *Christian formation* a hypostatic union between classical alienation and imperial becoming-at-home takes place. The Christian economist alienates himself from each and every imperial economy to become at home when communing with God in the society of believers in Christ's economy;[40] man becomes at home only in a perichoresis with some One whose nature is alien to him beyond recognition, and this ontological alienness is positioned at the heart of the society of believers. In the persona incarnated in the economy, *in Christ's body,* the Orthodox Christian is a member. Something whose nature is totally alien to man reveals itself, and despite his alienness he can contain its operation and be included in it.

3. The alternations in *man's enterprise for perpetuating himself* are somewhat parallel to the stages (as revealed in Diotima's questions) undertaken by the man who carries the seed of Eros in his soul, in his quest to perpetuate himself. In the classical moment men perpetuated themselves by pursuing the ideal mode of life, exceeding the boundaries of the economy; in the

imperial moment men did so by being governed in multiple economies; the Christians do so by partaking in the economy of the One who is multiple.

Alongside these alternations we witness a shift in the persona who composes the economic texts and to whom most of them are addressed: in classical texts this persona is the master/citizen who heads the oikos; in the imperial texts he is accompanied by the sage; both are replaced by the theoretical economist in Christian texts.

Compared with the minor changes in the definition of the economy, the Church Fathers radically altered the conception of the human condition as defined by Aristotle. As will be recalled, in the beginning of the *Politics* Aristotle presented the categorical imperative "to begin with talking about the economy" (*Pol.* 1253b). In my analysis of this imperative, I claimed that it implies an ontology in which the human condition that reveals itself is that the *economy begins with necessity*. Conversely, the human condition that reveals itself in the Orthodox ontology is that the *economy begins with freedom*. Tatian, who called this free act "economy," described God the Father as freely begetting his Son, a self-sufficient excess that willingly exceeds the Ontological Communion into created world. Unlike the personae who together constitute the Ontological Communion, humans, by their created nature, are faced with something that they cannot grasp with their mind which is bounded by space and time. The nature of that thing remains an ontological alienness for them: the Cappadocian Fathers describe it as the essence common to the modes of being of the Godhead, in what I termed the Ontological Communion. In accordance with the altered ontology of the economy, the categorical imperative changes too: Aristotle's imperative "*by necessity* to begin with talking about the economy" is replaced with "*by freedom* to begin with talking about the economy." The embarrassment occasioned by the fact that necessity lies at the beginning of every public speech was replaced with the mystery that is the hallmark of concerted speech and action originating in freedom. Hence the economy no longer begins with the embarrassment of necessity. It originates in the mysteries of freedom of which the economists are commanded to enlighten all (Ephesians 3:9).

The patristic perception of humans as created in the image and likeness of God is transposed into the concluding element of the human condition, formulated as follows: *ultimately, human action in concert necessarily generates surplus*. The phrasing of the concluding part of this formulation has not

TABLE 2.1   TRIAL BALANCE OF THE ECONOMY IN ITS THREE PREMODERN MOMENTS

PARAMETER/ MOMENT	CLASSICAL	IMPERIAL	CHRISTIAN
Origin of excess	nature's circularity	nature's circularity	the Ontological Communion
Alienation	the political community alienates itself from the economy	to avoid alienation by becoming at home in the world	alienation from the imperial economies in order to become at home in the society of believers in Christ's economy
Perpetuation	heroically exceeding the economy	being governed in multiple economies	communion in the economy of the One
Human condition: economy begins with	necessity	——	freedom
Ultimate human condition	by necessity human action in concert	——	by necessity human action in concert generates surplus
Categorical imperative	by necessity, to begin with "talking about the economy"	——	to freely begin with "talking about the economy"

changed, but its meaning has. What the Church Fathers see when recasting this condition is that human freedom lies in the choice of *what* surplus to generate and in *which* community. Humans are free to choose between two options: the first is to partake in sin, managed in an artificial sphere extending beyond the boundaries of the economy, a sphere encompassing everything that is solely human. The second choice is to commit the surplus to the generation of the growth of the economy, freely uniting hypostatically "like sea and land, by an interchange of their several gifts, (so) they might unite in promoting the one object, the glory of God" (Gregory of Nazianzus 1983a:Oration 43:62). In other words, a human, faced with the necessity of generating surplus, is free to choose either to partake in an alienness to which nothing is alien, in which the excess of the transcendental is economized, or to turn the surplus generated outside the boundaries of the economy. The latter option is considered by the Orthodox as the sphere of human sin. The economist, unlike the layperson, has yet another choice to make: whether to follow the dictates of law or to willingly include those *outside the economy and yet belonging*.

3
Economy and Philosophy

The Hermeneutics of the Subject

In his 1981–82 lectures on *The Hermeneutics of the Subject,* Michel Foucault (2005) inquired into a genealogy that attends to "the urgent, fundamental and politically indispensable task" of thinking and practicing the seemingly impossible and resisting "political power, situating it in the more general question of governmentality." The answer to this question, he argued, cannot "avoid passing through, theoretically and practically, the element of a subject defined by the relationship of self to self" for the simple reason "that power relations, governmentality, the government of the self and of others, and the relationship of self to self, constitute a chain, a thread, and I think it is round these notions that we should be able to connect together the question of politics and the question of ethics" (Foucault 2005:252).

In his genealogical search for a relation of self to self that can act as a fulcrum from which we will be able to reconstitute an art and theory of resistance to prevailing neoliberal governmentality, Foucault returned to "the period of the golden age of the culture of the self, of the cultivation of oneself, of the care of oneself" (2005:30) in the first two centuries CE. He did so while selecting Plato and Gregory of Nyssa as spokespersons for the classical and Christian—the before and after of the golden age of the care of the self. Though far from being developed, the Christian care of the self functions in the lectures as a reference point. In an attempt to advance Foucault's genealogy of the human subject, as well as our ability to answer the ever more urgent politico-ethical question, I will look in this chapter for an answer in Christian thought (rather than imperial thought, to which Foucault returns). I will do so by inquiring into a genealogy of the antique care of the self of my own. Like Foucault, I will start with Plato's Socrates, but instead of focusing on Stoic thought, the Christian philosopher Origen will serve as the missing link that connects Plato and Gregory.

As a consequence, I come up with a different understanding of Christian philosophical life from the one illustrated by Foucault on three crucial topics: while Foucault argued that Gregory professed a renunciation of the self, I hold that he professed renunciation of everything that is not truly part of one's self, defined as anything that does not participate in the truth of oneself. Second, Gregory stays loyal to the philosophical tradition of situating the appearance of this truth in the same place that the Greeks looked for it ever since Diotima taught Socrates what love is all about: in the erotic desire to beget in the good and the beautiful, translated by Gregory into the desire to beget in the spirit; third, in his reading of Gregory, Foucault seems to overlook the fact that the latter saw the self as always already appearing in a community,[1] that the Christian renunciation of the polis and oikos is done for the purpose of erecting a new philosophical community—the society of believers in Christ economy. Attending to the missing communal character in Foucault's account of Gregory adds accommodative and inclusive philanthropy as a third dimension to ancient spirituality beside the erotic desire for God and the ascetic labor of the self delineated by Foucault (Foucault 2005:16).

Platonic Self-knowledge

The maxim *"to discover the Maker and Father of this Universe were a task indeed; and having discovered Him, to declare Him unto all men were a thing impossible"* (Plato 1925, *Timaeus* 28c) was favored by Christian apologetics (Edwards 2005:569).[2] The maxim "was part of the tradition of Platonic anthologies, and so what every schoolboy knew" (Chadwick 1966:128) and was "perhaps the most hackneyed quotation from Plato in Hellenistic writers" (Chadwick in Origen 1980:429).[3] It "came to possess the force of an epistemological axiom" (Cooper 2005:17) as it was seen as binding two related axioms: an epistemological one concerning the human capability to know God and a discursive axiom concerning the limited capability of human language to describe him. While ancient interpreters agreed on Plato arguing that the knowledge of God couldn't be dispensed to all, they diverged as to whether Plato held that he is unknowable altogether or is knowable only to a handful of people.

The *Timaeus* maxim comes after a distinction Plato made between the sensual gaze and the theoretical one and their distinct objects: the ones that form the material world of becoming are given to the sensual gaze. This world is no more than a pale shadow of the things revealed to the theoretical gaze: the eternal ideas that feed on the light of the good (Plato 1925, *Timaeus* 27d–28a).

Plato's influence on ancient philosophers' perception of the mode by which divinity is given to the theoretical gaze can also be found in the discussion of divinity as the idea of the good in the sixth book of the *Politiea*. In it the good is presented as analogous to the sun in the sensible world (Plato 1969, *Republic* 508–9) and as such occupies a distinct and privileged ontological status compared to the rest of the *ideas*: "the Good itself is not essence but still transcends essence in dignity and surpassing power" (509b). Moreover, the rest of the ideas "not only receive from the presence of the Good their being known, but their very existence and essence is derived to them from it" (509b). It is the light shed by the *idea* of the Good that enlighten the soul (508) and functions as the condition of the latter possible knowledge of the rest of the *ideas*. Its nature is quite hard to apprehend (505e) and "when seen it must needs point us to the conclusion that this is indeed the cause for all things of all that is right and beautiful (517b–c).

As described in the Parable of the Cave, the soul originates in the sky of ideas to which it aspires to return and reunite with divinity (both as the idea of the Good and as Creator and Father). The return, conducted by turning the gaze from becoming to being, is conceived of as a journey of self-enlightenment (508d) that begins with turning the gaze from the sensed phenomena and setting the soul free from the bounds of the body. It is a time-limited journey of ascension and enlightenment that ends with descending to the body and to theoretical darkness upon her return to the human communities (both economic and political); it begins with embarrassment, it involves great pains, and ends, once more, with a sense of embarrassment.

The constitutive economic and political role of the soul's journey to its celestial origin (and back) is played out in Plato's Alcibiades A:132d–34e as Plato's response to the imperative "know thyself!," which, as Foucault noted,[4] is the first step toward taking care of oneself (Plato 1955, *Alcibiades* a 127–29). In it Plato situates the theoretical gaze inward as the gaze in which God is revealed as a mirror where the Good within man is reflected (a gaze that is described in *The Symposium* (Plato 1925) as an erotic gaze). To fully appreciate the soul's appearance in the mirror of the divine, we should bear in mind that ancient optics is quite different from contemporary optics. As told by Plato 1925 (*Timaeus* 46, *Sophist* 266), when looking in a mirror, the ray of light coming out of the eye meets a ray coming out of the perceived object, so that the image appearing in the mirror is formed by a mixture of both rays. According to this optics, the image seen in the mirror has real existence on its surface.[5] This means that the part of the soul that is reflected in the divine is the intellectual part that can gaze directly at God and enter into a partnership with him, which is seen by Plato as a necessary step toward acting with soundness of mind. Acquiring soundness of mind is, in turn, a prerequisite that qualifies the master/citizen to function in human communities, both economic and political.

Origen

Origen's thought, in which "Platonic Christianity" reached its culmination, sets the ground for Gregory's inclusion of knowledge achieved by the theoretical gaze and the discourse that accompany it in the economy. In his *Against Celsus* (*AC* VII:36–47) Origen offers his own interpretation of the *Timaeus* maxim (*AC* VII:42).[6] According to Origen, Plato held that the essence of God is given to the theoretical gaze of the few, while human discourse lacks the ability to make God known to all men (*AC* VII:42). Origen argues against Plato that the logos—the visible image of the invisible God—was incarnated so that the knowledge of God might be accessible to all people (who may become philosophers), and by doing so draws a line between Christian universally accessed communion in God and the Platonic (and Gnostic) exclusive one.

Origen's interpretation of the *Timaeus* maxim is quintessential as his reply to Celsus's accusation that Christians believe God is given to the sensual gaze and therefore renounces the theoretical gaze altogether. In *Against Celsus* Origen argues that the Christian sticks to the (Platonic) distinction between those phenomena given to the sensual gaze and those given to the theoretical. Referring to Romans 1:20, he argues that they "who live upon the earth have to begin with the use of the senses upon sensible objects, in order to go on from them to a knowledge of the nature of things intellectual, yet their knowledge must not stop short with the objects of sense" (*AC* VII:37).

THE THEORETICAL GAZE

In what follows, Origen moves on to an elaborated discussion on the object revealed to the theoretical gaze, arguing that the profane Platonic theoretical gaze cannot achieve true knowledge of God. The reason, according to Origen, is that such knowledge can only be obtained by turning one's gaze toward Christ-the-logos-incarnated—the visible image of the invisible God (*AC* VII:38–43). Because of that, every Christian, no matter how unschooled, practices philosophical life to a much greater extent than the most sophisticated (secular) philosopher (*AC* VII:44).[7] After establishing, against Plato, that everyone can become a philosopher (and thus know God) if, and only if, they follow Christ, Origen is quick to set an absolute limit to the reach of the theoretical gaze of the Christian philosopher. Origen distinguishes the theological gaze as a third kind of gaze, along with the sensual and the theoretical, saying that what makes God a unique object is that he reveals himself according to his will to the one who looks at the logos incarnated. Moreover, in order to gain the possibility of possessing a theological gaze, one must acknowledge a lack of ability to capture the sight of God against his will (*AC* VII:42). It should be noted that, his critique of profane philosophy notwithstanding, Origen reaffirms Clement's position that certain truths concerning God and world were revealed to the philosophers who did not turn their theoretical gaze to the logos incarnated. He then relocates the fallacy of profane philosophers, arguing that it stems from their arrogance, which causes them to fabricate a conceptual framework based on erroneous foundations. This is because God, the "founding father" of creation, is wholly missing from it (*AC* VII:46–48).

ETHICS, THEORY, THEOLOGY

Armed with the distinction between the three gazes, Origen moves on to define a Christian philosophical mode of conduct.[8] According to Origen's definition, the quest to know God begins with the purification of body and gaze, continues with the theoretical gaze, and a potential for the theological gaze emerges only at the last stage, achieved through the logos incarnated (*AC* VII:44–46). This threefold quest resembles the distinction Origen makes elsewhere between ethics, physics, and insight (*etike, physike, enoptike*), which he traces in the three books ascribed to Solomon.[9] Scripture functions as a locus in which traces of the revelation of divine nature can be found (*AC* II:71)—as a point of departure that distinguishes theology from philosophy (which departs on its journey following intuitions concerning the nature of the world). According to Origen, the theological quest begins by turning one's gaze to Scripture and embarking on an intellectual journey from its literal to its allegorical sense. Origen makes the analogy between this gaze and the one turned toward Christ's flesh as turning one's gaze from the literal to the allegorical follows the same pattern of turning the gaze from the sensual one directed at Jesus to the theoretical one directed at the logos incarnated, making God the Father visible.

Change in the Human Condition: Economy and Theology Are Set Apart

As described in his *Peri Archon*, the triple quest of ethics-theory-theology to know God was conducted within a two-stage economy of salvation (Trigg 1998:26–28). During the first stage of this economy, before the fall, there were only souls, rational beings who willingly chose to commune with God. At a certain moment all of them (with the exception of the one to be incarnated in Christ), experienced satiety (χόρος) from God (Origen 2006b, *De Principiis* II:8.3),[10] choosing to turn away from the divine fire, cooled down and fallen, which reflects Origen's belief that man can literally exhaust divine nature by knowing it all (Otis 1958:102).[11]

The second stage began with the creation of the cosmos and the sensual world, a time when a body was created for the purpose of stopping the soul's fall supporting its journey to reunite with God, who sent the logos incarnated to lead fallen souls on their journey. Despite the positive role ascribed to the created world and the human body in Origen's economy of salvation, it is conducted within a Platonic ontology that considers the body to be created, therefore belonging to the order of becoming, while the soul is perceived to belong to the order of being that persisted before the creation of body and world, aspiring thereafter to reunite with God. As may be seen, the threefold journey of ethics-theory-theology can remain in the framework of Platonic dualism only if the theological realm is not distinguished from the economic one (and, as a result, the distinction between the theoretical and the theological gazes is blurred). This choice is also reflected in the way Origen settles between Polybius's circular economy of history and Irenaeus's progressive economy of history,[12] narrating the soul's journey to return to God as moving in a "progressive circularity" where the circle of satiation-fall-return repeats itself each time some progress occurs toward full reunion.

The rise of the distinction between economy and theology—that is, between the Godhead in itself, the subject matter of theology, and divinity as it is given to the theoretical gaze in the economy, rendered Origen's philosophical mode of conduct inoperative, as the quasi-platonic ontology on which it was based could no longer sustain Christian philosophical life. This is because the new human condition dictates that man, *body and soul*, is conceived as subjected to the order of becoming.[13] As a consequence, the soul's journey toward God can no longer be thought of as a journey of return to its homeland in the order of being. Instead, it is illustrated as embarking on an eschatological quest for the fulfillment of the economy in the fullness of the ages when all, *body and soul*, will be recapitulated in Christ.

Gregory of Nyssa's Economy of Growth

Gregory of Nyssa took charge of the adaptation of philosophical life to the new human condition resulting from economy's being distinguished from theology (see Ware 1979:105; Louth 1981:81–83). In his *Commentary on the Song of Songs* (1987), Gregory repositioned the three steps ladder of ethics-theory-theology the Christian philosopher climbs on his way to know God. The first step remains the ethical one of external enlightenment achieved by cleansing the body, the soul, and one's conduct toward others (G2G 97); the second step is the theoretical one, which includes an internal enlightenment where God is reflected in the mirror of the soul. The radical change in the philosophical mode of conduct is found in the move from the second step to the third. The exclusion of economy from theology implies that humans can theoretically gaze at divinity only as mirrored in the image. If one were to reach the inaccessible light directly, that is, to climb up the ladder and practice the theological gaze, one would be surrounded by darkness, which is, according to Gregory, the way God reveals himself to the human gaze.[14]

APATHETIC ETHICS

As part of his project of adjusting Christian philosophical life to the new economic condition of becoming, Gregory distinguished between three types of desires. The *first* type is the natural bodily need that humans share with the rest of created beings. Fulfilling this need was conceived to be necessary in securing the species' existence. As such, it is neither good nor evil in itself. The second type of desire in this typology is the vicious perversion of natural desire that stems from self-enslavement to bodily desires without limits. Taken together, these vicious perversions comprise human sin. Against Gnostic tendencies, Gregory builds on the distinction between natural and unnatural desire to locate the origin of sin in man's free will (itself found in man's soul), arguing that "it is not the body that implants [in us an] impulse toward evil, but our faculty of choice, which perverts [the desire for] the object of need into unnatural lust" (Gregory of Nyssa 2009a:Concerning the one who has died).

In The Life of Moses Gregory allegorically calls the desire for food, beverages, and money "clay" (G2G 87),[15] paralleling the soul's enslavement in pursuit of these pleasures to the Israelites who were forced to mold bricks without being able to fulfill the quota set by Pharaoh (G2G 87). The subjugation of the "Israelites of the soul" to the despotic rule of "Pharaoh" causes the former to disavow God while relentlessly seeking more "clay" to mold, hopelessly trying to satisfy their despot and in so doing freely subjecting themselves to a circular economy of booms of satiation and busts of scarcity.[16]

Gregory here builds on the ethical standpoint that was shared by most pre-Christian schools of thought that self-enslavement to bodily desires is the vicious perversion of a virtuous economy.[17] And like most of them, Gregory positions the virtue of soundness of mind as in charge of drawing the distinction between the fulfillment of bodily needs and enslavement to excessive desire (Gregory of Nyssa 1967a, *On Virginity* 21). Borrowing from Stoicism, Gregory holds that one ought to become apathetic (Ludlow 2007:56) toward bodily desires.[18] It should be noted that apathy carried a different meaning in Stoicism than the one associated with it today. Stoic apathy meant economizing wants in accordance with nature's rationality, so that when demonstrating apathy one exceeds the utilitarian principle of maximizing pleasures by conducting oneself in accordance with a virtue that transcends the pleasure principle,[19] in this case soundness of mind. Using Origen's conception of humans as having two sets of senses— one bodily and one spiritual—Gregory argued that overcoming sin by apathetic self-purification is the first necessary step toward passing from the realm sensed by the bodily set to the realm sensed by the spiritual, so that only the purified soul can serve as a mirror in which the divine light is reflected in.

THE MIRROR STAGE

As described in the sixth sermon, *On the Beatitudes* (G2G 101–2), the second step in the quest to know God comes into play after apathy has been achieved and the philosopher eye's has been purified. At that moment the theoretical gaze (i.e., the gaze that appeared in Origen's as the theological gaze turned inward to man's soul), in which divinity reflects and participates in the mirror of the soul, comes into play.[20] As Gregory puts it, although humans are sentenced to gaze (Gregory of Nyssa 1967c, *On Virginity* 46), they are nevertheless free to choose between an economy of vice and one of virtue, that is, to choose whether to open their eyes and become enlightened or to shun the divine light. This choice in turn constitutes what is given to the human gaze: if one shuts his eyes he will be surrounded by darkness, and if he opens them he will see the light. In both instances his eyes keep on gazing, just as his soul never stops becoming, and this illustration enables Gregory to situate, once again, sin in the eyes of the beholder and not in the object of the gaze, be it his body, nature, or God.

INCORPORATING THE THEORETICAL GAZE
IN THE ECONOMY

The inclusion of the theoretical gaze in the economy surfaces when Gregory sets the theoretical gaze as a gaze that is *not* directed at the sun, i.e., divinity, but on its reflection in the mirror of the soul. "[This contemplation] has for object human realities, but seen in their celestial perspective. Knowledge takes then a precise sense. It is neither knowledge of God, *theologia*, for God remains inaccessible; nor is it any longer ordinary knowledge of human things: it is supernatural knowledge of God's plan, the *oikonomia*, the history of spiritual creatures" (Daniélou in Louth 1981:87). Unlike Plato's assertion that "the philosopher associating with the divine order will himself become orderly and divine in the measure permitted to man" (Plato 1969, *Republic* 500c–d), Gregory holds that in order to become a true philosopher, associated with the divine, a human needs to begin by becoming orderly, cleansing the body, the soul, and actions toward other humans (*G2G* 97), and, instead of the self appearing in the mirror of the divine, "so it is that the soul that has been purified by the Word and has put off all sin, receives within itself the circular form of the sun and shines now with this reflected light" (*G2G* 171).

Turning the gaze toward the mirror of the soul in which God is reflected is only the second stage on the way toward knowing him. At this stage the transition from the sensual gaze, which turned toward the phenomenal appearing in the world of becoming, to the theoretical gaze, which turned toward the invisible world, where the image of being is reflected, takes place. The latter gaze is constituted as a search for a *cataphatic* knowledge of God—that is, a knowledge of the divine as he is reflected and participates in the soul *in the economy* (contrary to a theological gaze, which turns directly to God). The difference between the objects given to the two gazes can be illustrated by using Plato's Parable of the Cave. In both Plato and Gregory we witness a journey of gazing. But while Plato set the pinnacle of his journey at the moment when the philosopher gazes directly at the sun, Gregory denies that such a gaze is possible altogether, as humans can only go so far as gazing at his reflection in their souls, suggesting that the climax of Platonic theory is only an intermediate stage in the quest to know God (Louth 1981:85). It seems that by doing so Gregory brings to light philosophical narcissism, as if saying to profane philosophers: "it may seem to you that you see God and your self reflected in Him. But the truth of the matter is that what you really gaze at is your own soul where you see the reflection of the divine (rather than the other way around). You may well ascend to the heaven of *ideas*, but it is cloudy, so you are disoriented and therefore mistakenly think that you surpassed the human condition of becoming and are gazing directly at God, when all you do is gaze into the mirror of your own soul. And you would agree with me if you were to turn your gaze from the light reflected in the mirror of your soul to find yourself in the darkness that is sensed in the true presence of God." And this self-love-making, according to Gregory, is the reason why profane philosophy is "truly barren . . . always at labor and never giving birth. For what fruits worthy of such pagans does philosophy show for being so long in labor? Do not all who are full of wind and never come to term miscarry before they come to the light of the knowledge of God" (*LM* 57).

THEOLOGICAL DARKNESS

While reaching the third stage in his quest to know God, man is covered in total darkness, as the "categories" by which phenomenal reality appears before his eyes (both sensual and spiritual) do not apply to God. In a description that resembles (and precedes) the Kantian situation of the phenomena as given in time and space, Gregory argues that God in himself is located outside the reach of (human) sight (*G2G* 126–27).[21] And much like (and before) Ludwig Wittgenstein's maxim of the mystical as the inexpressible that reveals itself, about which one must keep silent, Gregory argues that "in speaking of God, when there is the question of his essence, then it is time to keep silence. When however, it is the question of His operation, a knowledge of which can come down even to us, that is the time to speak of his omnipotence by telling of his work and explaining his deeds, and to use words to this extent" (*G2G* 129).

Unlike his modern counterparts, Gregory does not ignore Origen's "warning" that any attempt to describe time/space as given to our theoretical gaze by excluding the "sun" that nourishes and casts light on it is futile. Instead, on the one hand, he does not give up on the attempt to theorize (God) the unknowable. Moreover, he situates this erotic desire as the end of human life. On the other hand, he does not exclude the unknowable from theory, but situates it at the kernel of theoretical life and all human experience, as saying: there is always excess left outside the boundaries of the economy, one that by its nature is not given to the human gaze (both sensual and theoretical). But instead of pushing this excess outside its ontological boundaries, he situates it at its core and sets the end of human existence at constantly transcribing divine excess in time and space. Excess, which was excluded by Aristotle to the boundaries of theory, takes center stage. Moreover, divine excess is not limited to the bounds of theory but is conceived as the thing that binds members of the economy of the as with the previous change (see comment) society of believers in Christ, situated at the heart of each and every one of them, so that Christian society is constituted as a communion in divine excess. And, although human singularity is still conceived, as in Aristotle, as revealed in the eyes of others, its content has radically changed as man no longer makes his appearance as a singular being in the eyes of his fellows when submitting to the imperative "nothing in excess!" by acquiring a practical and theoretical disposition of prudence managed within the bounds of the economy. Instead of "nothing in excess," human singularity is conceptualized by Gregory as the mode in which excess is revealed to the gaze of the other members of the society of believers, so that, contrary to the Aristotelian excess-free political sphere, human singularity does not appear in the society of believers at the moment when excess ceases to do so. As a result, the persona is no longer the mask that man puts on when he enters the political sphere for the purpose of appearing in the eyes of his peers. The omnipresence of excess decrees that, on the one hand, man can never truly overcome the economic partnership (in truth itself) and, on the other hand, he is always already subjected to a gaze that participates in him, hence the persona, the singular mode in which excess operates in him, becomes the truth of the subject.

THE HUMAN CONDITION: BECOMING

Gregory circumscribed the quest to know God in an open-ended hermeneutical circle on both of its existential ends, so that the "circle of light" acts as a point of departure into a never-ending journey into darkness. Decreed by the human condition of becoming, human freedom is formulated as the choice between two journeys: from glory to glory or bad to worst. The incessant choice between a glorious economy and a vicious one is set as a choice that constitutes man and is seen by Gregory as an act of self-begetting (*LM* 55).[22] This act is not limited to the bounds of the worldly economy, as humans were natal creatures in heaven and will keep on being so in the future age to come (Harrison 1996:36–38). Moreover, it is this specific quality that is made present in every act of free choice that testifies to humans being created in the image and likeness of God. Unlike natality, being toward death is not seen by Gregory as a necessary by-product of the human condition of createdness, and of being subjected to the order of becoming, but as a result of man's fall: death did not exist in heaven, and it will not exist in the future age to come. Instead, death is conceived as the by-product of man's choice to bodily beget in the ages spanning the fall and the future age to come.[23] Furthermore, humans are capable of overcoming death by choosing to practice the ethical "eroticism of virginity," begetting in the spirit.[24] Again, the formulation of the new human condition as dictating free choice between the circular economy of the ancient oikos and the Christian growth economy is constituted as a choice between a necessity that *begins with* being born and *after all* to die and *to begin with* *and after all* the freedom to beget in an ontology in which to begin with the Father freely begets his Son and in the future age to come humans beget in the spirit eternality. Although it is a constitutive choice, it is not a once in a lifetime choice, but has to be made constantly because man, as a zoon oikonomikon, ceaselessly begets himself anew (Gregory of Nyssa 2004b:21).[25]

Unlimited Economic Growth

Coming to terms with the human condition of becoming and being given to constant change disqualifies the two modes of conduct that were conceived in antiquity as exceeding the boundaries of the economy: philosophy and politics. As we have seen, the philosopher can no longer surpass the boundaries of the economy. As for politics, generating a sphere that is solely human was considered by Christian philosophers to be the generation of an economy of vice in which man enslaves himself to the circularity of excessive bodily desires, described by Gregory as the free choice to live in freeless sphere.

Confronted with the insight that man is subjected to spend his entire life in the economy and that there is no way he can exceed its boundaries and perpetuate himself—whether by gazing at the Eternal or by (political) perpetuation in the memory of other humans, Gregory was in dire need of finding a way that people can become good and perpetuate themselves while being sentenced to spend their entire lives within the bounds of the economy. In order to do so, he reconceptualized the economy as a sphere in which everything that is born and grows is doomed to decay and perish. Forced to "destroy the equation: Good = immutability and evil = change" (Daniélou 1979:47), Gregory formulated a distinction between two kinds of movement: in and toward the good and in and toward the evil. While he posits the movement in and toward evil as the same old tiresome circular movement, Gregory was in uncharted territory seeking after a model of freely moving in and toward the good. Using the term *epektasis*,[26] Gregory was the first in the history of Greek philosophy to freely think of and enable an economy in which humans can desire without limits and was also the first who, instead of being preoccupied with setting a boundary to the economy, simply set economy's boundary beyond the reach of human consciousness. Moreover, he managed to shed a divine light on the destructive dimension that accompanies the limitless growth of the economy that made the ancients so worried, by describing it as "creative destruction" so that the end of the world that the growth of the economy is bound to bring in the fullness of the ages is sought after as the thing that will enable humans to perpetuate themselves in eternality. As a result of Gregory's discovery of unlimited growth, which is rightly considered his greatest contribution to Christian thought and, evidently, to the history of the economy,[27] each person and humanity as a whole faces the free choice of whether to partake in a growing economy in which freedom is exercised or to submerge in a circular economy in which anything that grows is destined to decay and perish.

THE LIMITLESS OBJECT GENERATES UNSATURATED DESIRE

Gregory insists that man cannot experience saturation from God (*LM* 31), in contrast to the ontology illustrated by Origen in which the fall originated in the satiety souls experienced from God. This is because God, as a limitless object of desire, generates unsaturated desire in that the gap between man, as a created being, and God is infinite (Sorabji 1983:150), so that man cannot exhaust divine knowledge. Gregory then turns nonsaturation into the quality that distinguishes between the virtuous economy of desiring God and the vicious economy of perverted carnal desires; thus the inclusion of philosophical life in the economy ultimately releases the latter from the ancient circularity of desire-saturation-desire. Gregory makes use of the second economic model when turning *bios theoretikos* into *bios praktikos* in which soundness of mind and fortitude, the two ethical virtues whose boundary is revealed in the absence of boundary "because [in them] the mean is in a sense an extreme" (*Eth.Nic* 1107a), are hypostatically united. The sheer brilliance and innovation of Gregory's theoretical maneuver of situating the productive paradox that accompanies the two virtues at the heart of theoretical active life is fully fledged when compared to the use Aristotle made of the same productive paradox. As may be recalled, Aristotle addressed the paradox by creating a spatial distinction between the two virtues, assigning soundness of mind with rule over the economic sphere and fortitude with the political one,[28] whereas by including philosophical life in the economy Gregory positions the productive paradox at the heart of an economic-philosophical sphere that knows no limits. All this comes down to a happiness, theorized as the economization of philosophical life in Gregory's thought, that is reached by a life in which there is no limit to the demonstration of soundness of mind in the pursuit of the ideal mode of life by begetting in the spirit within the bounds of a limitless economy.

Another productive paradox that sets the economy in motion is reached by defining the satisfaction of the desire to God in its dissatisfaction so that the desiring erotic act becomes itself the object of desire (see Ludlow 2000:63) and *epeketasis*, understood as growth in and toward the good, becomes in itself the end of the economy. As can be seen, Gregory's response to the question of how one can live a philosophical life as a virtuous one to its fullest degree in the economy is to become an eros who desires divinity incessantly when this mode of life becomes itself the object of desire (*LM* 115–16). As a result, unlimited economic growth becomes the only way humans can reach immutability in a life given to constant change, and the greater the rate of growth so does the economic stability increase. Economic growth hereby replaces economic circularity as the preferred mode by which the world of becoming resembles eternity in pre-Christian thought, when, beside economic growth, there is only one other option: falling from bad to worse. Two options then: economic stability achieved by unlimited economic growth or economic retreat into the abyss (see *LM* 133, 117).

THE CARE OF THE SELF

Plato interpreted the imperative "know thyself!" as a necessary step toward the attainment of the virtue of soundness of mind (Foucault 2005:71), a virtue whose attainment is a prerequisite for the master/citizen and the political ruler to be able to participate and excel in the "classical" human communities of the oikos and polis.[29]

Schematically summarizing Foucault's presentation of the care of the self in the three moments of antiquity (the classical, represented by Plato; the imperial, to which the lectures of 2005 are dedicated; and the Christian, represented by Gregory of Nyssa [Foucault 2005:83–84, 495]), one can draw the next scheme: in the classical moment the care of the self appears as part of the political project of perpetuation; in the imperial moment it appears as an end in itself; and in the Christian moment it appears as part of a perpetuation scheme that includes renunciation of the self and of the human communities of oikos, polis, and cosmopolis. It seems that Foucault's description of the Christian moment is in need of revision in light of Gregory's interpretation of the imperative to know thyself (*G2G* 159–63) as beginning with gaining knowledge of what is not truly part of the self, most importantly of what impersonates to form a part of it, as, for example, the political "persona," which he held to be mere impersonation. As Gregory saw it, anyone who wishes to complete his quest for self knowledge must shed this persona, as it is only after all masks are shed that the true self is revealed in the one thing that distinguishes the human zoon oikonomikon from the rest of creation: that they are the only ones in the world who were created in the image and likeness of God (this image is revealed, as shown earlier, in the act of free choice). The care of the self, then, is conducted in a gaze and action that allows the true self to appear as the reflection and participation of the image and likeness of God in the human persona. This is executed in a twofold manner: on the one hand, one has to purify oneself from anything that is not truly part of oneself, but only impersonating, while, on the other hand, one has to exert oneself by constantly becoming in the image and likeness of God. The implicit identification of the practice of virginity and philosophical life is made explicit at the beginning of Gregory's *On Virginity*[30] (where the latter is presented as necessary for the practice of philosophical life and is identified with it,[31] as becoming in the image and likeness of God) where virginity is described as a twofold practice of 1. self-*askesis* for the purpose of purification and 2. turning the erotic gaze toward God, i.e., to the mirror of the soul in which he is reflected and participates so that his image will get a hold on the soul, resulting in the person turning his gaze away from created world (*G2G* 163).

MODELING THE NEW SOCIETY

Hypostatically uniting communal and philosophical life is how Gregory answers the question Aristotle raised in the second book of the *Politics*, concerning the amount of sharing proper to the autarkic and happy community. As recalled, Aristotle attempted to solve the puzzle that on the one hand sharing wealth, as proposed by Plato, will harm the plurality that appears in the community and its autarky (*Pol.* 1261a), while, on the other hand, diverting from unity brings into action the threat posed by the vice of licentiousness to the conditions that enable the rise of a political community and (more important for Plato) the practice of a philosophical life (see Leshem 2014b). Gregory's answer to the immanent contradiction between plurality and unity, and evidently between an autarkic philosophical life and an autarkic communal life, is that the society of believers in the economy ought to reflect the first economic model of Ontological Communion between the three personae of the Godhead—in which there is no contradiction between unity and plurality—by miming it to the best of its ability. Such a "mimesis of the mirror" is to be performed in a mode of conduct that aspires to overcome the contrast between "economic" unity and "political" freedom and plurality, one that will enable living the philosophical life in the "polis set on the hill" (Mathew 5:14), a community that Gregory asserts is God's Polis (2004a, *Second Answer to Eunomius*) and the heavenly *politeuma* (on the baptism of Christ).[32]

This mimesis is concisely described by Gregory in the following manner:

> For he [Paul] says somewhere in the writing to the Ephesians, where he is explaining to us the great economy of salvation through the epiphany of God in the flesh. . . . If then the church is Christ's body, Christ is the head of the body, forming the countenance of the church with his own

features. . . . In her they see more clearly that which is invisible. It is like men who are unable to look upon the sun, yet they can see it by its reflection in water, so the friends of the bridegroom see the sun of justice by looking upon the face of the church as though it were a pure mirror, and thus he can be seen by his reflection.

(*G2G* 217–19)

Rephrasing the text in the conceptual language of the models, we may say that the Ontological Communion is transcribed in the persona of God the Son into the created world. The second phase is taking place in the economy of the incarnation when Christ's human nature is purified by the operation of the second economic model of the hypostatic union. In the third phase the Church is qualified, as Christ's sin-free body, to act as a mirror in which the persona of God the Son, a persona that essentially contains the Ontological Communion, is reflected.

As Gregory saw it, answering the question "who am I?" is possible only in a community that mimes the Ontological One, in my reflection in the image of my fellow members where I appear in somewhat mystifying "mirror relations"; on the one hand, the answer to the question Who Am I? is the true me as seen in the reflection of the divine in the mirror of the soul so that the singularity of a human, the divine light/darkness reflection, is revealed to the gaze of his or her fellow members among the society of believers.[33] On the other hand, this is a quality that is common to all humans, who are created in the image and likeness of God. Put differently, the singular persona of each human being—the unique mode of being in which the divine is reflected and participates—is fully revealed only when it is reflected and participates in the mirrors of the souls of his fellow members in the society of believers. The operation of the second economic model is made present in the transcription of the ontological communion into the human society when the "private" philosophical life and the "public" communal life are hypostatically united. As described by Gregory Nazianzus, who referred to the model, such a union took place in the persona of

the great Athanasius, who was always the mediator and reconciler of all other men, like Him Who made peace through His blood between things which were at variance, reconciled the solitary with the community life: by showing that the Priesthood is capable of contemplation, and that contemplation is in need of a spiritual guide. Thus he combined the two, and so united the partisans of both calm action and of active calm, as to convince them that the monastic life is characterized by steadfastness of disposition rather than by bodily retirement.

(Gregory of Nazianzus 1893a, Oration 21:19–20)

Practicing philosophical life in a community is Gregory's way of enabling humans, as *erotic, becoming, and communal creatures,* to turn their gaze toward God's reflection wherever they may be; whether inside, to the mirror of their own soul, or outside, to the souls of their fellow members in the society of believers. In both instances, the clarity of the image of the Ontological Communion incarnated in the economy is steadfastly growing without limits.

While such a growth is performed on a microlevel in each of the fellow members of society, it is also performed on a macrolevel in the society as a whole. Much like the microprocess, beginning with a purification that takes place in the mystery (sacrament) of baptism, its continuance is in the enlightened gaze and its summit is in the sensed mystery of the sacrament of the Eucharist when the future age to come is made present in the flesh. This homology between micro- and macroeconomics is very much present in economic growth theory, as the equivalent of personal growth (*theosis*) is the growth of the whole ecclesiastical body (soteria) and seems to posit, at first sight, the Church as the macroeconomic counterpart of the growth that is taking place in its members' souls at the microeconomic level. But the micro-macro relation exceeds the order of mere reflections of the micro in the macro, and vice versa, since the member, as a communal creature, is always already member of the economic body of society, that is, a member of the Church. As a result, economic growth at the macrolevel is dependent on the personal growth of each member,[34] and the virgin soul's search for the lost coin serves the interest of the whole of society as it affects its economic growth as a whole.[35] Yet another reason why the micro-macro relation exceeds the order of mere reflections is discovered when the person turns his theoretical gaze from his soul outward to the Church that functions as a body that mediates between the soul and God, which means that his personal economic growth is dependent on the growth of society as a whole.

The growth of the society of believers is pursued both "qualitatively" and "quantitatively." The first is by divinizing spheres of existence (beginning with the microlevel of the soul of each believer and up to the whole empire) and subjecting others to sustaining the growth of the economy, as in the case of imperial rule, which is discussed in the next chapter. Taking into account that the premodern economists of salvation (and other subjects, for that matter) were not as obsessed with measuring as contemporary economists and did not command the technical tools and dedicated concepts (such as GDP) for measuring growth rate, the inclusion of more people and sects into the Orthodox camp was one of the major preoccupation of the Church Fathers and qualified the use of the "principle of economy" as discussed in chapter 5.

CHRISTOMIMESIS: THE TRANSCRIPTION OF THE THIRD ECONOMIC MODEL

The Capadocians' attempt to found a model society in the monasteries, by bringing into existence a *politeuma* in heaven (Basil the Great 2003b, letter 223:2) that would replace the political community (Daley 1999:439; Azkoul 1968a, b; Downey 1964),[36] is pronounced in Gregory Nazianzus's eulogy of Basil: "Go a little outside the city (he says), and gaze on the new city: the storehouse of piety, the common treasury for those with possessions, where the superfluities of wealth as well as necessities lie stored away because of his persuasion—shaking off the moths, giving no joy to thieves, escaping struggles with envy and the onrush of time—where disease is treated by philosophy, where misfortunes are called blessed, where compassion is held in real esteem" (Gregory of Nazianzus 1893a: Oration 43.63). But the monasteries serve as more than just "model societies" as they intertwined into the chain of transcription that prescribes that anyone who begets himself constantly by practicing virginity (and who has achieved the desired immutability that accompanies economic growth in communion) has to mime the third economic model, that is, to reflect the Son's asceticism *and* philanthropy. Gregory noted that as erotic desire for God, executed by miming the model of the Virgin Mary, forms only one part of the care of the self: "whereas *askesis* may be described as the mode of God's salvific action in Christ, *philanthropia* is an Imation of its direction, i.e., toward mankind" (Winslow 1979:153). And Gregory makes sure to situate both in the economists gaze: "now the Holy Scripture . . . has various names to refer to those who guide us in the ways of truth . . . a seer, or one who see, and watchman . . . we are led to consider the eyes as referring to those who have been commanded to oversee . . . hence anyone God has set over his church as an eye, must wash away the rheum of sin if he is to oversee and superintend as purely as he should" (*G2G* 275).

The conduct of the conduct of the new society is entrusted into the hands of the economist-philosopher (and not the Platonic king-philosophers) whose entire operations, their theoretical life and their desired object not withstanding, are found within the bounds of the economy. As formulated by the Gregory Nazianzus: "Before a man has, as far as possible, gained this superiority, and sufficiently purified his mind, and far surpassed his fellows in nearness to God, I do not think it safe for him to be entrusted with the rule over souls, or the office of mediator (for such, I take it, a priest is) between God and man" (1893a:Oration 2.91).

As can be seen, the economist-philosopher functions as an Eros,

Interpreting and transporting human things to the gods and divine things to men; entreaties and sacrifices from below, and ordinances and requitals from above: being midway between, it makes each to supplement the other, so that the whole is combined in one. Through it are conveyed all divination and priestcraft concerning sacrifice and ritual and incantations, and all soothsaying and sorcery. God with man does not mingle: but he is the means of all society and converse of men with gods and of gods with men.

(Plato 1925c, *Symposium* 202e–3a)

4

Economy and Politics

The relations between the society of believers in Christ economy and the political sovereign began with hostility and distrust. For what can be expected of a society that transcribes a model persona that was executed by the political authorities? The hostility and mistrust must have developed when the Christians adopted Greek theoretical life, whose model philosopher, Socrates,[1] was himself executed by a political community. As if these two crucial moments in the history of the human trinity were not enough, after that came scores of martyrs who followed Socrates and choose truth over life and made this hostility and mistrust second nature.

But then again, how should a society that was transformed from a secret society to an imperial religion following the edicts of Galerius (311 CE), Milan (313 CE), and of Theodosius I (391–92 CE) approach the political sovereign? For sure, the Christianization of the empire transformed Christian political thought, which, as captured in one of Tertulian's maxims, firmly believed that "the world may need its Caesars, but the emperor can never be a Christian, nor a Christian ever be an emperor." These events, which many believed were caused by divine intervention, seem at first glance to revolutionize relations between the society of believers in Christ economy and the political sovereign. For one thing, it enabled the formation of Orthodoxy as emperors summoned ecumenical councils that unanimously declared creeds of faith and stipulated canons that Emperor Justinian ordered to be observed as imperial laws (Justinian 1932, codex novella 131).[2]

The miraculous events of the fourth century all suggest, as many scholars will agree, the portrayal of an age of resistance and persecution taking place in the three hundred years up to the baptism of Constantine, followed by an age of full merger between economy and politics in an empire headed by a caesar-pope.[3] But this picture is misleading. Reading the Apostolic and Apologetic Fathers, one finds positive evaluations of the empire despite the persecutions (Peterson in Williams 1951a:6), while Athanasius called Constantine's son the "modern Ahab" and Antichrist.[4] The Orthodox leaning against trusting rule over the Church in the hands of an emperor-pope strengthened as Constantius, son and heir of Constantine, supported their Arian opponents and even more when the empire was headed by "Julian the Apostate,"[5] a pagan emperor who forbade Christians from teaching classical literature.[6] The events that shaped the fourth century and the Orthodox realization that even after Constantine's conversion there was no guarantee that the support of the emperor was secured contributed to the reinforcement of the disposition of "respect and suspect" toward the latter, with the necessary adaptations to the living reality of a Christianized empire,[7] for "if the price of Imperial recognition was to be imperial domination, they [Church Fathers] would have none of it. It had suddenly become necessary to distinguish between *sacerdotium* and *imperium*" (Setton 1967:87).

All this is not meant to diminish the magnitude of the rupture in the history of the West and the Near East caused by the Christianization of the empire. For one, it forced Christians to think systemically about the organization of a social body that became wholly political and wholly economic. As Tertullian's maxim testifies, this was unthinkable before the fourth century. Yet the Christian attitude toward the political sovereign on both sides of the rupture is complex and much more nuanced than is usually admitted.

Another problem when discussing the political thought of the Greek Church Fathers is that none of the Orthodox political treaties, if existed, survived (Azkoul 1968b:191).[8] As a result, patristic thought was not only relegated from the history of economic thought but also from that of political thought, as most anthologies of political thought that ignore it or, at best, equate it with that of Augustinian thought, testify. But, as in the case of economic thought, that will be misleading. Patristic political thought, although scattered all over the texts, was a coherent system and of great importance to any genealogy of modern government, as I will show by reconstructing it from the Fathers' references to the "political verses" of the New Testament that form, according to Origen, the first step in the development of any Christian theory. Such a reconstruction is to be done in two ways: 1. analyzing homilies dedicated to exegesis of these verses and 2. following how these verses are used in homilies and treatises.

PHILIPPIANS 3:20–21: THE ECONOMIC CONTEXT OF ANY THOUGHT OF THE POLITICAL

A *politeuma*, according to Mary Smallwood, "was a recognized, formally constituted corporation of aliens enjoying the right of domicile in a foreign city and forming a separate, semi-autonomous civic body, a city within a city; it had its own constitution and administrated its internal affairs as an ethnic unit through official distinct from and independent of those of the host city. . . . Politemata were a regular feature of Hellenistic cities" (Smallwood 2001:225–26).[9] Seeing the society of believers in Christ's economy as a politeuma in heaven is fundamental to patristic political thought. What singles out the Christian politeuma from the earthly ones is that it is subjected to Christ (and not Caesar), as it is the savior (σωτήρ) and master (κύριος) who holds the power to subject all things unto himself (Philippians 3:21).[10] The politeuma in heaven gathers in the ecclesia—his body that has been purified from human sin—where the economy of the Holy Spirit is taking place. An early example of the attempt to define the politeuma in heaven appears in the *Epistle to Diognetus,* who argues that

> the Christians are distinguished from other men neither by country, nor language, nor the customs which they observe. For they neither inhabit cities of their own, nor employ a peculiar form of speech, nor lead a life which is marked out by any singularity . . . but, inhabiting Greek as well as barbarian cities, according as the lot of each of them has determined. . . . As citizens, they share in all things with others, and yet endure all things as if foreigners. Every foreign land is to them as their native country, and every land of their birth as a land of strangers. . . . They are in the flesh, but they do not live after the flesh. They pass their days on earth, but

they are citizens of heaven (εν ουρανώ πολιτεύονται). They obey the prescribed laws, and at the same time surpass the laws by their lives.

(Anonymous 2002, *Epistle to Diognetus* 5)

The economy of salvation, understood as social history, is the story of the
heavenly politeuma in created world and, as the *Epistle to Diognetus* demonstrates, this eschatological intentionality makes any thought of the political in itself already appear in an economic context.[11]

MATTHEW 22:21: THE SEPARATION OF POWERS

The heavenly politeuma cannot be rendered to Caesar, and one has to render it to God. The exegesis of Christ's maxim "render to Caesar the things
that are Caesar's; and to God the things that are God's" that appears in three
of the four gospels (Matthew 22:21; Mark 12:17; Luke 20:25; first and foremost by Paul) dictates a disposition of self-subjection to the political authorities and acknowledgment of a sphere that is subjected to these authorities[12]—one has to render to Caesar the things that belong to him—while
setting a limit to this subjection at the same time. Christ "sophistic" answer
needs to be understood in the proper context: using a coin that caries the
icon of Caesar ratifies his authority as well as subjection to him,[13] and with
that, at least implicitly, acknowledges his divinity.[14] In his answer, which
ratifies Caesar's authority while robbing him of his divinity, Christ avoids
the trap that was laid before him (either acknowledge Caesar divinity or revolt against him). Even more implicit in his answer is the claim that the
subject owns things that he should render to God, things that by definition
do not belong to Caesar in which the icon of the political sovereign does not
partake nor reflects, as one can assume that what is reflected and appears
in it is God. Christ's insistence on "the separation of powers" was followed
by the need to set limits of obedience to the political authorities vis-à-vis
obedience to God and the economists/bishops he has sent on his behalf.

ROMANS 13:1–7: THINKING THE POLITICAL IN ITSELF

The foundation of Christian thought of the political in itself is formulated in
two of the letters that are ascribed to Paul. In Romans 13:1–7[15] one can find
five of the main lines of thought that will guide the Church Fathers' attitude

toward the political sovereign: self-subjection to the governing authorities;[16] originating government in God;[17] presenting rulers as God's servants for the benefit of the believer; presenting the political sovereign as the one who, using the law, acts to prevent vice and to punish wrongdoers; presenting four different relations toward authority: tax, costume, fear, honor.

> Every person is to be in subjection to the governing authorities. For there is no authority except from God, and those which exist are established by God. 2 Therefore whoever resists authority has opposed the ordinance of God; and they who have opposed will receive condemnation upon themselves. 3 For sovereigns are not a cause of fear for good behavior, but for evil. Do you want to have no fear of authority? Do what is good and you will have praise from the same; 4 for it is a minister of God to you for good. But if you do what is evil, be afraid; for it does not bear the sword for nothing; for it is a minister of God, an avenger who brings wrath on the one who practices evil. 5 Therefore it is necessary to be in subjection, not only because of wrath, but also for conscience' sake. 6 For because of this you also pay taxes, for sovereigns are servants of God, devoting themselves to this very thing. 7 Render to all what is due them: tax to whom tax is due; custom to whom custom; fear to whom fear; honor to whom honor.
>
> (Romans 13:1–7)

An example of bringing together Christ's maxim and the Letter to the Romans can be found in Tertullian who, following a quotation from both, turns to set the limit of self-subjection to Caesar saying: "but man is the property of God alone. Peter, no doubt,[18] had likewise said that the king indeed must be honoured, yet so that the king be honoured only when he keeps to his own sphere, when he is far from assuming divine honours" (Tertullian 2006d:14). By mixing the verses, Tertullian redraws the amorphous borderline outlined by Christ between the sphere in which the Christian must subject himself to political sovereignty and the one that he ought to subject to the economy of God.

1 TIMOTHY 2:1–2: UTILITARIAN CALCULUS

First of all, then, I urge that entreaties and prayers, petitions and thanksgivings, be made on behalf of all men; for kings and all who

are in authority, so that we may lead a tranquil and quiet life
in all godliness and dignity.

—1 Timothy 2:1–2

1 Timothy 2:1–2 decrees prayer for those who are in (political) authority by using utilitarian reasoning, one that is absent from the "deontological" subjection of Romans 13. Later on the utilitarian logic will be used to argue why one should subject himself to the ruling powers. By doing so, the edict of self-subjection is circumvented yet again, this time by arguing that when the political sovereign does not contribute to the attainment of peaceful and virtuous life one is free to avoid subjection. 2 Timothy:1–2 also contributes another reason for the existence of political sovereignty, attributing to it its role of facilitating a tranquil and virtuous life that will be seen as a necessary condition for the growth of the economy of salvation.

Thinking of the Political Prior to the Christianization of the Empire

THE APOSTOLIC FATHERS

The Apostolic Fathers hardly referred to political authorities. The reason for this may well be their belief that the future age to come is at hand and that there is thus no point in treating an institution that soon will perish (see Dvornik 1966:594). In the few places where they do relate to the political authorities, the Apostolic Fathers embrace self-subjection to them. The most extensive treatment of political authorities is found in the longer version of three of the letters that are ascribed to Ignatius.[19] In the *Letter to the Antiochians* subjecting oneself to the political authorities is conditioned: one ought to "be subject to Caesar in everything in which subjection implies no [spiritual] danger" (Ignatius 2002a, *To the Antiochians* XI).[20] *The Letter to the Smyrneans* (Ignatius 2002d) decrees self-subjection to the political authorities alongside the edict to subject oneself to the economists of salvation, the latter ranking higher than the former.[21] If the longer versions were indeed written by Ignatius, or by a contemporary of his, they are the earliest texts that position economic pastorship and political sovereignty side by side, while creating a clear hierarchy between the two forms of government. In addition, the different relations toward authority in Romans 13 are being used to distinguish between the treatment that is given by the believer to his fellow person, the political sovereign, and God. The rest of the references to political sovereignty do not exhibit any real advancement from the one in Paul. Polycarp instructs the Christian to pray for kings, potentates, and princes (Polycarp 2002, *To the Philippians* XII) in spite of the persecutions, and the *Letter of Barnabas* instructs its addressees to "be subject to the Lord, and to [other] masters as the image of God, with modesty and fear" (Barnabas 2002:ixx).

APOLOGETIC TREATIES

Political sovereignty occupied the minds of the apologetic writers more that it did their predecessors, as the titles of many of their *apologiai,* that were addressed to emperors, testify. Romans 13:1–7 is the most quoted of the four passages (see Parsons 1940), a dominance that was maintained after the Christianization of the empire (Setton 1967:16). An example of the use of Romans 13 can be found in *The Address to the Greeks IV* (Tatian 2004) where Tatian plays with the four relations to authority to refine the distinctions between the ways that Christians should treat their fellow man, the sovereign, and divinity. While ratifying subjection to political authorities, Tatian presents a taxonomy of the relations mentioned in Paul: everyone should be treated with honor, tribute should be paid to the sovereign, while only God should be feared. In addition, he recircumvents subjection to earthly authorities, saying that one has to obey his political masters as long as they do not order him to deny God.

Theophilus of Antioch (1970) introduces three developments in the attitude toward political authorities: 1. explicit and unconditional denial of Caesar's divinity, since "he is not made to be worshipped, but to be reverenced with lawful honour, for he is not a God, but a man appointed by God, not to be worshipped, but to judge justly" (*Ad Autolycus* I:11); 2. that Christian loyalty to the political sovereign is based upon the utilitarian logic of 1 Timothy: they pray to God on his behalf, so that that they will live a peaceful life (*To Autolycus* III:4); 3. Theophilus uses the same logic to justify Christian subjection to the authorities (ibid). While administering Christian subjection to the political sovereign to utilitarian calculus, Theophilus also hints at a new way to circumvent political authority over the Christian subject by implying that whenever the commands given by the political sovereign pose a threat to the peaceful and virtuous communal life of the Christians they may disobey him. The innovation may become clearer by borrowing the terminology that was later developed concerning compliance to Church canons: suspending self-subjection to the emperor is no longer only in the case when doing so will be a scandal, but is justified also as a prudent act in order to achieve peaceful and virtuous communal life on earth in this day and age.

The dual political and economic government that the Christian must subject himself to can be found in Justin Martyr,[22] who professed that Christians can be loyal subjects of both God and Caesar by introducing a temporal distinction between the two: Caesar's kingdom is of the present age while Christ's kingdom is in the future age to come. Justin Martyr also sets an early example of the "tongue in the cheek" that the Church Fathers employ when declaring loyalty to Caesar alongside their subjection to God's economic government, arguing that the latter does not detract from their loyalty to the former but in fact strengthen it. In his apology Martyr "assures" Hadrian that when he hears the Christians declare their subjection and their expectation to another kingdom but his, they pose no threat to the fate of his own kingdom because the other kingdom is not headed by another human being. Putting it differently, if Caesar will "only" be willing to give up his claims of divinity, he will come to terms with the fact that the Christians are the most loyal subjects a human sovereign can find. The reason for this hyperloyalty is that their subjection to the other kingdom makes them lawful abiding subjects who act virtuously at all times in all spheres of existence (see Justin Martyr 2002a: 1st apology).[23] Signs of this extreme form of loyalty can be found in the decree of the "other king" to pay Caesar "both ordinary and extraordinary" (Justin Martyr 2002a:xvii) tributes and taxes. The naive persona Martyr puts on is unmasked when taking into account that this declaration of loyalty is accompanied by a denial of the emperor's divinity,[24] which troubled Caesar much more than a Christian tax mutiny. Another strategy that the apologists used to rob Caesar of his divinity was to posit him as the closest man to God and as having his authority ordained by God. As captured by another of Tertullian's maxims: "To call him God, is to rob him of his title" (Tertullian 2006b, Apology XXXIII), as he explained to Caesar:

> For we offer prayer for the safety of our princes to the eternal, the true, the living God, whose favour, beyond all others, they must themselves

desire . . . ; they are convinced that He is God alone, on whose power alone
they are entirely dependent, to whom they are second, after whom they
occupy the highest places, before and above all the gods. . . . They reflect
upon the extent of their power, and so they come to understand the highest; they acknowledge that they have all their might from Him against
whom their might is nought. Let the emperor make war on heaven; let him
lead heaven captive in his triumph; let him put guards on heaven; let him
impose taxes on heaven! He cannot. Just because he is less than heaven, he
is great. For he himself is His to whom heaven and every creature apper-
tains. . . . Without ceasing, for all our emperors we offer prayer. We pray
for life prolonged; for security to the empire; for protection to the imperial house; for brave armies, a faithful senate, a virtuous people, the world at
rest, whatever, as man or Caesar, an emperor would wish.

(Tertullian 2006b, Apology XXX)

Tertullian here brings key passages from the New Testament into play to
design the limited subjection of the Christians to Caesar by drawing a clear
distinction between political and economic government.[25] In addition to
the distinction between the two governments and the circumvention of
the political sphere, Tertullian also defined a raison d'être of political sovereignty, suggesting "that a mighty shock impending over the whole
earth— in fact, the very end of all things threatening dreadful woes— is
only retarded by the continued existence of the Roman Empire (Tertullian
2006b, Apology XXXII, see also Tertullian 2006c, On the Resurrection of the
Flesh XXIV).

Here, as elsewhere, *Irenaeus* mark a new development in the exegesis of
Romans 13:1–7:

For since man, by departing from God, reached such a pitch of fury as
even to look upon his brother as his enemy, and engaged without fear in
every kind of restless conduct, and murder, and avarice; God imposed
upon mankind the fear of man, as they did not acknowledge the fear of
God, in order that, being subjected to the authority of men, and kept under restraint by their laws, they might attain to some degree of justice,
and exercise mutual forbearance through dread of the sword suspended
full in their view, as the apostle says: For he bears not the sword in vain;
for he is the minister of God, the avenger for wrath upon him who does

evil. And for this reason too, magistrates themselves, having laws as a clothing of righteousness whenever they act in a just and legitimate manner, shall not be called in question for their conduct, nor be liable to punishment. But whatsoever they do to the subversion of justice, iniquitously, and impiously, and illegally, and tyrannically, in these things shall they also perish; for the just judgment of God comes equally upon all, and in no case is defective. Earthly rule, therefore, has been appointed by God for the benefit of nations, and not by the devil, who is never at rest at all, nay, who does not love to see even nations conducting themselves after a quiet manner, so that under the fear of human rule, men may not eat each other up like fishes; but that, by means of the establishment of laws, they may keep down an excess of wickedness among the nations.

(AH V:24.2)

In the foregoing "Hobbesian" quotation, Irenaeus ties together two assertions from Romans 13: first, that political authority originates in divinity; second, that political rule by law is established in order to prevent vice and to punish evildoers. Irenaeus binds the two together by arguing that God appointed political institutions as a punishment for original sin as a tool to manage vice. Conceptualizing the political this way, Irenaeus introduces yet another revolution to Greek thought, as the boundary that the ancients labored to sustain between the political community and the management of excessive desire in the economy is erased. Instead of a virtuous sphere of freedom, the political community is conceived by Irenaeus as just another sphere where human vice is performed, and for this reason it ought to be subjected to despotic rule. And since politics is no longer the sphere where one is enabled to pursue the ideal mode of life and pass judgments, it becomes a sphere in which people should exercise soundness of mind.

ORIGEN

Origen, who is considered to be the forerunner of both Athanasian orthodoxy and Arian heterodoxy, stipulated a political theory that situates him at the militant extreme of the orthodox camp. Many of his references to the political authorities can be found in his reply to Celsus's accusation that Christians pose a threat to the political community by "enter(ing) into secret associations with each other contrary to law. . . . Since, then, he [Celsus] babbles about the public law, alleging that the associations of the Christians are in violation of it" (AC I:1).

By condemning the subversive element that accompanies the Christian "secret society," Celsus makes use of the received (Roman) view that any partnership that exceeds the oikos that is not legalized must, by definition, pose a threat to the public order. In his reply, Origen avoids stating the obvious, namely, that the Christians gather their ecclesia in the oikos[26]—the most private of all places—because the political authorities denied them the right to manage their heavenly politeuma in public. Instead, Origen justifies the existence of the Christian community outside the legal framework by relying on an age-old philosophical argument that one can transgress the law and go as far as "revolt from a government which is, as it were, Scythian, and despotic" in the name of truth.[27] This claim is translated into a "Kantian" argument that one has to obey the political law only when it does not conflict with the divine law,[28] for if the two stand in conflict one must always obey divine law (AC VIII:26). Origen adds a utilitarian hedging to the legal one arguing that one has to obey political sovereignty only when it acts to promote the good against evil (Chrysostom 2002a on Romans IX:27). Commenting on Romans 13, Origen establishes an "anarchistic" approach (Parsons 1940:348) by reading Paul as saying that every *soul* (Ψυχή) must subject itself as freeing the *spirit* from such obligation, advocating that any person who has reached a full spiritual com-union with God has nothing to render onto Caesar.[29] Liberating the spirit from subjection to Caesar frees any person who has reached a full spiritual com-union with God from subjection to political authorities.[30] By presenting the possibility of living a life devoid of subjection to these authorities, by practicing a sin-free life, Origen takes Irenaeus's assertion that the source of political sovereignty is human sin one step further. He does so by setting the apostles who had no (earthly) possessions whatsoever to render to Caesar as a model.[31]

It should be noted that, by releasing the spiritual person from subjection to political authorities, Origen does not release humans from subjection in itself, as there are two distinct forms of government—the political and economic (identified with the imperial and the ecclesiastical administrations)—to which humans are subjected. While the political one lawfully subjects any person who (still) communes in the sphere of human vices and sin as part of the role ascribed to it in sustaining the ecclesiastical-spiritual government (in the same way that the despotic rule over bodily desires is used to enable communal theoretical life), all are subjected to the other government, whether directly as a member of the society of believers or indirectly through political rule, which is itself subjected to God, who appoints the kings (*AC* VIII:68).

Origen[32] made yet another contribution that was embraced after the Christianization of the empire (Setton 1967:48–49),[33] this time to thought on the role of political sovereignty in promoting the economy of salvation, arguing that "God preparing the nations for His teaching, that they might be under one prince, the king of the Romans, and that it might not, owing to . . . the existence of many kingdoms would have been a hindrance to the spread of the doctrine of Christ throughout the entire world" (*AC* II:30), as it was part of the divine economy "that Christ was born in the reign of Augustus, who, so to speak, fused together into one monarchy the many populations of the earth" (*AC* II:30).

It is only after he establishes how the empire serves the economy of salvation that Origen turns to discuss how Christians contribute to the well-being of the former, demonstrating why they are loyal citizens of the empire in spite of the fact that they evade military and civil service. This is done by bringing together Paul's call to pray on behalf of political sovereigns and Christ's imperative, saying that the Christians render to Caesar a prayer on his behalf, which in turn brings peace, and that this prayer is a far greater service to Caesar than the one rendered by those who serve in his army. The reason being is that they recruit the help and might of God himself for the safety of the empire (*AC* VIII:73) and, contrary to the latter, they freely choose to do so. In reply to Celsus's accusations that the Christians evade holding politico-governmental positions, Origen replies in the same spirit saying that "it is not for the purpose of escaping public duties that Christians decline public offices, but that they may reserve themselves for a diviner and more necessary service in the Church of God—for the salvation of men" (*AC* VIII:75).

Summing up pre-Nicean Christian political theory, it is based on the following three principles:

1. Limited self-subjection to political powers. Alongside the acceptance of the Pauline imperative of self-subjection, the Christian writers labor to circumvent it, arguing that the Christian subject is allowed to avoid compliance to the sovereign when it doesn't pose a spiritual threat, demand of her that she deny God, and when it is in accordance with the divine law. Another kind of limitation depends on the believer's judgment of the

sovereign action in general: one can avoid self-subjection when the sovereign does not strive to achieve peace for his subjects and when he acts in the service of the Evil One instead of the Good One.

2. Christ's maxim is interpreted as creating a distinction between economy and politics. As summarized by Wilfrid Parsons:

> The fundamental quarrel between the Roman Empire and the Christian Church was that the Church refused to identify the two orders and in fact separated them. The empire demanded the absolute union of religion and political government, while the Church insisted that each be confined to its proper sphere. This separation, of course, was based on Christ's own dictum about the separate duties owed to God and to Caesar. On the other hand, Saint Paul elevated Caesar, that is, political government, to a higher plane, since he derived Caesar's powers from God Himself. This duality of Christian thought—separation of the two orders and their common origin from the same God—must be remembered in all that follows.
>
> (Parsons 1940: 341–42)

3. There's an attempt to define the role of political sovereignty in the economy of salvation. Political sovereignty is considered in different manners: first, a punishment for human sin; second, as the one that is entrusted with its management using despotic rule, third, as passing just trials, and last, as keeping the peace that is essential for the growth of the society of the believers in Christ's economy.

Following the Baptism of Constantine

The Christianization of the empire in the fourth century CE radically altered relations between economy and politics as the Christian ecclesia ceased being a "secret society" that congregated outside the boundaries of the law and, as such, poses an immanent threat to the security of the empire. Although not the first to exceed the boundaries of the oikos into the public sphere,[34] the Christian society was indeed the first public partnership that was entirely dedicated to function as economy's space of appearance. As happened in previous events when the economy exceeded its boundaries into a new sphere, the problem the Fathers of the fourth century had to deal with was reestablishing new boundaries, a problem that was formulated this time as how the economy should function in the same ecumenical space that was already occupied by the imperial polity. This gets translated into a series of questions: is the ecclesia included in the empire, does it exist alongside it, or does it contain the empire in its bounds? Should the Christianized empire adapt the ready-made Hellenistic model in which Caesar-God functions as the head of both political and religious communities to its need?[35] And, if not, how can two different social bodies—the Christian and the imperial—coexist in the same space, or should there be only one social body, one legal persona, that is subjected to two distinct establishments and two different wills that are hypostatically united? The answers to these questions was framed by the Christological debate between the orthodox and the heterodox that revolved around the first economic model, and particularly the question whether the Son is of the same essence (ὁμοούσιος) as the father, or is he "just" of a similar essence (ὁμοιούσιος)? As argued by Athanasius, who championed the orthodox camp, the subordination of the Church to the rule of Caesar goes in tandem with the denial of the Son's full divinity.[36] That is because the transcription of Christ's full subjection as the one who is similar to the Father, but does not share his essence, dictates the unconditional subjection of the Church's economists to Caesar, as held by the Arians.

The two models that competed over the hearts of both Caesar and the economists are described by George H. Williams in the following way:

> Schematically we may call the two contending concepts of Christ dominating the dogmatic history of the fourth century, the Catholic and the Arian. . . . Roughly speaking these two Christologies gave rise to, or are at least associated with, two main views of the Empire and the relationship of the Church thereto. According to one view the emperor is bishop of bishops. According to the other, the emperor is within the Church. . . . That Christology, in the broadest sense of the word, was a matter of political concern in the fourth century needs, of course, no demonstration. . . . In brief, the possible connection (1) between the Catholic insistence upon the consubstantiality of the Son and the championship of the independence of the Church of which he is the Head and (2) between the Arian preference for Christological subordination and the Arian disposition to subordinate the Church to the State.
>
> (Williams 1951a: 9–10)

"To sum up, then, the Arianizing view of the divine authority of the Christian emperor, as we have been able to reconstruct it from the meager and disparate remains: the emperor is either the imitator or the interpreter of either the logos or the Supreme God (in Arian Christian terms, the Father), himself a kind of god coordinated in function with the demigod Christ, and as such the living law in a monolithic, monotheistic Church-empire opposed alike to divisive polytheism and disruptive Nicene Trinitarianism" (Williams 1951a:25).[37] At this initial stage in the development of the economic models, the model was translated into equating the status of the Church—the transcription of God the Son with that of Caesar—who was seen as the transcription of God the Father.[38]

It took some time for the orthodox model to gain traction, as the enthusiasm steered by the Christianization of Constantine did not pass over them. Even Athanasius, the champion of orthodoxy, approved in his earlier texts of the subjection of the church to the rule of Caesar (Dvornik 1966:735). Such approval can be found in *Against the Heathen* where he states that God's rule of the cosmos, political rule, the soul ruling over the body, the harmony of a chorus, and the division of labor in the polis are all administered by one sovereign (Athanasius 2004b, *Against the Heathen* 38, 43). It was only after Constantius (Constantine's son and heir) sided with the Arian heterodoxy in the Christological debate that Athanasius began fighting against surrendering the Church to Caesar by proclaiming a clear-cut distinction between economy and politics. He did so by zealously protecting the independence of the Church from any political intervention in the economy of the mysteries, allowing its subjection to Caesar solely in profane matters (Murphy 1967:129). Athanasius stressed this position in his Arian history, while quoting the following letter that Hosius sent to Constantius:[39]

> Remember that you are a mortal man. Be afraid of the day of judgment, and keep yourself pure thereunto. Intrude not yourself into Ecclesiastical matters, neither give commands unto us concerning them; but learn them from us. God has put into your hands the kingdom; to us He has entrusted the affairs of His Church; and as he who would steal the empire from you would resist the ordinance of God, so likewise fear on your part lest by taking upon yourself the government of the Church, you become guilty of a great offense. It is written, Render unto Caesar the things that

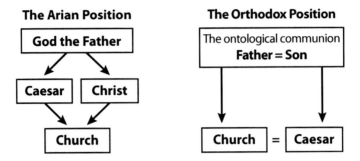

FIGURE 4.1. THE TRANSCRIPTION OF THE FIRST ECONOMIC MODEL INTO THE ECUMENICAL SPHERE

are Caesar's, and unto God the things that are God's. Neither therefore is it permitted unto us to exercise an earthly rule, nor have you, Sire, any authority to burn incense.

(Athanasius 2004c:44)

In the text Athanasius combines the Pauline assertion that political sovereignty originates in divinity and Christ's imperative for the purpose of reestablishing the distinction between the two forms of government that humans are subjected to. Like many before him, Athanasius chooses to point to the divine source of sovereignty in order to "remind" Caesar that he is human and not divine. To this "reminder" Athanasius added the claim that government, either political or economic, was entrusted into the hands of those in authority in the service of a higher cause, as implied in Timothy 1.

If we translate the debate into the economic models terminology, the origin of the Arian "fallacy" is the denial of the Ontological Communion, instead viewing the transcription principle as the substance of what is transcribed (and not "merely" as the mode of transcription). Putting it differently, the Arian claim is that what is transcribed in the economy of the incarnation is the Father's rule over the Son. The orthodox response is best formulated by Gregory of Nazianzus in Oration 29:2.[40] In it, Gregory sheds light on a crucial difference between the Father's monarchy in the Ontological Communion and human monarchies, arguing that the former does not result solely from the persona of the Father, but is created by the communion between the three persons of the Godhead, who generate it as an equal partnership of harmony of will and identity of action. This kind of monarchy cannot be transcribed into the human communities that are subjected to the condition of becoming.[41] this implies that anyone who chooses to embrace the monarchy of a single human persona betrays the Godhead.[42]

John Chrysostom

Patristic political thought reached its culmination in John Chrysostom,[43] who adapted and developed political thought to doctrinal developments and to the living reality of an empire in which it was most likely, although there was no guaranty, that both Church and empire would remain orthodox.[44]

THE SON'S SELF-SUBJECTION TO THE FATHER: THE TRANSCRIPTION OF THE MODEL FOR BEING GOVERNED

Chrysostom's theory of government can be found in his exegesis of first Corinthians 11:3: "Christ is the head of every man, and the man is the head of a woman, and God is the head of Christ."[45] In the Ontological Communion, he claims, there was only one form of government. In it the Father being an ultimate source—mon-arche—is accompanied by the son's being governed by the Father, a governmentality that is characterized by the Son's free choice to subject himself to the Father: "as the obedience of the Son to the Father is greater than we find in men towards the authors of their being, so also His liberty is greater. . . . We ought to admire the Father also, that He begot such a son, not as a slave under command, but as free, yielding obedience and giving counsel. For the counselor is no slave. But again, when you hear of a counselor, do not understand it as though the Father were in need, but that the Son has the same honor with Him that begot Him" (Chrysostom2004d, homily 26 on First Corinthians 3).

EVE'S PUNISHMENT

The monarchical relationship between God the Father and his son are transcribed into the relationship between Adam and Eve, who before committing her sin subjected herself to Adam willingly as equal partner.[46] The

divine punishment bestowed on humanity in response to Eve's sin introduces into the world the other form of government, a despotic one that
subjects the governed by brute force, fear, and limitations on life.[47] As described by Elaine Pagels,[48] "Eve's subjection, once voluntary, now took on
the quality of punishment, becoming mandatory and hence oppressive.
Wherever sin enters, Chrysostom explains, fear and coercion displace the
dynamic energy of love. Spreading from that first government, man's rule
over woman, fear and coercion have infected the whole structure of human relationships, from family to city and nation.... Imperial rule, above
all, epitomizes the social consequences of sin" (Pagels 1985:71).[49]

According to Chrysostom, the truly original form of subjection re-
emerges into created world in the economy of the incarnation when the
Son willingly subjected himself to death as an equal partner to the Father.
Ever since, there are two forms of subjection that takes place in the world:
the political one that is originated in Eve's sin and ruled by necessity and
the economic one that is freely chosen by its subjects and is transcribed
into the Church, which is Christ's sin-free body.

SETTING THE MATRON FREE

Implicit in Chrysostom's governmental theory is that the basic human
condition is to be governed[50] so that there is no sphere of human life that is
devoid of subjection.[51] Chrysostom adds another transgender imperative
to the one promulgated by Gregory of Nyssa (who instructs the philosopher to desire to give birth in the spirit in accordance with the model of
the Virgin Mary), instructing every man to subject himself to human authorities in the same way that the Eve subjected herself to Adam.[52] That is,
as an act of free will, as equal by nature, and as a persona who is subjected
to him. Reading the two imperatives together portrays the "heavenly politeuma" as a community in which a "real and true drag show" is enacted
in both theoretical and practical life, so that all are expected to put on display a persona of a graceful matron reflecting the persona of the Son as
governed in the eyes of their fellow members who gaze at their actions and
souls. Although setting the persona of the matron free by offering a clear
governmental model in which she partakes in government as an equal
partner who willingly subjects herself to her master, Chrysostom did not
free females from their subjection. For any man can become a matron, but

no women can become more than a matron, including the one whose "name expresses the entire mystery of the economy,"[53] the God bearer Virgin Mary,[54] who, in a nonsaturated desire to give birth in the good and beautiful, gave birth to God in the flesh.

Chrysostom further explores his governmental theory in his homily on Second Corinthians (15:4–5), arguing that "there are (these) species of rule; one, that whereby men rule peoples and states, regulating this the political life. . . . A second there is whereby every one that has understanding rules himself. . . . There is yet another rule, higher than the political rule. And what is this? That in the Church." The three species coalesce in the final account into the political and the economic. "For as the rule over the many is in a manner twofold, so also is that which each one exerts over himself. And again, in this point also the spiritual rule transcends the political. . . . As great then as the difference between soul and body, is that which separates this rule again from that."

According to Chrysostom, politics is the kingdom of necessity and suppression, while the society of believers in Christ's economy is modeled as a sphere in which humans practice their freedom imitating the Son's self-subjection as a mode of participating in government. Equating the economy with the soul and seeing it as the sphere of freedom, alongside paralleling Caesar's despotic rule over his subjects with the soul's rule over the body, overturns economy and politics positioning in Aristotle. As described in Leshem 2014a, in Aristotle the *oikodespotic* rule of the master over the slave is paralleled with the soul rule over the excess of the nonrational part in man, and the political community is seen as the sphere in which the masters rule over themselves and others pursue the ideal mode of life.[55]

Based on his genealogy, Chrysostom introduces a distinction between two forms of government, a "good" and a "bad" one, conferring the free choice between the two upon the governed subject. The revolution in politics-economy relations is reflected in the modeling of the political sphere as a sphere that contains nothing except despotic rule that forces itself by necessity. As a result, the question of human freedom is no longer the classical question of how one can exceed the human condition of subjection. Instead, the question that is posed before each human by Chrysostom is to what form of government to subject herself, as it is evident that life devoid of subjection is out of the question. The problem of human freedom is translated into a choice between two optional subjections:

Classical Moment	Imperial Moment	Christian Moment
The political sphere is distinguished by exclusion	*Economy is everywhere*	*Economic growth by inclusion*
Politics is the freedom of the nonsubjected	Governmentality is being at home in the	Economy is willingly subjecting oneself as an equal
——*law*——	• Cosmopolis	——*law*——
	• Polis	
Economy is despotic rule over excessive necessity	• Household	**Politics is despotic rule over excessive necessity**
	• Self through familiarization	
Icon: master-citizen	Icon: the wise man	Icon: the matron

FIGURE 4.2. THE RELATIONSHIP BETWEEN ECONOMY AND POLITICS IN THE THREE MOMENTS

willingly subjecting oneself to the divine will, an act that is a stepping-stone into a true life of freedom, or a forced sinful life in which man is subjected to a despotic political government. Such free choice is taken both in the initial decision as to which form of government to subject oneself, a choice that repeats itself over and over again, and in the freedom that results from living virtuously. Once again, the mode in which Chrysostom designs the answer to the question of how to be governed in community transcribes the same model that Gregory of Nyssa designed as an answer to the problem of freedom in its ethical context, in the space between me and myself (a homology that Chrysostom is well aware of, pointing to the similarity between the rule over the many and the rule over oneself).

Based on the changeover of the sphere of freedom, Chrysostom argues that "of governments there are some natural, and others which are elective;— natural as of the lion over the quadrupeds, or as that of the eagle over the birds; elective, as that of an Emperor over us; for he does not reign over his fellow-servants by any natural authority. Therefore it is that he oftentimes loses his sovereignty. For such are things which are not naturally inherent; they readily admit of change and transposition" (Chrysostom 2004a, Homilies on the Statutes to the People of Antioch 7:3).

Comparing Chrysostom's claims that the cyclical rise and fall of political regimes result from their artificial nature to Polybius's claim that the rise and fall of political regimes are a by-product of their conditioning by the cyclical economy of nature is yet another demonstration of the novelty of Christian political thought. Once again, the resemblance between the way Gregory of Nyssa connects circularity to the artificial deviation of natural desire in the sphere between man and himself and the way Chrysostom ties circularity to the artificiality that is produced by the rule of one slave over his fellow bondsperson in community is clearly seen.

THE SEPARATION OF POWERS

Chrysostom held that the duality of government (over the virtuous free and over the sinful) was transcribed at first into the earthly oikos and only later into political government, and although Chrysostom is clearly in favor of people managing a virgin oikos (monastery in this context) in which every human can become a truly God-fearing matron, he acknowledge that a free and equal government can subsist in the earthly oikos. By admitting that marriage and bodily begetting is not necessarily sinful (see *homilies on Isaiah*),[56] he establishes the ethical and free choice in the earthly oikos as a choice of the form of government that it is governed by. Unlike the oikos, which is subjected to only one form of government, the public sphere is governed by the two modes simultaneously that differ in two ways.[57] First, each form of government applies a different code of conduct, so while political sovereignty enforces the law over its subjects, economic government persuades them to self-subject (Chrysostom 2004b, On the Priesthood 2:3).[58] The distinction between the two forms of governmental reason is expressed in Chrysostom's discussion of the role of the emperor as a "bishop of extra ecclesiastical affairs," arguing that it is not "right for Christians to eradicate error by constraint and force, but to save humanity by persuasion and reason and gentleness. Hence no emperor of Christian persuasion enacted against you [pagan] legislation such as was contrived against us by those who served demons" (John Chrysostom 1985:83).[59]

The two forms of government rule over two distinct spheres are discussed in the fourth and fifth oration (of six) on Isaiah 6. In it Chrysostom takes great liberty in commenting on Isaiah 6:1: "In the year of King Uzziah's death (I saw the Lord sitting on a throne, lofty and exalted)," as if it was a mere excuse to present his theory of the relation between the economic and the political forms of government. In the oration he rushes to discuss the circumstances of Uzziah's death from a leprosy that broke out on his forehead upon entering the Temple with the intention of burning incense

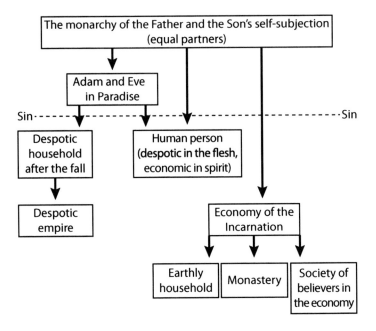

FIGURE 4.3. GENEALOGY OF SOVEREIGNTY

on the altar. The story of the political sovereign's attempt to exceed the boundaries of the sphere that is given to his authority into the one that is handed to the economists of salvation and the divine punishment that was inflicted in response to this transgression is used by Chrysostom to redraw the line between the spheres that are governed by each authority, as well as to establish a hierarchy between them:[60]

> The limits of kingship are of one kind, the limits of priesthood another—but the latter surpass the former. . . . He (the king) is in fact appointed to economize things on earth; the institution of priesthood, on the other hand, is established on high. . . . The king is entrusted with things here below, I with heavenly things (when I say "I," I mean the priest). . . . The king is entrusted with bodies, the priest with souls; the king remits the balance of debts, the priest the balance of sins; the former obliges, the latter exhorts; the former by pressure, the latter by free will; the former has material weapons, the later spiritual weapons; the former wages war on savages, the latter on demons. The latter office is higher;

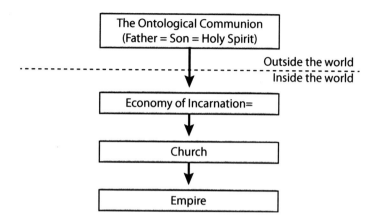

FIGURE 4.4. THE TRANSCRIPTION OF GOVERNMENT

hence the prince submits his head to the priest's hands, and at all points the old dispensation [economy] priests anointed kings. . . . So that you may learn that priesthood is greater than kingship.[61]

(John Chrysostom, homily 4 on Isaiah)

Chrysostom also traces the demarcation line between economy and politics in the human soul, along the "undefined by definition" borderline (see Leshem 2014b) between the sphere of bodily desires that must be subjected to despotic rule and the ethical and theoretical sphere that participates in communal philosophical life.

THE DISTINCTION BETWEEN GOVERNOR AND GOVERNMENT[62]

In his exegesis of Romans 13 Chrysostom introduces a distinction between the particular sovereign who happen to be in power and the institution of sovereignty.[63] Based on this distinction, Chrysostom interprets the Pauline imperative as decreeing subjection to the institution of sovereignty as long as it works in the service of the economy. In so doing, he sets a limit on obedience to any particular sovereign while arguing that, although humans must subject themselves to the institution of sovereignty, they nevertheless are continually confronted with the choice whether to subject themselves to the particular sovereigns that are in power at the present time.[64] Chrysostom generalizes the limits of self-subjection to authorities by employing the same distinction in his discourse on subjection to pastoral economy in general and to a specific bishop.[65] Thus he entrusts humans as governed creatures, subjected to authorities and having a share in government, with a responsibility to examine each edict and free choice whether to comply or not.

THE ROLES OF POLITICAL GOVERNMENT IN THE SERVICE OF THE ECONOMY

Although Chrysostom draws a clear distinction and a hierarchy between the two forms of government,[66] he does not identify any inherent conflict between empire and Church. On the contrary, he sees harmony, as the purpose of the economic government of the Church is not to annihilate political government but to complete and improve it.[67] Although sharing Origen's assertion that "spiritual persons" have no need for a political government,[68] Chrysostom acknowledged that until the fullness of the ages political sovereignty is very much needed: "For anarchy, be where it may, is an evil, and a cause of confusion . . . so if you take away the sovereigns of the state, we will live a life more irrational than the beasts. For what the joists are to buildings, that sovereigns are in cities" (homily 21 on empire power and glory), without which there can be no economy.[69] By situating "adamic" politics as chronologically prior and a precondition for Christ economy,[70] Chrysostom turns once again to the classical economy-politics formation—in which the orderly management of the economy was considered a precondition for the emergence of politics—on its head. The role reversal can also be detected in the multiple modes of conduct that Chrysostom assigns the political sovereign in his attempts of keeping public order, as he adds positive incentives to the political sovereign toolbox along with the negative ones. A somewhat detailed discussion of the different roles of political government can be found in Chrysostom's exegesis of Romans 13. Not neglecting to mention the "traditional" roles of political government, he presents, in a tone that does not lack sarcasm, political sovereigns as wage earners and public servants:

But also because he (Caesar) is a benefactor to you in things of the greatest importance, as he procures peace to you and the blessings of political economy [οἰκονομίας πολιτικῆς] and the blessings of civil institutions. For there are countless blessings to states through these authorities; and if you were to remove them, all things would go to ruin, and neither city nor country, nor private nor public buildings, nor anything else would stand, but all the world will be turned upside down, while the more powerful devour the weaker. And so even if some wrath were not to follow man's disobedience, even on this ground you ought to be subject, that you may not seem devoid of conscience and feeling towards the benefactor. . . . Without going one by one into the benefits done to states by the sovereigns, as that of good order and peace, the other services, as regarding the soldiery, and those over the public business, he shows the whole of this by a single case. For that you are benefited by him, he means, you bear witness yourself, by paying him a salary. Observe the wisdom and judgment of the blessed Paul. For that which seemed to be burdensome and annoying—the system of imposts—this he turns into a proof of their care for men. What is the reason, he means, that we pay tribute to a king? It is not as providing for us? And yet we should not have paid it unless we had known in the first instance that we were gainers from this superintendence. Yet it was for this that from of old all men came to an agreement that governors should be maintained by us, because to the neglect of their own affairs, they take charge of the public, and on this they spend their whole leisure, whereby our goods also are kept safe. . . . For it is in no small degree that they contribute to the settled state of the present life, by keeping guard, beating off enemies, hindering those who are for sedition in the cities, putting an end to differences among any.

(John Chrysostom 2002a, homily 23 on Romans 13)

Chrysostom here continues the tradition of conceptualizing sovereignty in its economic context and of judging its function by the services it renders to the economy.[71] As was demonstrated, patristic political thought accounts for great variation of these services, beginning with the night watchperson state of Irenaeus, who assigns it with the legal use of violence and limits its involvement to keeping public order while using its punishing capabilities as written in law. Chrysostom enriches the sovereign toolkit in the service of public order by adding positive incentives to the negative ones. Besides protecting internal order, Chrysostom also follows Tertullian and entrusts the sovereign with the role of forestalling an imminent catastrophe in the form of the Antichrist (see John Chrysostom 2002c, homily 4 on Second Thessalonians 1–2).[72] A significant development of the political sovereign function sanctions its active involvement in the life of its citizens as the protector of the economy by securing the environmental conditions for its growth, as a "bishop of extra-ecclesiastical affairs."[73] Following Origen, the mere subjection of all of the inhabited world—the *ecumenia*—to the same political sovereignty was considered to be an essential contribution to economic growth.[74] This role is defined by Karl Friedrich Hagel as "free church under the protection of Emperor" (Hagel in Setton 1967:74), which can be rephrased as "free economy under the protection of Caesar." Caesar's protection of the society of believers in Christ's economy is not solely a passive one. The political sovereign is expected to play an active role in the persuasion of those who refuse to partake in the economy to join the society of believers. The last role given to political government is that of care for the welfare of its citizens. One can find echoes of such a role in the writings of Basil the Great and John Chrysostom (Reilly 1945:8–9).[75]

The Distinction Between Economy and Politics as Mirrored by the Models

The economic models design both economic-political relations and the thought of the political in itself. This was already demonstrated by Athanasius, who translated the Nicean formulation of the first economic model (of the ontological communion) that depicted God the Son and God the Father as equal by nature into the view that the Church ought not to be subordinated to Caesar. Chrysostom followed suit and translated the "Cappadocian Settlement" into the subjection of political sovereignty to economic government in this manner: Following the purification of Christ's (human) body by its inclusion in the economy of the incarnation and his ascension, the Church became the purified body that serves as the space of appearance of the economy of the Holy Spirit. At the next stage, the Church acts as the purified soul while the political body is conceived as the one in need of purifying. Here, as elsewhere, purification by inclusion is operated by a mimesis of the mirror. In this case, the Church functions as the mirror in which the persona of God the Son partakes and reflects. The mirror of the Church is polished by a mimesis of the operations of the Son in the third economic model, which are reflected in Church actions toward the carnal and impure political sphere. These operation enable the inclusion of the political body into the sphere of holiness by the operation of the second economic model (of the hypostatic union). As can be seen, political sovereignty serves as the sinful body purified by the Church by its subjection to it in the hierarchy of transcription.

The hypostatic union of *imperium* and *sacerdotium* also dictates that the two do not unite into one principle of action (*energia*), in the same way that in Christ the human will appeared alongside the divine one, notwithstanding their mutual eschatological goal to "recapitulate all in the economy at the fullness of times"; moreover, each of the wills (fully identified with the political institution and the ecclesiastical one respectively) acts through its distinguished principle of action: the Church persuades and Caesar lawfully enforces positive and negative incentives. As may be seen, the second economic model inspires the formulation of a theory that will retain economy and politics wholly distinct in the same social body while acting in prefect harmony.

The by-product of the use of the models in the design of the economic-political relations is a role reversal of their classical formation, as politics becomes a sphere of coercion while the economy becomes a sphere of freedom. This freedom is not the negative freedom that will characterize our modern economy, namely, freedom from political coercion. Instead, it is a positive freedom to pursue the ideal mode of life in the bounds of the economic sphere. And while the political sphere is classified as a sphere of coercion that was meant to maintain order in the service of the ever-growing economic sphere, the latter is governed in accordance with the third economic model (*Christomimesis*), in which coercion is practically useless, as any use of it will turn it into a political sphere. Instead, the new society is governed by the use of the (once) political art of rhetoric, as the oikonomos is required to persuade the multitude to agree to certain things, first and foremost to a mode of conduct that mimes the third economic model by practicing erotic desire of God, self-askesis, and inclusive philanthropic condescension (*sugkatabsys*). The economy that was handed to Paul and, by apostolic succession, to all the economists is to persuade those who are subjected to their authority to willingly choose to partake in a free association, doing so by using his entire rhetorical arsenal, not excluding "economy of truth," as any form of coercion by force, as novel at its intentions may be, will necessarily corrupt the economy.

THE REFLECTION OF THE ECONOMIC MODELS IN POLITICAL LAW

> And yet, despite this [pastoral being a terrestrial power], and leaving aside the Eastern Church, in the Western Church it has always remained a power that is completely distinct from [political]* power.... I think pastoral power, its form, type of function, and internal technology, remains absolutely specific and different from political power, at least until the eighteen century.... The reason for this distinction is a big problem of history and, for me at least, an enigma. Anyway, I make absolutely no claim to resolve the problem, or even to set out its complex dimensions.... How did it come about that these two types of power, political and pastoral, thus maintained their specificity and their physiognomies? My impression is that if we examined Eastern Christianity we would have a different process, a quite different development, a much stronger intrication, and perhaps some different development, and perhaps some form of loss of specificity on both sides. I don't know.
>
> (Foucault 2007:154–55)

The answer to Foucault's "Eastern enigma" is that the two types of power maintained their specificity and their physiognomies while fully united in an attempt to transcribe the second economic model in imperial law and in what can be termed, anachronistically, the mechanism of security of the Christian Empire of the East.

The models are clearly reflected in the introduction to the Sixth Novella of Emperor Justinian, which "was at once a summary, and a program" (Florovsky 1957:141), and "one of the most important texts defining the basic ideas of Byzantine political thought" (Dvornik 1956:83), which prescribed relations between imperial authority and the Christian priesthood (see Baynes 1955:50):[76]

> The greatest gifts given by God to men by His supreme kindness are the priesthood and the empire, of which the first serves the things of God and

the second rules the things of men and assumes the burden of care for them. Both proceed from one source and adorn the life of man. Nothing therefore will be so greatly desired by the emperors than the honour of the priests, since they always pray to God about both these very things. For if the first is without reproach and adorned with faithfulness to God, and the other adorns the state entrusted to it rightly and competently, a good symphony will exist, which will offer everything that is useful for the human race. We therefore have the greatest care concerning the true dogmas of God and concerning the honour of the priests ... because through this the greatest good things will be given by God—both those things that we already have will be made firm and those things which we do not have yet we shall acquire. Everything will go well if the principle of the matter is right and pleasing to God. We believe that this will come to pass if the holy canons are observed, which have been handed down to us by the apostles, those inspectors and ministers of God worthy of praise and veneration, and which have been preserved and explained.[77]

(Barker 1957:57–76)

As explained by John Meyendorff, the novela bares witness to the incarnation of the second economic model in the political law of the East:

In the west, this famous text [the sixth novella] provoked an institutional struggle between two legally different powers, the sacerdotium and the Imperium; but in Byzantium it was understood in a Christological context. In Christ, the natures are united, without separation or confusion, into one single hypostasis, or person, who is the unique source of their united (though distinct) existence. The adoption of the Christological model as a pattern for the organization of society illustrates quite well the contrast between the legally minded West and eschatologically oriented East.[78]

(Meyendorff 1979:123)

THREE SPHERES OF ACTION: HUMAN, DIVINE, PERICHORESIS BETWEEN THE TWO

The third economic model, in which a perichoresis between the Divine Persona of the Son and sin-free human nature takes place, is transcribed into

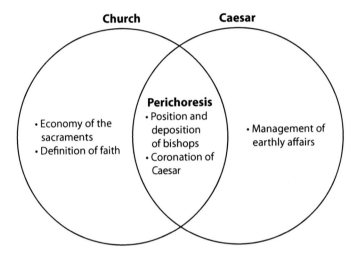

FIGURE 4.5. THE HYPOSTATIC UNION BETWEEN ECONOMY AND POLITICS

Eastern Christian imperial security mechanisms by a "double-edge limita-tion" that sets an absolute limit to imperial involvement in ecclesiastical affairs and to the economists' involvement in politics together with the generation of a perichoretic sphere in which Caesar partakes in ecclesiasti-cal affairs and the economists in the political ones.

Deno Geanakoplos, who examined the "double-edge limit" formation from its political point of view, sketches three distinct spheres of imperial involvement (Geanakoplos 1965).[79] The profane sphere of politics is the first one. Being nothing but human, it is subjected solely to Caesar's rule. The second sphere is dedicated to the administration of ecclesiastical af-fairs such as summoning ecumenical councils;[80] redistribution of patri-archates and the nomination and deposition of patriarchs was jointly ruled by Church and empire, when, in cases of disagreement and confrontation, Caesar had the last word.[81] Caesar's entrance into the third sphere, which includes the economy of the sacraments and the definition of dogma, is strictly forbidden. Dividing the social body into three spheres transcribes the economic models: The profane sphere is dedicated to the economy of vice and does not partake in the hypostatic union. As such, it is governed by Caeasr, the most human of all humans in the service of the economy, which seems to be the reason why Emperor Constantine called himself "bishop of extra-ecclesiastical affairs." The just and prudent government of the empire renders the same services to the society of believers in Christ economy as the ones produced by the ethical management of bodily desires, as both are seen as necessary for economic growth of personal theosis and communal soteria. Even though they lacked any institutional authority, the economists made sure to criticize political government when it diverged from sound-minded management of the political sphere, as the many orations that the Cappadocian Fathers and Chrysostom dedicated to what is now termed social justice testifies.

The imperial involvement in the management of the earthly affairs of the ecclesiastical body is justified by the presence of both human and divine wills in Christ. The use of the models also explain orthodox insistence (as well as the imperial concession) on keeping the third sphere,[82] in which the mysteries (sacraments) are economized free from imperial interference at all costs, for if that were so, "the Orthodox faith would have long since come to an end."[83]

5

Economy and the Legal Framework

The Two Paradigms

Upon the publication of *The Kingdom and the Glory: For a Theological Genealogy of Economy and Government* (2011), Giorgio Agamben completed his inquiry into the genealogy of the two paradigms that political power has assumed throughout the history of the West. The first of these paradigms, discussed by the "political" Agamben in *Homo Sacer* and *State of Exception,* is sovereign power. In his exploration of this concept, Agamben further developed the work of Carl Schmitt, who traced its origins in political theology. Agamben elaborated upon this foundation by inquiring into the revelation of sovereign power in the state of exception, arguing that we are living in an age in which the exception has become the norm. The second paradigm studied by the "economic" Agamben, which forms the subject matter of *The Kingdom and the Glory*, is governmental power. Here Agamben attempted to complete the work of Michel Foucault, who described pastoral economy as "the art of all arts, knowledge of all knowledges" (Foucault 2007:151), which "must bear on the whole Christian community and on each Christian in particular" (Foucault 2007:192), conducted in relation to three concepts: salvation, truth, and law. According to Foucault, governmentality came into being with the accommodation of these concepts as raison d'état in the sixteenth and seventeenth centuries (Foucault 2007:261–78) and its application to the whole of society and each individual via the apparatus of the police (Foucault 2007:278). As described by Foucault in his lectures from the following year (Foucault 2008), governmental reason was criticized and transformed into liberal governmentality in the eighteenth through nineteenth centuries, later denaturalized into neoliberal governmentality in the second half of the twentieth century.

While sharing Foucault's sense of urgency (2007:165; Agamben 2011:1) in inquiring into the genealogy of the Christian origins of governmentality, due to the latter's preeminence over all other paradigms of power, sovereignty included, and accepting his general scheme positing early Christianity as the origin of contemporary governmentality, Agamben argues that Foucault was prevented from "articulating his genealogy of governmentality all the way to the end and in a convincing way" (Agamben 2011:112–13). Foucault fails to account for the implications in consideration of the fact that "the very secularization of the world becomes the mark that identifies it as belonging to a divine oikonomia" (Agamben 2011:4). Agamben's genealogy of government differs from Foucault's in two ways.[1] Methodologically, he argues that Foucault fails to subscribe to his own rule, and as a result his archaeology of government does not "need to be able to follow the signature that displaces the concepts and orients their interpretation towards different fields" (Agamben 2011:112).[2] Based on this critique, Agamben labors on a corrective genealogy of theological economy, arguing that Foucault's historical situation of the original appearance of the distinction between being and acting should be moved back in time—from the sixteenth to the second century (Agamben 2011:111). Substantially, he argues that oikonomia was first displaced onto Trinitarian theology, to be translated only later as the art of pastorship. Thus, in order to be able to argue that one can recover the meaning of economy in the pastorate, one has to identify the way in which it belongs to a divine oikonomia (Agamben 2011:110), as I do in chapter 2.

The Christological Origins of Pastoral Economy in the State of Exception

The economic models and the transcription principle described in chapter 2 fully answer Agamben's substantial critique within the bounds of canon law as it describes how the pastoral economy reflects that of the divine. In order to tackle it outside the boundaries of the canon, I will draw on Hamilcar Alivisatos's typology of divine and pastoral economy. The first sort of economy in Alivisatos's typology is divine. He writes that "this is the incarnation of the Divine Logos for the salvation of humanity from sin, according to the all-wise and all-holy Will of God. After the completion of the Saviour's redemptive work, the divine 'economy' is continued through the Church instituted by Him and governed by the Holy Spirit" (Alivisatos 1944:31). The second aspect of economy in Alivisatos's taxonomy relates to the Church. He describes it as "*The spiritual and moral administration of the Church*—either of the whole Church or of a particular Church. . . . Thus the Apostles and their collaborators, and consequently their successors who continue their work are called οἰκονομοι του λογου και των μυστηριων (stewards of the word and of the mysteries)" (Alivisatos 1944:31). Foucault describes the secularization of this type of economy in his genealogy of governmentality. Finally, the third aspect of economy is more directly administrative. Alivisatos claims that it concerns "the regulation of the condition of Church life, order and administration according to circumstances" (Alivisatos 1944:31). Such an economy forms a continuation of the second kind, and, as George Maloney (1971:95) argues, it "is used wherever a strict application of the law would put in peril the essential aim of the church, i.e., the salvation of souls according to the spirit of the gospel." This third aspect is the one that canon law literature terms "the principle of economy."

The second and third economies, namely the two types of pastoral economy, are preformed by what Nicholas the Mystic defined as "an imitation of divine philanthropy" in the form of "accommodation unto salvation" (Nicholas Mystikos 1973, Letter 32).[3] The distinction between these two is found in their relation to canon law: the second aspect of economy is conducted within the bounds of canon law, while the third is applied whenever the suspension of canon law is called for. When this third aspect of economy is applied, the boundaries set by canon law are lifted by pastoral authority, and the Church's domain is extended, generating a liminal sphere at its boundaries. This usually takes place whenever acting according to the strict letter of canon does not allow for such an extension, and it requires the exclusion of (potential) believers from the body of the Church.

Other scholars of canon law have further complicated this typology. Constantine Tsirpanlis (1987:30) divides what came to be called the principle of economy (the third aspect of pastoral economy) into two subcategories. The first of these is doctrinal economy, originating in the writings of Athanasius and Gregory of Nazianzus. The term is used by Tsirpanlis to denote "terminological flexibility" or a "terminological compromise and concession of love over a matter of faith" (1987:30–31). The latter is applied for the purpose of preserving the unity of the Church, and for allowing as many people as possible to become members of the living body of Christ. Put differently, doctrinal economy allows for flexibility in the use of words, particularly technical terms, as long as the essence of the doctrine remains unharmed. The second category within the principle of economy is termed either ecclesiastical, sacramental, or disciplinary economy. It originates in the first canon of Basil the Great and is applied in order to confirm the validity of sacraments conducted outside the boundaries of the Orthodox Church—the most important of which is baptism. Its focus on validating baptism—most important since the great schism, Latin baptism—means that this aspect of economy deals above all with the question of the boundaries of the ecclesial body.

A Genealogy of the Principle of Economy

BASIL THE GREAT: PHENOMENOLOGY OF THE OUTSIDE

Economy as an explicit digression from strict adherence to canon made its debut in the first canon of Basil the Great, "the father of sacramental economy" (Tsirpanlis 1987:31), which is identified by Agamben as "the origin of the evolution that leads the term oikonomia to assume the meaning of 'exception'" (Agamben 2011:50). It formed part of a letter concerning the validity of baptism conducted outside the canonic boundaries of the Church. Basil's first canon is to be read against an ecclesiastical and canonic background. Following the baptism of Constantine, Christianity underwent a process of consolidation: emperors summoned bishops from all across the ecumene to canonize a doctrine concerning the nature of the Godhead and of Christ as well as the conducting of the sacraments. At the same time, all across the Christianized empire, Orthodox bishops labored to strengthen their dioceses in their struggle for eminence among the many sects by incorporating both laity and clergy of various creeds who wished to join the Orthodox camp. As part of this effort, Basil wrote a letter to tackle the convention that limited a bishop's authority to the canonical boundaries of the Church. This convention could be traced back to Cyprian, the third-century bishop of Carthage who asserted that "outside the church there is no salvation" and, therefore, that the sacraments, most importantly baptism, conducted by non-Orthodox clergy were null and void. In order to do so, Basil defines two modes of conduct of pastoral authority toward those baptized outside the canonic boundaries of the Church: According to canonic akribeia (Cyprian's stance), their baptism is considered invalid, and any digression from the canon is defined as falling within the confines of economy. Basil thereby entrusts bishops with the authority to decide which of these paths to follow: if they so wish, they will acknowledge a person's membership in the body of Christ; if not, let him or her be (re)baptized.

Nevertheless, by breaking canonic shackles placed on pastoral authority, Basil does not mean to grant bishops full-fledged freedom in inscribing the borders of the Church, and he is quick to set new limits on pastoral authority with respect to economy. He does so by grouping those who are located on the fringes of canonic boundaries into three kinds: "Heresies is the name applied to those who have broken entirely and have become alienated from the faith itself. Schisms is the name applied to those who on account of ecclesiastical causes and remediable questions have developed a quarrel amongst themselves. Parasynagogues is the name applied to gatherings held by insubordinate presbyters or bishops, and those held by uneducated laities" (Nikodemos and Agapios 1957:773–74). Basil designates a special procedure through which each of these groups may become members of the body of Christ: parasynagogues have to repent, heretics are in need of (re)baptism, and schismatics are considered as "being outside and yet belonging" and have to undergo chrismation. Basil's distinction between the treatment of schismatics and heretics introduces a novelty in the attitude toward baptism conducted outside the Church in which both heretics and schismatics are treated the same way, and both need to be baptized (Nikodemos and Agapios 1957:485).

Basil's phenomenology of the outside, as we may refer to it, redraws the boundaries of the Church. Its absolute boundary, which Cyprian identified with its canonic boundary, is pushed back, and the canon is now seen as

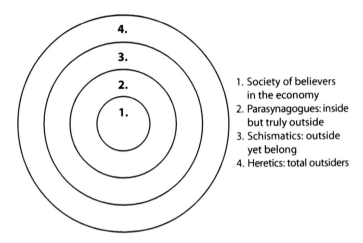

1. Society of believers
   in the economy
2. Parasynagogues: inside
   but truly outside
3. Schismatics: outside
   yet belong
4. Heretics: total outsiders

FIGURE 5.1. BASIL'S PHENOMENOLOGY OF THE OUTSIDE

setting only a relative boundary. It no longer demarcates the beginning of the outside world. Within its bounds there may now be found parasynagogues, who do not form part of the body of the Church, and outside it are the schismatics, who may well be introduced into the Church. The canon does not delimit the exercise of pastoral economy, but only testifies to its whereabouts. In so doing, it also generates a liminal sphere in which pastoral authority is not governed by the dictates of canon.

This liminal sphere that emerges in Basil's canon, and which lies between the approximate boundary and the absolute one, has three characteristics:

1. The liminal sphere is exceptional: One does not have to apply the principle of economy to the schismatics—the inhabitants of the liminal sphere. The bishop enjoys full discretion with respect to whether or not to apply economy to them. The exceptional quality of this sphere is shown by the way Basil treats the Catharoi and the Encratites, two sects identified as schismatics: while he allows for the application of economy toward the former group, with the result that their baptism is validated, he demands that the latter group be (re)baptized. If, as Andre de Halleux suggests (1987:57), the two groups function as "canonized models," then we may assume that Basil's mention of them and their differing treatment is meant to signify that the bishop holds the power to exercise economy in a state of exception.

2. The liminal sphere is anomalous: Acting according to economy in the liminal sphere is temporally delimited and can be changed in an instant according to the circumstances. This can be deduced from the fact that Basil is quick to restrict the harsh treatment of the Encratites, stating that whenever their treatment according to akribeia "is to become an obstacle in the general economy [of the Church], we must again adopt the custom and follow the Fathers who economically regulated the affairs of our Church" (Nikodemos and Agapios 1957:774).[4] Another testimony can be found in Basil's forty-seventh canon (Nikodemos and Agapios 1957:823). Basil argues that, against the economy exercised by the Church of Rome, both the Encratites and the Catharoi ought to be (re)baptized. By altering his decision, Basil clearly demonstrates that in the liminal sphere there are in fact no precedents whatsoever.

3. The liminal sphere is regulated: pastoral economy cannot be exercised without limits. It does not allow for the unconditional inclusion of the schismatics, not even through the procedures applied in the case of the parasynagogues. Local authorities enjoy full discretion in whether to apply economy in this matter, but it is the discretion to follow a specific economic procedure.

CYRIL OF ALEXANDRIA: ECONOMIC RATIONALITY

The question of how to exercise pastoral economy outside the boundaries set by canon arises time and again in the letters of Cyril of Alexandria (1987).[5] It is in these letters that a systematic thought concerning the principle of economy appears for the first time (Rai 1973).

Reading Cyril's letters, it seems clear that he fully embraces the existence of a sphere in which pastoral authority is unchecked by canon law. In a letter to Proclus, the archbishop of Constantinople, he goes even further and suggests that this sphere is generated on purpose by the canon. Cyril argues that the Council of Ephesus refrained from anathematizing Theodore of Mopsuestia "by economy, in order that some by paying heed to the opinion of the man might not cast themselves out of the churches. Economy in these matters is the best thing and a wise one" (letter 72). Thus, according to Cyril, pastoral economy was practiced in the formation of canon law itself: it meant to constitute a liminal sphere in which those in authority are endowed with the discretion to apply economy.

Taking the existence of this liminal sphere for granted, Cyril's main concern is the rationality that ought to govern the conduct of pastoral authority within it, as well as serving as a basis for criticizing the practice of such authority. Cyril is certain that one cannot simply economize at whim. In those cases when pastoral power is not checked by canon law, the need arises to find a way to regulate it, so that it won't be exercised arbitrarily. Cyril stresses three dimensions of pastoral economy: economy is a means to a higher end, its enactment is determined by the circumstances, and it is subject to prudent calculations.

1. The ends of economy: Cyril mentions several ends toward which economy is practiced: the peace and general good of the Church as a whole (letter 76); avoidance of a scandal that will pose a threat to the Church's stability (letter 82); and the one he favors—the graded inclusion of new members in the Church (letters 56, 57, 58, 72, 82). Thus, for example, in letter 82 he states that: "economy is the best and wisest course in these matters [involving repentant heretics], for akribeia generally disturbs many, even of the wisest."

2. The circumstantial nature of economy: The principle of economy is not to be applied automatically. As Cyril puts it, "it is the task of economy to appear sometimes to depart somewhat from the proper position with foregoing of loss in useful circumstances" (letter 76). A scandal is an example of a circumstance in which pastoral economy is exercised, but Cyril shows preference for practicing economy in peaceful times than in a state of emergency. This is most evident in Cyril's correspondence with Atticus, archbishop of Constantinople. The latter tries to justify his decision to allow the inclusion of John Chrysostom in a triptych as a legitimate exercise of pastoral economy, arguing that he had been forced to do so. In response, Cyril neither rules out the application of economy in general nor in the state of emergency, yet argues that the case in question does not qualify. After disqualifying the application of the principle of economy on account of a scandal, Cyril goes on to argue that, had Atticus prudently calculated his actions, he would not have needed to economize in the first place. As can be seen in other letters, Cyril regards the use of economy in the state of exception as an opportunity to be seized, rather than as something forced upon Church authorities. Cyril's antagonism toward emergency-based reasoning—an antagonism of which we can find other historical examples

as well—may be due to the fact that it is not subjected to prudent calculations. A scandal must be avoided at (nearly) all costs: it is something that altogether escapes the domain of prudent deliberation and therefore cannot be rationally criticized. As such, it can also be used to license economy under almost any circumstances. It seems that Cyril's antagonism toward using scandal, as other "arkribeists" do, is the result of his attempt to regulate the liminal sphere. Much like Basil, who defines that sphere in spatial terms, Cyril defines it in governmental terms: it is a sphere that is not governed by the dictates of canon law, yet is nonetheless prudently regulated.

3. Prudent calculations: Under exceptional circumstances, one has to prudently calculate the benefits and losses that would be achieved by diverting from the course of action dictated by the letter of canon. In his letter to Atticus, Cyril makes his position clear: the ultimate end of economy is the sheer size of the Church, and it is this end that serves as an arbitrator for evaluating its use. According to Cyril, Atticus's bad judgment can be measured in numbers: his imprudent use of pastoral authority not only did not bring as much as a single soul to join the Church, it also disturbed its peace and distanced many regions fromIn addition, Cyril's emphasis on the prudent-calculative nature of economy is evident in his use of two metaphors: the helmsperson and the physician. Here is an example of how he uses the former (letter 56): "Economies sometimes demand that a little be lost in order that more may be gained. Just as sailors in a storm, when their ship is in danger, throw overboard some of their cargo in order to save the rest, so we in matters where it is not possible to keep everything, we surrender some in order that we may not lose all." The use of the helmsperson metaphor demonstrates several qualities of pastoral economy: it is practiced for the benefit of the entire Church (the ship); it is enacted under exceptional circumstances (cargo is not thrown overboard under normal circumstances, namely when the sea is peaceful); and its exercise is a prudent and calculated act, which takes into account the benefits gained and the costs suffered by it. The same holds for Cyril's use of the physician metaphor, which stresses the prudent mode of economic conduct. In letter 57 he uses this metaphor to prescribe the application of economy rather than akribeia to those who are sick in their souls (in an analogy to treating a sickness of the body). In letter 72 he compares Nestorian heresy to a chronic disease that resists medical treatment and thus demands a patient and economically prudent treatment.

EULOGIUS: REGULATING THE EXCEPTION

Eulogius (patriarch of Alexandria 580–607) wrote a treatise dedicated to the principle of economy as part of his polemic against the monophysites, who enjoyed great popularity in the East, and it played an important role in furthering the principle's systemization (Rai 1973). While the treatise itself was lost, its summary appears in codex 227 of Photius's *Bibliotheca*. The codex summarizes Eulogius's analytic framework, through which pastoral economy can be prudently exercised and regulated. As such, his treatise is the first manual to guide pastoral authorities economizing in the liminal sphere.

As with any good manual, this one begins by stating who is licensed to make use of the methods it prescribes. In the case of pastoral economy, such a license is solely in the hands of the "servants of Christ and economists of the Mystery of God,[6] and those to whom the government of the Episcopal thrones were entrusted" (Photius 2003). Following this, Eulogius classifies pastoral economy into three types. The first is what is now called sacramental, disciplinary, or ecclesiastical economy. The second has to do with speech, later to be called "doctrinal economy." The third, which may be termed communal economy, deals with entering a communion with non-Orthodox Christians, when it goes against a decree promulgated in order to prohibit such activity. Based on this classification, Eulogius supplements the licensed exercises of economy with some directions on how to do so with respect to each of these types:

1. Sacramental economy: thematically speaking, sacramental economy may be practiced as long as "the dogma of true faith is not endangered. For if that dogma remains pure and unadulterated, economy is found to be in charge of the area outside and around it" (Photius 2003). Temporally, this exercise economy is limited: the "upholding and protecting of what ought not to be" (Photius 2003) is allowed for a short time under three conditions: it must be grounded in unshakable truth; it must be used for the reinforcement of canonic order; and, once its limited period is over, the Church must return to the preexisting canonical order.

2. Doctrinal economy: unlike sacramental economy, time limits are not an issue when making use of doctrinal economy. The use of different terms to proclaim the Christian faith is allowed, as long as they are meant

to confess the true doctrine. In Eulogius's listing of the various technologies of doctrinal economy, he writes that one may allow the use of certain words instead of others and may also keep silence or avoid the use of certain words.

3. Communal economy: the third type of economy has to do with entering into communion with people who, according to akribeia, are under a decree of excommunication. As in the case of sacramental economy, this can be done as long as the dogma remains unharmed, and, as in the case of doctrinal economy, it is not time limited. The only restriction placed on communal economy is that nothing new should be added to the dogma, which means that, when applying such an economy, promulgated decrees are not revoked.

Salvation, Truth, and Law

As we have seen, Agamben criticized Foucault's genealogy of government for not establishing its origins in theological economy. Thus far I answered this critique by focusing on the operations of economy outside the boundaries of canon law. In particular, i begun by showing how the pastorate forms part of the divine economy, and then how the conceptual triad of salvation, truth, and law, whose relation to pastoral economy was identified by Foucault, is clearly presented outside the canonic boundaries of the Church. As defined by Basil, the economist of the divine mysteries is not subjected to the dictates of law, as the economy transcends the boundaries set by the latter. Economy itself is defined by Nicholas the Mystic as "accommodation unto salvation," which is conducted by the ecclesiastical authorities in a pastoral manner, as its rationality is described by Cyril. As for truth, economy is defined by Eulogius as regulating the area outside and around the dogma of true faith, which remains unchanged.

Agamben's focus on pre-Nicean Christian thought leads him to charge modern scholars to insert "a caesura between two senses of the term oikonomia that are clearly different, the first referring to the articulation of the single divine substance into three persons, the second concerning the historical dispensation of salvation" (Agamben 2011:51). But, as described in former chapters, that caesura was introduced in the fourth century when the concept of oikonomia could no longer sustain the two doctrines and a distinction between theology and economy was established. As a result, the Trinity, the history of salvation, and the relation between the two underwent reconceptualization in the era between the Councils of Nicea (325) and Chalcedon (451). Following the expulsion of the economic paradigm from the Trinity, the latter was reconceptualized by "the Cappadocians [who] introduced a revolution into Greek ontology" (Zizioulas 2006:186) by their use of the concepts of essence, modes of being, and persona (*ousia, hypostasis, propsopon*) to articulate the inner organization of the Godhead. A few decades later, the Chalcedonian Definition declared that in the "mystery of the economy" of Christ (a phrase repeated three times in the declaration), divine and human nature are united "unconfusedly, immutably, indivisibly, inseparably . . . without the distinction of natures being taken away by such union." Thus the economy of the mysteries denotes a different relationship between being and acting than the one portrayed by Agamben, as divine being is actuated in the economy when the latter is conceived of as always already an accommodation of the divine mode of being toward salvation.

Agamben criticizes Foucault's genealogy of governmental power for not verifying its theological meaning by analyzing how it refers to the original (archaic) denotation of oikonomia to the Trinity to which it was first displaced (Agamben 2011:21). This censure can be dismissed when taking into account the way that the economic model of the Trinity was transcribed into the model of hypostatic union and then into the one of the perichoresis, as presented in chapter 2. Framing Foucault's investigation into the genealogy of government by the economic model and pointing to its theological origins arguably demonstrates that his work is indeed persuasive, as it shows how the signature of secularization displaces the concept of economy from the ecclesiastical field and orients its interpretation toward the institution of the market.

Focusing solely on Hypolitus and Tertulian's indiscriminate use of oikonomia in the Trinity and in history may have caused Agamben to overlook the fact that oikonomia was thought of as a human-divine enterprise actuated by human economists as a mimesis of divine love, in the mode of an accommodation toward salvation. Agamben's disregard for the essential role played by humans may cause him to dismiss the suggestion that the economists of divine mysteries actuated the economy, in a semantic field defined by economy's relation to truth, salvation, and the law. As this chapter suggests, each of the three concepts identified by Foucault has its own *energia*, or principle of action: growth in the case of salvation, accommodation in the case of truth, and obedience to higher authorities in the case of law (Foucault 2007:174–80). Pastoral power founded in divine oikonomia, then, is an art and science, the knowledge of all knowledges, of the conduct of zoon oikonomikon, a person who is not fully subjected to law by an authority who accommodates the ways of the governed for the purpose of generating economic growth. If there is such a thing as "the signature of secularization," it may be better to speak of secularizations in the plural, just as Foucault described plural formations of governmentalities. As implied by Foucault's genealogy of government, each of the modern governementalities (police state, classical liberalism, neoliberalism) constitutes an orthodoxy of its own and has its own peculiar way of generating growth by accommodating itself to the ways of the governed, who are not fully subjected to the law. The conjectural nature of the economy suggests that when circumstances change, so do the ways in which *economy* refers back to its denotation in the fourth century.[7]

Economic Pastorship and Political Sovereignty in the Exception

It is hard not to notice the striking resemblances between the operations of pastoral economy in the state of exception, as discussed earlier, and both Schmitt's and Agamben's critical analysis of the political state of exception. As previously noted, Agamben, basing himself on Carl Schmitt's famous epigram that "sovereign is he who decides on the exception" (2005:5), argues that the essence of political sovereignty is to be found in its authority to suspend the law in order to exclude, so that "the original political relation is the ban" (1998:181).[8] In the same vein, the prominent twentieth-century Orthodox theologian Georges Florovsky equates the suspension of canon law by Church authorities with pastoral economy, saying that "economy is pastorship and pastorship is economy" (1933:117). The resemblance between Agamben's conception of political sovereignty and Florovsky's conception of economic pastorship goes further. Both authors direct the attention of their audience to a sphere generated when the law is suspended: Florovsky argues that when suspending canon law by exercising pastoral economy, the Church "bears witness to the extension of her mystical territory even beyond her canonical borders: the 'outside world' does not begin immediately" (1933:134). Thus a liminal sphere is generated on the boundaries of the Church (Florovsky 1950). As shown, the liminal sphere generated by the exercise of economy is characterized by the use of pastoral authority unchecked by canon law. When describing political sovereignty, Agamben argues that the suspension of law leads to the generation of a new sphere, termed "the camp." Human life in the camp loses the protection granted by law and is, as a result, exposed to (sovereign) violence. Agamben further argues that the sphere generated by the decision to suspend the law is where we should look for "the hidden matrix and nomos of the political space in which we are still living" (1998:166). In the same manner in which Agamben argues that the "camp" encapsulates the political formation of sovereign power, I will attempt to show that this is also true in the case of the governmental formation of pastoral economy as revealed in civil society.

In advancing our inquiry into the resemblance between political sovereignty and economic pastorship, we can name the Catharoi (literally, "puritans") as the premodern figures analogous to *homo sacer*.[9] The latter is described by Agamben as "an obscure figure of archaic Roman law, in which human life is included in the juridical order [ordinamento] solely in the form of its exclusion (that is, of its capacity to be killed)" (Agamben 1998:8). In Basil's first canon, canon law can be suspended so as to allow the Catharoi to be included in the body of the Church by validating their baptism (against the canon that dictates their exclusion). Like a mirror image of the homo sacer, whose life becomes expendable due to the suspension of the law, the suspension of canon law grants the Catharoi what is believed to be an opportunity for eternal life. It is here, indeed, that a stark difference arises between Agamben's conception of political sovereignty and the Orthodox Christian conception of economic pastorship. While the two formations of power are both fully revealed when law or canon is suspended, they move in opposite directions: sovereignty operates by inclusive exclusion by banishing from the political body, while pastorship includes those who were excluded by validation of membership in the living body of Christ as a kind of exclusionary inclusion. Moreover, contrary to Agamben's assertion that the boundary set by law is removed when it obstructs the political sovereign's use of violence, canon law is suspended

when, according to Nicholas the Mystic, it obstructs the pastoral economist's "imitat[ion of] divine philanthropy" by "accommodation unto salvation" (letter 32).

The relations between the economic exception and norm are different
from those portrayed by either Schmitt's or Agamben's inquiries into the
political state of exception. Schmitt observed that political sovereignty is
exercised in the state of emergency "on the basis of its right of self-preser-
vation, as one would say" (Agamben 2005:12). While this is also the raison
d'être of the suspension of canon law by means of pastoral economy, there
is a crucial difference in the way the exception and the norm interact.
Schmitt informs us that in the political state of emergency "the two elements of the concept legal order are ... dissolved into independent notions and thereby testify to their conceptual independence. Unlike the
normal situation, when the autonomous moment of decision recedes to a
minimum, the norm is destroyed in the exception" (Agamben 2005:12). A
different relationship between canon law and authority is constituted in
the texts dealing with pastoral economy: as established in Basil's first canon, both canon law and authority remain intact even in times when they
do not coincide. When the pastoral economist deems it right to incorpo-
rate believers into the Church, he can suspend canon law by following certain procedures listed in Eulogius's "manual." This is achieved in a way
that keeps both canon law and pastoral authority intact: under no circumstances is the first reduced to a bare minimum or the second destroyed.
The radical gap between authority and canon law is made present at all
times, and not just in the state of emergency, the latter being no more than
one instance when pastoral economy is exercised. Hence there is no attempt to insert the autonomous moment of decision into the norm or to
codify authority in law.

On the other hand, keeping both canon and authority distinct at all
times prevents the liminal sphere from receding into a zone of indistinc-
tion between the exception and the norm, as Agamben conceived of the
political camp. Thus the pastoral-economic relationship between authority
and canon does not entail the exception operating as the norm, a state of
affairs that, according to Agamben, prevails in liberal democracies over
the past few decades. This may be due to the fact that, as demonstrated in
Cyril's letters, the application of economy does not require the existence
of a state of emergency in order to be applied and does not necessitate the

maintenance of such a continuous state of affairs in order to persist. That being said, the balance of power between pastoral authority and canon is not immune to threats posed to the legal order by the state of emergency. Following its inception, all major contributions to the formation of the principle of economy were made in response to its abuse in a state of emergency (whether real of imagined), and all resulted in further limitations on the application of economy. Beside the contributions of Cyril and Eulogius, the three most important later contributions took place between the eighth and the tenth centuries, when the application of economy was justified by a state of emergency. The first of these involved applying economy toward repentant iconoclast clergy, and the other two were applied with respect to the emperor. All three met harsh opposition, driving the Church to the brink of schism. Despite their resemblance to the political state of emergency, what was frowned upon during these events was the extension of the liminal sphere by applying economy toward those who were considered to be complete outsiders and not the canonic boundaries of the Church. Consequently, the akribeists' aversion to the use of a state of emergency to validate the application of economy can be understood as an attempt to avoid the corruption of pastoral authority and the infringement of what Florovsky regarded as the "mystic body of the church" rather than its canonic boundaries.

The Modern Power of Exclusive Inclusion

Criticizing Foucault, Agamben is unclear about how his methodological "lacuna" is to be blamed for the transposition of his investigations into how the conceptual triad of salvation, truth, and law from the ecclesiastical to the political field by the signature of secularization in the sixteenth and seventeenth centuries is theorized "in all truth, in not terribly convincing a way" (Agamben 2011:111). One can only assume that, if Agamben had elaborated more on this point, he would have criticized Foucault for allowing the signature of secularization, that is, the shift of the field for the denotation of the economic paradigm from church to state, to alter the meaning of these concepts (namely, economy and politics). Foucault achieved this with the introduction of a permanent coup d'état (2007:334), that is, the suspension of law (261) and the penetration of violence into

economic rationality (262–63) by the mechanism of selection and exclusion (263). This seems to be implied in Foucault's (otherwise obscure) assertion that "our societies proved to be really demonic since they happened to combine those two games—the city- citizen game and the
shepherd- flock game—in what we call the modern states" (Foucault
1999c:143). The latter assertion may be interpreted in light of the genealogical inquiry into the archaic denotation of oikonomia in the era between Nicea and Chalcedon in comparison with Schmitt and Agamben's
investigation into political sovereignty in the state of exception as the way
in which the modern state happened to combine pastoral economy's inclusive quality and political sovereignty's exclusive one in the form of inclusive exclusion, the demonic effects of which were thoroughly described by
"political" Agamben and the ensuing literature that followed the publication of *Homo Sacer.* Disregarding Agamben's methodological critique and
allowing, as Foucault did, the signature of secularization to alter both concepts of economy and politics by the hybrid of political economy suggests
that inclusive exclusion, which "political" Agamben traced back to antiquity, may be forward-dated to the sixteenth through seventeenth centuries and seen as an effect of the signature of secularization.

6

From Ecclesiastical to Market Economy

B oth a historical and a genealogical reason sent me inquiring after the Christian oikonomia: the historical reason was that this chapter in the history of the human trinity has been relegated from most accounts of the history of the economy, philosophy, or politics. Rewriting this chapter from the economic perspective into our history was done by showing how 1. a human condition is manifested in the economy (chapters 1 and 2); 2. the internal organization of the economy is modeled and constituted (chapter 2); 3. the nature of the thing economized is rendered intelligible (chapters 2 and 3); and 4. how its relations with philosophical life (chapter 3), with politics (chapter 4), and with the legal framework (chapter 5) are remodeled.

The genealogical reason for studying the Christian oikonomia was guided by my intuition that doing so carries far-reaching implications for a critical engagement with the present ordering of the human trinity. First, it may well improve our critical understanding of this particular ordering. Second, once a sufficient level of understanding is reached, we will be able to rethink and reorder the three-dimensional human space of economy, politics, and philosophy in which we live. Accordingly, this chapter will first present a condensed history of oikonomia in the classical oikos, the imperial *cosmopolis,* and the Christian ecclesia in the one thousand years following its inception. Following a summary of the revisions of Foucault's genealogical inquiry into patristic economy and philosophy, it then revises two key concepts in Hannah Arendt's genealogy of politics, namely the social and the economic human condition. This is followed by a genealogical inquiry into the marketized neoliberal economy by delineating how 1. the economy is redefined; 2. the human condition manifested in it is rendered intelligible; 3. the nature of the thing is economized; 4. economic growth is marketized; 5. the relationship of the economy with philosophy and politics is redrawn; 6. a new ethics of the governed is formulated.

A Condensed History of Oikonomia in Greek-Speaking Antiquity

The definition of the economy: as demonstrated in some detail in the trial balance at the end of chapter 2, the definitions of the economy in the classical moment and in the Christian moment appear to be somewhat similar. In each of these moments, *faced with the human condition of excess, the human has to acquire a theoretical and practical disposition of prudence in order to fulfill the economy and to generate surplus.* Contrary to these two moments, in the imperial moment what is common to the many different applications of "economy" is the absence of either excess or surplus (and usually of both) from the various definitions. In this moment, "economy" is understood as *the acquisition of a theoretical and practical disposition of prudence.* Excess and surplus can be found in the "economic imperialism" itself, in the totality of all the various applications of the concept of economy. The surplus generated by imperial man in his dealings with the economy was, in fact, an ever growing number of definitions and economic applications in all spheres of human existence and human thought. It seems to me that such a "metaphysical" hypothesis finds reinforcement when we look at the history of the economy between the sixteenth and eighteen centuries. As Germano Maifreda's encyclopedic review of economy in early modernity shows (Maifreda 2012:183–212),[1] in that period the term *economy* was used in various spheres and fields of knowledge—including the ecclesiastical—political economy being only one among them, and not the most common.[2] This similitude is attested by the fact that political economy, at least in its first modern appearance, is used to describe the state as an absolute monarchy (and not a form of knowledge),[3] much like its usage in the imperial moment describing Ptolemaic Egypt.[4]

Moving from the classical moment to the Christian moment, a change occurred in *the condition manifested in the economy*. While in the classical moment the economy was seen as originating in and subsequently corresponding to the human condition of necessity, in the Christian moment it was seen as corresponding to the condition of freedom. Common to the understanding of the economy in both these moments is the notion that, ultimately, human action in concert *necessarily generates surplus*. As for the imperial moment, due to the lack of excess and surplus from the various definitions, I was unable to identify a human condition manifested in its economy. The greatest transformation occurred in *the nature of the thing economized*. Whereas in the classical moment the needs of the life process itself, common to humans and all other living beings, are economized, in the Christian moment the divine within humans—that which humans and God hold in common—is economized. In between these two moments stands the imperial moment, wherein all spheres of life and various sciences and theories received their own economies.

TABLE 6.1   BASIC PARAMETERS OF THE ECONOMY IN ITS THREE PREMODERN MOMENTS

PARAMETER/ MOMENT	CLASSICAL	IMPERIAL	CHRISTIAN
Nature of the thing economized	the lower part of man, common to man and animal	each thing according to its nature	the divine in humans, common to God and humans
Initial human condition	necessity	——	freedom
Ultimate human condition	by necessity human action in concert generates surplus	——	by necessity human action in concert generates surplus
Excess	of nature		of divinity
Required disposition	prudence	prudence	prudence
Surplus	outside the boundaries of the economy	of applications	within the economy

ECONOMY'S RELATIONS WITH POLITICS, PHILOSOPHICAL LIFE, AND THE BOUNDARIES SET BY LAW IN GREEK-SPEAKING ANTIQUITY

The relations between economy, politics, philosophical life, and the legal framework underwent far-reaching changes in the premodern era. After philosophical life and political community were distinguished from economic life, establishing the economy as a distinct sphere, in the classical moment the law was used as a framework that excluded the economy from the political sphere, much as the walls of the polis were used to ward off cosmological nature. Economy now appeared in a sphere located outside the legal framework and was regarded as a sort of slave laboring in the service of both politics and philosophical life. In the imperial moment we witness the economy moving beyond the confines of the oikos. This move was a by-product of the spread of politics beyond the walls of the polis. Alongside its appearance in a variety of theories and scientific fields, the term *oikonomia* was used in this moment to define governance in all spheres of life, beginning with man's rule over his body and self, through the oikos and the polis, up to the cosmopolitan sphere. Despite its appearance as governance in the political sphere, the economy retains its slavish status in its relations with politics and, with the exception of one text, remains behind the scenes of political activity and is not allowed to appear in public (speech). As part of the services rendered by the economy to the political community, the law itself is economized at this moment. Economy's relationship with philosophical life also undergoes changes in the imperial moment, with the products of philosophical life economized before they can appear in public speech (*lexis*).

The Christian moment witnessed the advent of a new realm of life, the society of believers, whose economic activity takes place in the ecclesia. This new sphere, in which the economy of the Holy Spirit is dispensed, is an ever growing sphere that is "neither public nor private, strictly speaking." The growth of the Christian economy is seen as diachronically limited, so that, in the fullness of the ages, when all things are recapitulated in Christ, it will encompass both the private sphere and the political sphere. At this moment the law once again serves as economy's boundary, but with two decisive differences relative to the classical moment: 1. canon law is not responsible for excluding the economy from the public sphere, but rather demarcates the borders of the society of believers in Christ's economy; 2. canon law serves only as a relative border, which the economy transgresses whenever the economist concludes that the benefits of suspending the law outweigh those of observing it.

The relationship between the economy and philosophical life also underwent changes in the fourth century, as philosophical life has come to be contained within the economy. This containment accompanies a segmentation of space into three distinct parts, as follows: the theological "space," which up until the fourth century was the object of philosophical inquiry, is "found" outside of space and time and beyond the reach of human knowledge (gnosis); the economic space, where the divine reveals itself and philosophical life is economized in the society of believers; and the space of secular life, which includes the political community and the earthly oikos. This new way of dividing space occurs in tandem with a dramatic change in the relationship that holds between economy and politics as compared with their relation in classical moment. Politics is now seen as a sphere of necessity that slaves in the service of the economy, which is where people exercise their freedom.

TABLE 6.2   ECONOMY'S RELATION TO LAW, POLITICS, AND PHILOSOPHY IN ITS
THREE PREMODERN MOMENTS

MOMENT	SPACE OF APPEARANCE	RELATION TO LAW	RELATION TO POLITICS	RELATION TO PHILOSOPHY
Classical	the oikos	outside the boundary of law	subjected to politics	subjected to philosophy
Imperial	economic government in all spheres of life	economy of law	in the service of politics	organizes the products of philosophical life
Christian	society of believers in the economy	exceeds the boundaries set by canon law	subjects politics	contains philosophical life

A Genealogical Inquiry Into the Neoliberal Marketized Economy

The genealogical inquiry conducted in this book was framed by Michel Foucault's genealogy of the economy and of philosophy. The bearings of its finding on Foucault's genealogy of philosophy are discussed in chapter 3 and of his genealogy of the economy in chapter 5. These chapters amend crucial aspects of Foucault's genealogies: adding the communal dimension of Christian philosophical life, drawing the distinction between economic and political power formations (chapter 4), redefining the relationship of self to self in Christianity, introducing the macrodimension of pastoral economy, modifying Foucault's formulation of the secularization of political economy, and introducing the missing link between theology and economy. These amendments and additions resituate Foucault's pastorship as the origin of governmentality in a broader context from which it appeared by showing how pastoral economy was originated in theology and enacted in the "society of believers in Christ's economy," a society in which philosophical life is economized, the principle of economy is enacted on the macrolevel vis-à-vis the law, and politics is subjugated to the economy. As argued against Agamben in chapter 5, doing so does not discredit Foucault genealogy of the economy in which we now live, but lends it much needed support.

THE RISE OF THE SOCIAL, REVISED

The genealogy of the economy portrayed in my study is also framed by Arendt's genealogy of politics. The following pages address the manner in which this volume changes two of Arendt's main convictions. *First*, it shows how the birth of the society of believers in Christ's economy in the fourth century adds a new dimension to Arendt's description of the rise of the "social" in modernity—a phenomenon that she presents as an effect of world alienation and the expropriation of the Church's material possessions. *Second*, it demonstrates the ways in which adding the Christian chapter to the history of the economy changes the human condition as it is revealed in the economy.

In *The Human Condition* Arendt presented Western history as spanning between two crucial moments: the first occurred in the classical era, when politics and philosophical life distinguished themselves from the economy, thereby constituting it as a distinct sphere; the second takes place in modernity, with the expansion of the economy beyond the boundaries of the oikos and into society—a novel sphere of life that is neither public nor private and whose infinite growth threatens to take over both the public and the private (HC 28–33). Arendt's focus on the history of political theory and the fall of the political, from its elevated status in the classical era to its virtual disappearance into the economy in modernity, was designed to offer ways to reestablish political community (and philosophical life) under the modern human condition. She considered this project urgent, fundamental, and politically indispensable for the purpose of halting what she called "the modern growth of worldlessness, the withering away of everything between us, [which] can also be described as the spread of the desert" (Arendt 2005:200); it was essential so as to avoid the "danger [that] lies in becoming true inhabitants of the desert and feeling at home in it" (2005:200) when political and philosophical life would cease to exist and the earth would be ruled by sandstorms in the form of "totalitarian movements whose chief characteristic is that they are extremely well-adjusted to the conditions of the desert" (2005:200–1). Given the urgency of the task she took upon herself, one can imagine why Arendt chose to focus on the defeat of the political instead of attempting to tell the story of the evident victory of the economy.

Nonetheless, the urgency of reconstructing the latter narrative can be deduced from Arendt's own logic, advocating the sort of historiography first introduced in Homer: a historiography that recounts history as seen from the points of view of both the victor and the vanquished (2005:162–68). The importance of writing history from the winners' point of view emerges clearly when we recall the crucial role Arendt ascribed to historiography as a pre-political action that contributed to the first successful attempt by the polis to create a political realm (2005:162–68).[5] It seems that Arendt's focus on the political side of our history accounts for the fact that her dating of the moment the economy exceeded the boundaries of the oikos was off by more than fourteen hundred years. As shown, the outstanding feature of the economy in the imperial moment was its expansion beyond the boundaries of the oikos into all spheres of life and all branches of knowledge while the society of believers in Christ's economy makes its debut on the world stage in the fourth century CE.

The importance of supplementing Arendt's (hi)story with the economic side may become clearer when taking into account that the fourth-century debut by the society of believers in the economy was not a solo act; as described in the previous chapters, it was accompanied by several other new phenomena whose appearance is usually attributed to modernity. Among these the distinction between economy and theology, the subjugation of politics to the economy, the migration of freedom from the realm of politics to that of the economy, the conception of politics as possessing a monopoly over the legal use of violence, the economizing of philosophical life, the conception of the law as acting in the service of the economy and as demarcating the outer borders that economy (sometimes) oversteps, economic growth, and the birth of a novel form of pastoral government, of which, according to Foucault, individualization and totalization are both inevitable effects.

THE EXPROPRIATION OF THE SOCIETY OF BELIEVERS IN THE ECONOMY

Of the three historical events that Arendt lists as standing at the threshold of the modern age and determining its character—the discovery of America, the Reformation, the invention of the telescope—she views the Reformation, with its attendant expropriation of Church property, as the most closely related to the emergence of the social (HC 248–51). Her claim, in other words, is that the appearance of a society dedicated to economic activity "grew out of Luther's and Calvin's attempts to restore the uncompromising otherworldliness of the Christian Faith" (HC 251). In *The Human Condition* Arendt suggests two routes—a material-Marxian and a cultural-Weberian—along which the efforts of the Reformation led to the rise of the society of believers in the modern economy. Relying on the thought of Karl Marx, Arendt claims that "the Reformation . . . by expropriating ecclesiastical and monastic possessions, started the twofold process of individual expropriation and the accumulation of social wealth" (HC 248). This twofold process came to fruition with the appearance of the society of believers in the modern economy, in which the economy based on expropriation and accumulation became "'the life process of society,' as Marx used to call it" (HC 255). Supported by Weber's explanation, she asserts that "world alienation, and not self-alienation as Marx thought, has been the hallmark of the modern age" (HC 254).[6] It is precisely here that backdating to the fourth century the rise of the society of believers in the economy stands to contribute to the Arendtian story of modernity. This contribution will demonstrate that in addition to the expropriation of the Church's worldly possessions, which Arendt mentions, a further expropriation took place, for which Arendt does not fully account: the Church was stripped of the society of believers in the economy.

ECONOMY AND POLITICS, REVISED

Arendt's own presentation of the way politics was altered by Christianity suggests that the idea that the economy first appeared in public in the society of Christian believers is not foreign to the overall framework of the Arendtian story. In *The Promise of Politics* she describes the Christians as "[constituting] within the world a totally new, religiously defined public space, which, although public, was not political. The public nature of this space of the faithful . . . was always ambiguous" (2005:138). She notes that "Augustine explicitly demands that the life of the saints unfold within a 'Society'" (138).[7] Later Arendt makes the following claim:

> What changed with the advent of the modern era was not a change in the actual function of politics; it was not that politics was suddenly assigned a new dignity peculiar to it. What changed were the arenas for which politics seemed necessary. The religious realm sank back into the private sphere, while the realm of life and its necessities, which both in antiquity and in the Middle Ages was considered the private sphere par excellence, now attained a new dignity and thrust itself into the public arena in the form of society.
>
> (140)

Arendt more than implies that the Reformation played a part in the changing of the guard (from the Christian to the modern economic society), saying that "when the Reformation finally succeeded in removing everything connected with appearance and display from its churches . . . the public character of these ecclesiastical spaces disappeared as well" (139). Given Arendt's description, it seems that the only thing preventing her from removing the inverted commas and plainly calling the Christian public space, the Christian ecclesia, a *society* was the recognition that the activity taking place (the activity appearing and being displayed) in the Christian society of believers was an economic one. The realization that alongside the expropriation from the Church of its worldly possessions it was also stripped of its most important, if intangible, asset—the society of believers in Christ's economy—adds an important facet to the process described by Arendt: the expropriation from the Church of this intangible asset left it free to be overtaken by another economic activity, as indeed happened in modernity. The (re)appearance of a society dedicated to economic activity, which Arendt describes in some detail, differs from the Christian economy first and foremost in the nature of the thing economized. Introducing the society of believers in Christ's economy into the narrative amounts to more than a mere philological correction to Arendt's terminology. That is partly because the similarities between the two societies of believers in the economy go far beyond the way in which both these societies subject politics to their economy: the addition of this chapter to the story alters the very definition of economy as well as our understanding of the nature of the human condition manifested within it.

THE ECONOMIC HUMAN CONDITION, REDEFINED

Following Gregory of Nyssa, Christian art and theory grounds the phenomenon of economic growth in microfoundations. Then as now, the growth of the economy is conceived as the product of the free choices of each and every member of society. This is a crucial point for the significance of introducing the society of believers in Christ's economy into the Arendtian story of modernity, altering her story for the simple reason that, if its second crucial moment is said to be the inception of a society of believers in the economy, this moment is now backdated by more that fourteen hundred years. That the economy that grows in a society of believers first appeared against the background of the economizing of philosophical life (and not as a by-product of the liberation of labor from the bounds of the private sphere)[8]—in other words, that the economy first exceeded the proto-oikos of the Godhead, and only much later the earthly one—changes our understanding of the human condition manifested in the economy. This condition is not, as Arendt claims at the beginning of *The Human Condition*, the human need to labor and consume in order to exist. Instead, the human condition that finds its way into the economy is the excess that humans face and that, either by necessity or freely, they economize. This economy by necessity generates surplus.

A Condensed History of Economic Growth

Foucault traced the essential role of economic growth in the police state,[9] classical liberalism (2008:54), and neoliberal postwar economics where it is the only social policy (144) that is perceived as that which creates liberty (86).[10] According to Arendt:

> The answer, on the lowest level, says: let us develop what we have into something better, greater, et cetera. The, at first glance, irrational faith of liberals in growth, so characteristic of all our present political and economic theories, depends on this notion.
>
> (Arendt 1969b:27).

> And I think it can be shown that no other human ability [humans' faculty of action, the ability to begin something new that guaranties the essential human quality of the political realm] has suffered to such an extent from the progress of the modern age, for progress, as we have come to understand it, means growth, the relentless process of more and more, of bigger and bigger.
>
> (Arendt 1969b:82–83)

While both Arendt and Foucault saw the attainment of economic growth as crucial to modern economy, society, and politics, they did so by disregarding its origins. The following pages will show how setting the origins of economic growth in the Christianity of Late Antiquity adds a crucial dimension to the genealogy of the human trinity.

A DESIRE FOR A LIMITLESS THING GENERATES UNLIMITED GROWTH

As presented in Leshem 2014a, the first persona to practice its freedom in a growing economy was the matron of the classical oikos, while full theorization of the concept of economic growth appeared in the fourth century in the writing of Gregory of Nyssa. It is in Gregory's thought that we witness an "epistemic break" within Greek thought, with being human appearing for the first time as a becoming creature whose desire by nature knows no limits in the economy. In light of this new condition, Gregory embarked on a phenomenology of human desire, distinguishing between three kinds of human desires. Like many of his Greek predecessors, the *first type* he discerned included the basic carnal needs that humans share with all other creatures. These needs he regards as defining the human condition as a species, a condition whose fulfillment to the proper degree is seen as necessary for ensuring the existence of the species. As such, it is neither morally "good" nor "evil" in itself. The *second type* is the vicious perversion of the natural carnal desires. This type originates in the unchecked self-enslavement to these carnal desires. In line still with his predecessors, Gregory appoints soundness of mind as the virtue in charge of drawing the line between these two types, borrowing Stoic indifference (apathy) as the governing principle of action in relation to both kinds. Gregory's novelty lies in the claim that indifference toward these desires, when practiced well, relieves man's erotic energy to practice a *third type* of desire—the erotic desire for God, which generates unlimited growth. The reason that man's desire for God generates growth and does not, like the former types, incarcerate him in a circular economy of desire-saturation-desire has to do, according to Gregory, with the unique nature of the Godhead as an object of desire: it knows no limits and, as such, generates in people an insatiable desire. Paraphrasing Arendt's description of the origin of modern economic growth in the unleashing of the life process from the boundaries of the earthly oikos, we can say that "the growth element *unique to humans* had completely overcome and overgrown the processes of decay by which organic life is checked and balanced in nature's household."[11] Eventually, Gregory concludes that the insatiable desire for the divine object becomes itself the object of desire, and growth for its own sake becomes the ultimate test and goal of the economy generated by the society of believers.[12]

Gregory's "microfoundations" of personal economic growth take place in the Christian ecclesia, which by then ceases to be a "secret society" that gathers in the private sphere of the oikos, hidden from the public eye, and convenes instead on an ecumenical scale. As shown in chapter 2, the use of economic models and the principle of transcription enables the growth of the society of believers in Christ's economy through a mechanism of inclusion by purification. This mechanism, as shown in chapter 5, is enacted on the macrolevel using the "principle of the economy." Once enacted, all legal barriers to economic growth are removed.

AN UNLIMITED DESIRE GENERATES LIMITLESS GROWTH AND AN INFINITE NUMBER OF OBJECTS

The process through which contemporary economic art and theory came to be governed by the ethical disposition of desire for more of the same thing regardless of the nature of the thing occurred in three steps. *First,* the domain of inquiry of economics was diverted from *an investigation into the nature and causes of the wealth of nations* to an investigation of a human persona that Aristotle called "licentious" (ἀκόλαστος),[13] people whose

> desire for life is unlimited, they also desire without limit the means pro-ductive of life. And even those who fix their aim on the good life seek the good life as measured by bodily enjoyments, so that inasmuch as this also seems to be found in the possession of property, all their energies are oc-cupied in the business of getting wealth; and owing to this the second kind of the art of supply has arisen. For as their enjoyment is in excess, they try to discover the art that is productive of enjoyable excess.
>
> (*Pol.* 1258a)

This is the persona that appears in John Stuart Mill's definition of political economy's domain:[14]

> [Political economy] does not treat of the whole of man's nature as modi-fied by the social state, nor of the whole conduct of man in society. It is concerned with him solely as a being who desires to possess wealth, and who is capable of judging of the comparative efficacy of means for ob-taining that end. It predicts only such of the phenomena of the social state as take place in consequence of the pursuit of wealth. It makes en-tire abstraction of every other human passion or motive.... Political Economy considers mankind as occupied solely in acquiring and consum-ing wealth; and aims at showing what is the course of action into which mankind, living in a state of society, would be impelled, if that motive ... were absolute ruler of all their actions.
>
> (Mill 1874:137)

Despite the apologetics that accompanied the positing of the person who desires wealth as the object of inquiry of political economy,[15] a discourse that took great pains to show that such persons need not lose their soundness of mind, history has proved Aristotle right in his statement that a human is either "sound minded or licentious" (*Eth.Nic.* 1148a). In the first stage, as clearly demonstrated in the forgoing, political economists disregarded Aristotle's warning concerning the threat of licentiousness embedded in the market, focusing their inquiries on what was then viewed as the vicious perversion of the virtue of soundness of mind.

In the *second stage*, partly influenced by the "social problem" that emerged in the nineteenth century as a consequence of the licentious management of desires, the nature of the thing that appeared in the domain of political economy seems at first glance to be identical to that of the classical oikos (i.e., existential need). In what came to be known as the neoclassical turn, economic theory shifts its attention from the "licentious persona" who pursues wealth to the persona of the consumer. At this stage the persona of the pursuer of wealth is overshadowed by the other type of licentious person[16]—the one who typifies, according to Aristotle, those whose "interests are set upon life but not upon the good life; as therefore the desire for life is unlimited, they also desire without limit the means productive of life" (*Pol.* 1257a). This is the exact type to appear in Alfred Marshall's definition: "Political Economy or Economics is a study of mankind in the ordinary business of life; it examines that part of individual and social action which is most closely connected with the attainment and with the use of the material requisites of well-being. Thus it is on the one side a study of wealth; and on the other, and more important side, a part of the study of man" (Marshall 1920:1). Marshall's definition illustrates how the focus of economics had by then shifted to an examination of the ways in which the limitless pursuit of wealth influences the unlimited desire for life itself, both of which considered as social phenomena taking place in society. It is at this stage that the "life process" first occupies center stage, and it is "as though the growth element inherent in all organic life had completely overcome and overgrown the processes of decay by which organic life is checked and balanced in nature's household. The social realm, where the life process has established its own public domain, has let loose an unnatural growth, so to speak, of the natural" (*HC* 47). What was left uneconomized for the time being in the modern society of believers in the economy was political life and the desire for God. William Stanley Jevons, a contemporary of Marshall and one of the three "neoclassical fathers" (together with Leon Walras and Carl Menger), acknowledges their absence, as well as the absence of any limits to those desires that economics does address, when he states that "a true theory of economy can only be attained by going back to the great springs of human action—the feelings of pleasure and pain" (Jevons 1866:282); and elsewhere: "My present purpose is accomplished in . . . assigning a proper place to the pleasures and pains with which the Economist deals. It is the lowest rank of feelings which we here treat" (Jevons 1888:26). A decade later, Francis Y. Edgeworth wrote that economics deals with "the lower elements of human nature" (Edgeworth 1881:52–53).

In the *third stage* all limitations whatsoever on the desires that form the domain of economics are withdrawn. People's lives as a whole, including their political lives and their desire for God, are now economized. The discipline's loss of distinction appears most clearly in Lionel Robbins's definition of it: "Economics is a science which studies human behavior as a relationship between ends and scarce means which have alternative uses. . . . It follows that Economics is entirely neutral between ends, that, in so far as the achievement of any end is dependent on scarce means, it is germane to the preoccupations of the economist. Economics is not concerned with ends as such" (Robbins 1935:16–24).[17] In other words, as long as the need/desire for a thing cannot be saturated, regardless of its nature, this need/desire lies within the economic domain. And as concluded forty-odd years later by Gary Becker, all human desires are economized in a unified (psychic) space that knows no distinctions between types of desires.[18] Here we see that humans, as modeled by contemporary economics, are so licentious as to render meaningless the distinction between types of licentiousness; in contemporary economics there is absolutely no distinction between a need originating in the desire for life itself and one that originates in the desire for the (vicious) good life.

THE MARKETIZATION OF THE ECONOMY

From this presentation of the three stages of the modeling of humans in economic theory, culminating with the construction of their image as creatures who act in a unified space in which everything is economized in order to attain more of the same, we may draw further conclusions. First, that the loss of the virtue of soundness of mind is just as crucial as the expropriation of the Christian society of believers in the economy. It seems, in other words, that what occurred was not a clear and simple secularization of Christian society but a radicalization of the Christian theory of economic growth, which now hold that each and every object (and no longer only the Divine One) possesses the ability to generate in humans an unlimited, unsaturated desire. Put differently, the shift that occurred with the marketization of Christian economy is not the expulsion of God from economy but rather the indiscriminate ascription of His divine ability to generate insatiable desires, which, in turn, generate an unlimited growth. What we are witnessing, therefore, is not the exclusion of the desire for God from the economy (if only because this desire is analyzed by economists).[19] Given this picture, we should consider the hypothesis that instead of the exclusion of God from the economy what we are really confronted with is the divinization of each and every object of desire; if we unmasked the a-theistic persona that contemporary economy has taken on, we would come face to face with is an *anarchic* pantheism (anarchic because it excludes Christ as the economic *arche* of the Father). If so, it would be more accurate to describe this double-edged displacement of Christ's excessive quality to the interplay between, on the one hand, a desiring subject and, on the other hand, each and every object of desire.

Second, attributing the origin of growth to the economy can help us rethink how the two elements of the concept "market economy" dissolve into independent notions and thereby testify to their conceptual independence. Thus far, the inclusive quality of market economy, namely that it is constantly growing by including more and more spheres of existence within its bounds, was attributed (most notably by Marxists such as Rosa Luxemburg, Ernest Mandel, and Fredric Jameson) to the "market" and not to "economy." Attributing the origin of this inclusiveness to economy by revealing its origins in fourth-century Christianity clearly suggests that the well-recorded tendency of market economy to grow by inclusion is a quality of the economy rather than of the market. It also suggests that the marketization of Christ economy ought to be understood as the transposition of the excess found in the economy from Christ to the desiring subject and desired object.

PRUDENCE IN THE FACE OF THE HUMAN CONDITION OF EXCESS IN ORDER TO GENERATE SURPLUS

As described, in its third stage, contemporary economic theory situates one pole of the human condition of excess within humans themselves; the theory models people as creatures whose desire for more of the same thing, regardless of the nature of the thing, cannot by definition reach saturation.[20] The theory defines the domain of economic inquiry as encompassing all human behavior that is enacted in relation to man's excessive desires while also claiming that any and every human action can be explained as carried out in relation to this excess. Contemporary economic theory also models people as acting, by necessity, in a *prudent* (i.e., "rational" in the terminology of the social sciences) manner.[21] Faced with their excessive desires, people strive to maximize their satisfaction—a type of rationality that economic theory suggests can be inferred from their revealed preferences. Finally, economic theory regards people's prudent actions (in the face of their excessive desires) as a prime source of *surplus*.[22] Moreover, the ideal toward which the political sovereign ought to strive is what economic theorists term *general equilibrium:* a condition in which the prudent acts of each and every individual faced with the human condition of excessive desires reach what is known as "Pareto optimality"—the maximum aggregated surplus possible given the initial allocation of resources. In other words, the answer offered by contemporary economists to the puzzle posed by the "greatest happiness principle"—how to measure and how to attain the greatest happiness for the greatest number—is the greatest surplus, disregarding the number of people and the distribution of the generated surplus. This accounts for growth being the sole test of any socioeconomic policy, understood as the ability of a policy to generate a continuous and solid growth in surplus.

THE MARKETIZED ECONOMY, REDEFINED

The definition of the economy: from the foregoing analysis we can deduce that the contemporary definition of the economy shows a surprising resemblance to the definition of the economy in the classical and Christian moments. According to this definition, the economy involves *a prudent disposition in the face of the human condition of excessive desires, which is translated into a practical and theoretical knowledge. The outcome of this prudent action is the generation of a surplus that is endogenous to the economy. Maintaining the generation of this surplus necessitates the existence of the political sovereign.* The human condition that manifests itself in the contemporary economy can be described as follows: *initially, desires are necessarily economized and, ultimately, human action in concert necessarily generates surplus.* Paradoxically, though the conception of the economy today resembles the Christian one in that both treat it as the sphere in which humans practice their liberty, the human condition appearing in our economy resembles that which appears not in the Christian economy but in the classical one, namely, from beginning to end, the human condition of existential necessity. The nature of the thing economized in the contemporary economy is a combination of sorts, which is distinguished from the earlier moments by none other than the lack of distinction between the natures of the things economized in them. All things—understood to include every need and object of desire—are insatiably desired and indiscriminately economized.

Comparative Politics

Aristotle defined politics as a form of knowledge that aims at obtaining a certain degree of scientific precision concerning the qualitative (rather than quantitative) difference between the natures of the following personae of rulership: the *politcos*, the monarch, the economist, and the despot (πολιτικὸν, βασιλικὸν, οἰκονομικὸν, δεσποτικὸν).[23] If we were to schematize this book's finding concerning the distinction made between these authoritative personae in the first three moments of the history of the human trinity, we may present this history in the following manner:

In the *classical* oikos/polis the persona of the *politicos* is distinguished from the rest of the ruling personae, as he governs as well as being governed in the public sphere of the polis. When the citizen returns to his oikos and puts on the persona of the *oikodespotes,* he governs the wife economically, the children monarchically, and the slaves despotically. In the political economy the virtuous king is distinguished from the vicious one by the persona they take on, as the political monarch puts on the economic persona, and the political despot the persona of tyrant.

The expansion of both politics and the economy beyond their relative boundaries in the *imperial moment* together with the introduction of the new cosmopolitical sphere took place along a change in the ordering of the personae: the government of the cosmos by nature/god, the political sphere by the monarch, the household by the *oikodespots*, and the self by the sage were all reckoned to be governed economically. The economization of government brought along with it the birth of an ethical art and theory on how to be governed by becoming at home (*oikeiosis*) in each sphere according to its economized nature.

In the *Christian moment* the distinction between political rule and economic one is reestablished. At that time the persona of the despot is distinguished for the first time from the one of the economist and is solely attached to that of the politicos;[24] the emperor rules by political means over the despotic sphere of earthly desires while economy becomes the art and theory of government of self and others by following the example of *the Governed*: this art include erotic desire for God, self-askesis, and accommodative (*sugkatabasis*) love for humans (*philantthropia*) in accordance with their nature. The ethical art and theory of how to be governed is also transformed. Oikeiosis is now understood to dictate fleeing from the imperial human communities for the purpose of becoming at home communing in Christ together with the rise of a new ethics of the governed who is held accountable for her decision whether or not to comply with the dictates of the persons who occupy political and economic authority.

THE LIBERAL TRIAD: POLITICAL MONARCHIC RULE, CIVIL SOCIETY, AND MARKET ECONOMY

As we have seen, one of the consequences of backdating Arendt's rise of the social to the fourth century is that its rebirth in modernity can be described as the transposition of the society of believers in the economy from the ecclesia to the market by changing the origin of the excess economized and thereof the nature of the surplus generated by it. But this explanation of what took place in the liberal moment with the rise of civil society and the market economy, and later by the marketization of the economy by the neoliberals, still calls for further elaborations, of which I can only give a few summary indications at this stage.

If we are to schematize the rise of civil society in tandem with that of the market economy, we may say that classical liberalism challenged the modes by which the monarch of early modern Europe exercises his political power when governing the economic sphere. The liberal political economists argued for the constitution: first, of the market economy as a sphere free of sovereign oversight in which the bourgeoisie may freely practice purchasing power; second, of civil society as a sphere in which the political monarch and the governed multitude of economic men interact. The first of these claims is stated as such in Adam Smith's interpretation of the definition by Thomas Hobbes of economic power:

> Wealth, as Mr. Hobbes says, is power. But the person who either acquires, or succeeds to a great fortune, does not necessarily acquire or succeed to any political power, either civil or military.... The power which that possession immediately and directly conveys to him, is the power of purchasing; a certain command over all the labour, or over all the produce of labour, which is then in the market. His fortune is greater or less, precisely in proportion to the extent of this power; or to the quantity either of other men's labour, or, what is the same thing, of the produce of other men's labour, which it enables him to purchase or command. The exchangeable value of everything must always be precisely equal to the extent of this power which it conveys to its owner.
>
> (Smith 1904:book 1, chapter 5)

Returning to Michel Foucault's final, dense lecture of the 1978–79 series may help us further refine this story by introducing a clear distinction between civil society and market economy. The demand for a civil society appears in the form of laying down a critique of the monarchical rationality of economic government by, arguing that the "rationality of those who are governed as economic subjects . . . [that] must serve as the regulating principle for the rationality of government" (Foucault 2008:312). The liberal challenge was clear and simple: the political economists asserted that the aggregated judgments of the multitude that dare to know (the price of things) far exceed the insight of the One who yields political power over the economic sphere. As a result of the political monarch being proven to hold no supravision and thus being inadequate to oversee the market economy, this sphere, in which people put into action their purchasing power by exercising economic rationality, ought to stay sovereign free. And, as argued by Smith, better to be left free for the owners of wealth to exercise their economic power.

In the sphere of civil society, the liberal political economists presented the sovereign with a new problem—"how not to govern like that and at that price"—which was translated into the problem of "how not to govern too much," that is, into the question of how and to what extent the political monarch ought to restrict, willingly, the exercise of despotic power (2008:13–17). What was demanded of the political monarch is a new form of political technology by which he limits his exercise of power by accommodating the rationality of the governed economic multitude. As can be seen, a radical gap is introduced between the political sphere ruled by the One in power and the economic one inhabited by the governed multitude that pursues its interests by rationally exercising economic power. As Foucault saw it, civil society fills this gap when serving as "a new plane of reference" (2008:295). Within its bounds, the governed economic multitude and the political monarch engage in a critical discussion of *the problem* of political economy as just described, that is, how the political monarch accommodates to the will of the governed not to be governed "like that and at that price," which is translated into the problem of "how not to govern too much."

THE NEOLIBERAL MARKETIZED ECONOMY AND POLITICS

The process of the marketization of the economy from Mill to Becker described earlier is concluded in Becker's notions of "Human Capital" and "Economics of Crime and Punishment." Becker reformulates the ethical modes by which one governs one's self by theorizing the economic self as human capital that generates labor in return for income. Such self-government is conducted by economizing one's *earning power*, the form of power that one commands over one's labor. Theorizing self-government as a form of command over one's own labor, Becker inserts the power relations of the market, which Smith identified as purchasing power over other people's labor, into the *ethical* sphere of the relationship between a person and herself. Becker's theory of self-government also entails a transformation of the technologies of the self into an *askesis* of economizing the scarce means of the marketized self that have alternative uses for the purpose of maximizing the earning and purchasing power one commands in the marketized economy.

The marketization of the self that turned zoon oikonomikon into a power-craving homo economicus also makes him governable by the political monarch, as demonstrated in the Economic analysis of *Crime and Punishment*. Economic man is governed through the legal framework of the market economy. Human action is controlled by tweaking a matrix of punishments and incentives that make the governed subject, as a prudent creature who craves to maximize his economic power, *freely* choose the desired course of action that will ensure economic growth. At the same time that Becker's technologies of the conduct of the marketized self establish a neoliberal self-mastery, they also enable the governmental technology of conducting one self conduct in the all-encompassing and ever growing marketized economy. Although Becker seems to reverse the age-old ethical question, that is, how can a human, as a governed subject, become free in the economy, into the technological one of how one can make a free human governable, the end result is pretty much the same, as the economy is reconstituted as a sphere in which the subject is seen as free and governed.

A neoliberal interpretation of Hobbes's economic power is found in Tullock and Buchanan's use of economic theory to "deal with traditional problems of political science," that is, to trace the works of Smithian economic power that have by now been transposed onto the political sphere:

> Incorporat(ing) political activity as a particular form of exchange; and, as in the market relation, mutual gains to all parties are ideally expected to result from the collective relation. In a very real sense, therefore, political action is viewed essentially as a means through which the "power" of all participants may be increased, if we define "power" as the ability to command things that are desired by men. To be justified by the criteria employed here, collective action must be advantageous to all parties.
>
> (Tullock and Buchanan 1962:23)

One can trace in the foregoing a pattern of marketization of the economy in two ways: first, the transposition of the definition of economic power from command over labor to the command over things desired by men; and, second, that political action is marketized and defined as a form of exchange that is viewed essentially as a means to the growth of economic power of all citizens. As recalled, Foucault (2008:118–20, 147) identified the turn from classical political economy to neoliberal economics with the shift from exchange as the regulatory principle of the market to that of competition, and of the economic subject from man of exchange to that of Becker's entrepreneur of the "marketized self" (Foucault 2008:175). Taking Tullock and Buchanan's economic approach to political behavior into account, it seems as if it would be more accurate to say that the neoliberal economic man marketized the split person that we already encountered with ancient zoon koinonikon (between political and economic life). The latter was split, as a political and economic creature, between being a *polites* in the public sphere and an *oikodespotes* in the private one. Neoliberal economic man is split between liberalized politics and marketized economy: his labor is governed in the competitive market and he participates in politics as a Smithian subject of exchange.

On the macrolevel, this split enables the demise of liberal civil society as a plane of reference between the economic multitude and the political One. "The king's head is cut off," or, more accurately, the political monarch is anarchized: *first*, by changing his role from liberal noninterference in the market economy to the proactive one of recalibrating the legal framework in which marketized economic men interact. Second, by constituting sovereign action as resulting from the collective relation between the politization of the liberal "man of exchange," it is supposed to nullify the need for an extraeconomic and extrapolitical plane of reference in which the economic multitude freely expresses its will as to how not be governed at that price.

A NOTE ON ECONOMY AND PHILOSOPHY

In the dialogue in which Diotima instructs Socrates in the different kinds of erotic desire for self-perpetuation, she hierarchizes these desires: the crude and lowly way to perpetuate oneself is by begetting offspring that fulfill the human animal's natural desire for the "immortal element in the creature that is mortal" (Plato 1925c: *Symposium* 206c).[25] Above the bodily desire are means by which people perpetuate themselves in spirit. The lesser of them is self-perpetuation in the memory of others. It is achieved by demonstrating virtues such as courage, soundness of mind, and righteousness as a zoon koinonikon. The loftiest mode of self-perpetuation is the theoretical life, in which the human soul strains to beget in the "ever-existent and neither comes to be nor perishes, neither waxes nor wanes . . . existing ever in singularity of form independent by itself " (210e–11b). Later these types were scaled by the students of Diotima's student in the following order: self-perpetuating by bodily begetting offspring, demonstrating soundness of mind in the economic sphere, passing judgment on the work of the poet, pursuing the ideal mode of life in politics, liberally engaging in philosophy.

In the imperial cosmopolis Hermagoras led the rhetorical charge on philosophy that elevated political self-perpetuation and downgraded the philosophical self-perpetuation by embedding the latter in the economy. Reestablishing the primacy of philosophy over politics, the Christian philosophers accepted Hermagoras's insight that philosophy's only way to appear in public is within the bounds of the economy and constituted the philosophical-ethical disposition of caring for oneself as conducted in an ever growing economic society in which every person erotically desires a nonexhaustive truth by means of body and soul. This was achieved by internalizing Diotima's distinction between forms of erotic desire into the economic sphere, so that displaying an ethical soundness of mind toward bodily desires released erotic energies for the desire for God.

Triumphant as the Christian philosophical reply to Hermagoras's challenge was (as it outlived the classical polis and the imperial cosmopolis by millennia), the cunning of history had proven to hold the upper hand and "philosophy and politics, their old conflict notwithstanding, have suffered the same fate" (Arendt 2004:453). This happened when the "worldly philosophers" took control over the economy and society by cashing in on the two prices the Christian philosophers had to pay on their way to saving philosophy be embedding it in the economy: the *first* is that the philosopher governed society as an economist instead of as a political monarch; the *second* was the immanentization of both truth and soul into a world given to constant change. As we have seen, in the first stage the liberal political economists took charge over the economy and society from the early modern political monarch. In the second stage the neoliberal economists denied the theoretical object of desire its unique ontological status of nonsaturation on their way to erasing all distinctions between desired objects whatsoever. The loss of distinctions through the marketization of

TABLE 6.3   BASIC PARAMETERS OF THE ECONOMY IN CLASSICAL, CHRISTIAN,
AND CONTEMPORARY MOMENTS

PARAMETER/ MOMENT	CLASSICAL	CHRISTIAN	CONTEMPORARY
Origin of excess	nature's circularity	the Godhead	human wants
Surplus	noneconomic	economic growth	economic growth
Limit	in space; the law	in time; the fullness of times	no limit
Action	prudent	prudent	prudent
The thing economized	needs	the desire for God	each need and every desire indiscriminately
Initial human condition	by necessity	by freedom	by necessity
Freedom	to exceed the economy	practiced within the economy	practiced within the economy
Relation to law	outside the boundary of law	exceeds the limits set by canon law	multiple: framed by; exceeds; an economy of law
Relation to philosophy	subjected to philosophy	contains philosophy	democratizes philosophy
Relation to politics	subjected to politics	subjects politics	subjects politics

the economy of everything threatens to annihilate philosophy, at least as we have come to know it. This is so because its mere existence depends on the elevated and distinct status of its object of desire (and of the desire itself) from the rest of human-desired objects.

Economic Ethics: Practicing Freedom as a Governed Subject

For over one hundred and fifty years, critical thought on the left has been preoccupied with demonstrating how the liberal project of turning the market economy into the primary sphere in which people practice their freedom actually masks their enslavement to it. The authors typically go about this by detailing the multiple ways in which humans are governed within the economy. Doing so seems to be based on two misrecognitions. First, by assuming that the economy, as a sphere in which freedom is exercised, necessitates the absence of rulership (*archeh*), they misidentify the object to be criticized. As shown, the economy as a sphere in which freedom is practiced in no way necessitates the absence of subjection, only the absence of a government that imposes itself upon its subjects. This kind of freedom was demonstrated by the matron from the classical oikos, by the sage of the imperial cosmopolis, by the members of the society of believers in Christ's economy, by the liberal use of wealth in the market economy, and by neoliberal mastery of the marketized self. Moreover, the Christians and the liberals had identified this sort of despotic imposition with the political rule of the monarch. In other words, the critique from the left tends to overlook that, ever since Xenophon's Ischomachus and his matron established their common oikos and right up to the present marketized economy, humans have found various ways of practicing their freedom while being governed in the economic sphere. The *second* misrecognition of this line of criticism is, like the first, due to the tendency to embrace the conception of economic freedom as a freedom from any form of government. The result of this uncritical stance, as Foucault sharply pointed out (Foucault 2008:91–94),[26] is that these critics form the left thereby avoid the task of developing an ethics, theory, and art of a (post)modern economics in which humans would be able to practice their freedom while being subjected to the rule of a nonoppressive government.[27]

Both Arendt and Foucault sidestepped the double trap of masking the fact that the economy is always already governed and that economic freedom does not necessitate freedom from being governed. Arendt did so by altogether circumventing these claims and returning to the persona of the master/citizen of the classical moment. In this model the citizen practices his freedom as a communal creature by economizing his desires with soundness of mind and partaking in an unruled sphere outside the boundaries of the economy. Foucault did so by returning to the persona of the imperial sage (while disregarding the classical matron) in search of models that would serve the critique in its attempt to articulate "the art of not being governed so much."[28] As can be inferred, these two attempts to criticize modernity by offering models for the reconstruction of freedom are clearly distinct; whereas Arendt searches for a freedom from economic government through the limiting of the economic sphere, Foucault seeks freedom within its bounds as a governed economic subject. Bearing in mind this fundamental difference, we can trace at least three features that these attempts share in common. 1. Both authors sought their models in an age that preceded the rise of the society of believers in Christ economy; while Arendt relies on the polis of the classical moment, Foucault returned in his lectures from the years 1982–84 to "the golden age of the culture of the self" in the imperial moment. 2. Despite the great many differences between the classical master/citizen and the imperial sage, both subject the economy to the rule of soundness of mind. As I describe elsewhere,[29] ever since the political community and philosophical life were distinguished from the economy, a display of soundness of mind in the economy was considered a prerequisite for the maintenance of a virtuous life and for the joint practice of freedom. Exhibiting soundness of mind in the economy was demanded both from those who, like the master/citizen, wished to practice their freedom outside the boundaries of the economy and those who, like the matron, were destined to practice it within the bounds of an ever growing economy. The urgent need for restoring soundness of mind to the contemporary economy of needs and desires appears, then, to constitute a necessary condition for both parties: politicians who tend, like Arendt, to believe in the possibility of reconstructing the political sphere and philosophers who, like Foucault, have given up on this possibility, attempting instead to theorize and practice freedom within the economy. 3. Finally, both Arendt and Foucault share the belief that, against all odds, we can live a virtuous life and practice our freedom either outside the economy or within it. Moreover, both claim that, in order to enable this, politics and philosophy must join hands in formulating new norms for the economy. Foucault presents such a claim in its theoretical context:

> I think we may have to suspect that we find it impossible today to constitute an ethics of the self, even though it may be an urgent, fundamental and politically indispensable task, if it is true after all that there is no first or final point of resistance to political power other than in the relationship one has to oneself. . . . if we take the question of power, of political power, situating it in the more general question of governmentality . . . then I do not think that reflection on this notion of governmentality can

avoid passing through, theoretically and practically, the element of a subject defined by the relationship of self to self. . . . Quite simply, this means
that in the type of analysis I have been trying to advance for some time
you can see that power relations, governmentality, the government of the
self and of others, and the relationship of self to self, constitute a chain, a
thread, and I think it is round these notions that we should be able to connect together the question of politics and the question of ethics.

(Foucault 2005:252)

While Arendt presents it in its historical context: "We live today in a world
in which not even common sense makes sense any longer. The breakdown
of common sense in the present world signals that philosophy and politics,
their old conflict notwithstanding, have suffered the same fate. And that
means that the problem of philosophy and politics, or the necessity for a
new political philosophy from which could come a new science of politics,
is once more on the agenda" (Arendt 2005:38).

As shown, politicians and philosophers alike used and abused the economy for their own ends more than once during their "old conflict." This
conflict, as described in the introduction, began with the execution of *the*
Philosopher, Socrates, by the political community, in response to which his
student Plato ridiculed Rhetoric and introduced the idea that the legal
framework that distinguishes politics from the economy should be removed. In the imperial moment it was Hermagoras of Temnos, who, in reply to the Platonist insult, pointed out the fact that the products of philosophical endeavor must, by necessity, be economized if they are to appear
in public speech. The philosophers' overwhelming response was delivered
by the Christians, whose economizing of philosophical life in communion
"constituted within the world a totally new, religiously defined public
space, which, although public, was not political," and in which they exercised their freedom while placing politics in the service of the society of
believers in the economy. Philosophical life fared no better than politics as
political economists (followed by neoliberal economists) fully expropriat-
ed the society of believers in the economy, granting it indiscriminate control over all spheres of life. Faced with this constant expansion, "the private and intimate, on the one hand, and the political (in the narrower
sense of the word), on the other, have proved incapable of defending themselves" (*HC* 47).

I do not know if it has always been the case, but in the current state of affairs it seems to me that politicians and philosophers need to return to Aristotole's categorical imperative "to begin with speaking of the economy" (*Pol.* 1253b2)—whether of necessity, as he orders at the opening of *The Politics*, or willingly, as implied by the Church Fathers—in an attempt to reconstitute a new political philosophy. If Aristotle's categorical imperative is still valid today, then the genealogy of the neoliberal marketized economy conducted in this book may help us in the search for new ways to define the economy, to contend with the human condition that appears within it, and to reorganize its relations with politics, philosophical life, and the boundaries set by law. It is suggested that such a new political philosophy, although feeding on Arendt's and Foucault's critical genealogies into the present human trinity of politics, philosophy, and economy, must transcend both. This need goes beyond introducing the necessary corrections to their genealogical inquiries in order to exact the critique of neoliberalism, as performed throughout this book.

Can this be achieved in the present? That is the question I tried to put once more on the agenda by conducting a genealogy of the human trinity from the economic perspective.

Notes

Introduction

1. Agamben's critique of modernity by introducing Christian oikonomia was preceded by Mondzain 2005.
2. Arendt 1958:38.
3. Ibid., 47.
4. Of all the Greek Church Fathers, Arendt refers to Origen on two occasions and is quick to reject (Arendt 1977:287) Oscar Cullmann's (1964) conception of the history of salvation.
5. Classical Greek economy is referred to in Foucault 1990:141–84, in which the third part is dedicated to economy. References to imperial moment appear in Foucault 1988b, 2005, and 1988c, where economy is referenced many times, from the classical age, through the imperial, and up to Christianity. Christian oikonomia is dealt with in lectures 5–9 in Foucault 2007:114–254, 2014a, 2014b, 1999c:52–135, 1999a:81–158, and 1988a:57–85. Foucault dealt with mercantile and classical economies twice. At first, it appeared as part of Foucault 1973 and later in his genealogy of governmentality in Foucault 2007:255–363 and in the first part of Foucault 2008:1–100. Neoliberal economics (both German and American) is treated in the second part of Foucault 2008:101–317.
6. Elsewhere he argues that "the essential issue of government will be the introduction of economy into Political practice.... The transition in the eighteenth century from a regime dominated by structures of sovereignty to a regime dominated by techniques of government revolves around population and consequently around the birth of political economy.... Political economy as both a science and a technique of intervention in this field of reality ... political economy as its major form of knowledge." Foucault 2007:95–108.

7. For an excellent discussion, see Singh 2015.

8. For other examples and discussion, see Leshem 2013a:57–58.

9. Agamben 1998:120.

10. In Leshem 2014c I venture on doing so by reinterpreting Arendt's claim that the holes of oblivion do not exist. This interpretation casts Arendt as offering a new concept of secularization that enables a reconceptualization of the economy of human nature as described by the Church Fathers. Based on a comparative analysis of the Jewish, Christian, and Arendtian persona of the witness, I look for a new political philosophy that 1. posits morality as ontologically prior to utility when it comes to the economy, and 2. proposes a return to the different modes of "begetting on a beautiful thing by means of body and soul" enumerated by Diotima.

11. For a detailed discussion, see Leshem 2014b.

12. Xenophon's *Oikonomikos* is the earliest text preserved. It was preceded by a lost treatise by Antisthenes. A generation later, Aristotle dedicated large portions of the first book of his *Politics* (Aristotle 1944) to the study of the economy. Students of Aristotle composed three texts on economics, all ascribed to Aristotle himself. Philodemus of Gadara ascribed the first of these texts to Theophrastus. Treatises dedicated to the economy as household management from later periods were preserved as well: a dialogue named *Eryxias*, tackling the question of wealth; a summary of Stoic and Peripatetic thought by Arius Didymus (1999) preserved in Stobaeus; and texts by Dio of Prusa, Callicratidas, Herocles, Phlodemus of Gadara, Bryon, and Plutarch. Other texts, of which only fragments have survived, are ascribed to Theano II, Perictione I, Phyntis, Myia, and Aesara, all female members of the Pythagorean school; the original date of their composition is under debate (Waithe 1987:61, 65, 72–73). Another genre of literature that touches on the economy deals mostly with marital problems and their remedies.

13. As stated by Arius Didymus (1999) in his summary of Stoic economic thought, "an oikos with necessities. These necessities are twofold, those for communal life and those for a good life. For the *oikonomikos* needs first to have forethought about these things, either increasing his revenues through free means of procurement or by cutting down on expenses."

14. Xenophon 1994.

15. *Xen. Ec.* 2:10, 11:9–10; see also *Xen. Ec.* 1:4, 21:9.

16. Ibid., 2:4.

17. Ibid., 11:9–10.

18. For other examples and discussion, see Leshem 2013a:57–8.

19. The original Greek text was lost. Its translation into Arabic (later to be translated into Hebrew) was preserved. All translations of Bryson are mine, from the Hebrew version.

20. It is not a partnership in which there is an ordinary political government, since the ruler and the ruled do not interchange. It is also not an ordinary aristocratic government, since the wife is charged with spheres and activities that she rules by herself.

21. Arendt 2005:178–86.
22. Tarn 1952:325; Shaw 1985:16–54.
23. Kennedy 1999:1.
24. Plato 1925:262b.
25. Meijering 1989:135.
26. Plato 1925:266d.
27. Swanson 1992.
28. Ibid., 270–71.
29. Aristotle 1926:1–2.
30. Ibid., 3.1.1.
31. See, for example, Diogenes Laertius 1853:43, who presented the common Stoic division.
32. This is the common Latin translation of *oikonomia*, alongside *dispensatio* and *oeconomia*.
33. Anonymous 1996:163.
34. Aristotle 1926:3.3.3.
35. Ibid.
36. Aristotle 1932:23.
37. Murphy 2003:131; Kennedy 1995:67.
38. Tacitus 2006:109; Kennedy 1999:99.
39. Bennett 2005:187.
40. Ibid.
41. On philosophy as a private affair, see Swanson 1992.
42. Quintilian 1920–44:3.
43. Kennedy 1994:100.
44. Reid 1997:12.
45. Dionysius of Halicarnassus translated ibid.
46. See Meijering 1989:137.
47. Reid 1997:5.
48. Anonymous in Reumann 1957:378. For a discussion and other examples, see ibid., 378–83; Meijering 1989:141–42; Reid 1997.

1. From Oikos to Ecclesia

1. In Isaiah 22:21, where it is a translation of הלשממ, "government."
2. Jastrow 1926.
3. According to Mondzain, economy is "the very concept that is responsible for linking them [the real and the ideal] with a minimum of contradiction, by means of the imaginal and iconic system": Mondzain 2005:11.
4. Marie-Jose Mondzain argued that "[Hyppolytus . . .] starting as all the Church Fathers, from the usage Paul makes of the term *economy* (Mondzain 2005). See also Meyendorff 1982:34–5; and Reumann 1992:9. Oikonomos appears also in Luke 16:1, 3, 8 and 12:42, where it refers to a household economist, translated as steward or

manager. In Romans 16:23 *oikonomos* appears in its political context, translated as city treasurer or chamberlain. *Oikonomia* appears in Luke 16:2, 3, 4 as household management. Subtracting these appearances, we are left with only eleven appearances in the New Testament.

5. See Mondzain 2005:21; Markus 1958:92; Quinn and Wacker 2000:74–78.

6. A distinction is made between "special" and "general" economy and sometimes between providence (πρόνοια) and economy.

7. Discussed in Leshem 2013b:29–51.

8. See also Ephesians 3:2.

9. ἐπίσκοπος: literally, "overseer."

10. The Apostolic Fathers are Ignatius, Clement of Rome, Policarp, and the unknown authors of the *Didache* and *The Shepard of Herms* from the second half of the first century and the beginning of the second. They are supposed to have been in direct contact with one (or more) of the apostles. The apologists from the second and third centuries wrote tractates in defense (ἀπολογία) of Christianity against other sects, the empire, and Greek philosophy. These defenses were usually meant to demonstrate the coherence and rationality of the Christian faith and their absence in opponents.

11. Justin Martyr was born in the year 100 CE, becoming Christian in the year 130 and martyred in 165. He is considered to be the most prolific and the influential among the early apologists.

12. See Leshem 2013b.

13. As well as to Cain and Abel.

14. Leshem 2013b.

15. See, for example, Clement of Alexandria 2004b:6:15.

16. Gregory of Nazianzus (1893:oration 29:2) makes the lack of necessity that accompanies excess one of the crucial points that distinguish Christianity from Neoplatonism.

17. I here follow Otto Lilge; see Reumann 1957:88.

18. With the exception of Richter, modern scholars hold that Irenaeus understood oikonomia as the fulfillment of God's salvific plan. Richter (2005:115–35) argues that this misconception originates in Loffs, repeated by Lilge and Widmann.

19. On recapitulation in Irenaeus's thought, see Osborn 2000:12–31.

20. For a detailed discussion see Pagels 1972 and Pagels 1974:35–53.

21. Its materialization can also be seen in by the replacement of the Pauline economy of the mysteries by the mysteries of the economy (Agamben 2011).

22. ἐκδιηγεῖσθαι τὴν πραγματείαν καὶ οἰκονομίαν τοῦ Θεοῦ τὴν ἐπὶ τῇ ἀνθρωπότητι γενομένην.

23. For a comparative discussion of the incarnation in Irenaeus and Clement of Alexandria, see Behr 2000.

24. In the *Histories* Polybius argued that the economy is managed by fortune, and the historiographer has to follow this economy and render it intelligible (1.4). Polybius hints that there is a divine ordering of history and in it the divine intervention is prudent (Reumann 1957).

25. Tertullian does not limit the economy and his (Latin) translation of it (*dispensatio, dispositio*) to the inner organization of the Godhead. As argued by Mondzain (2005:25–27) and by Richter (2005:168), each of the Latin translations is saved for the description of a different facet of the economy: while *dispositio* describes the inner organization of the Godhead, *dispensatio* describes the revelation of God's mysterious plan throughout history. According to Basil Studer, Tertullian held that the economy existed before creation and the incarnation sought to reveal the mysteries of the original economy (Studer 1993).

26. Markus 1958: 98–102 argued against the received view (influenced by Prestige 1964:106–11) that in Hippolitus *economy* does not describe the inner organization of the Godhead, but is solely used to describe the incarnation. For this reason I will limit myself to Tertullian's use of *economy*.

27. Osborn refers to *AP* II.

28. According to Botte (1980:59–72), Tertullian's use of *economy* was itself influenced by Gnosticism.

29. My presentation of Clement's thought relies, in addition to the Otto Lilge thesis, on Behr 2000 and Kovacs 2001:1–24, both arguing that economy is rendered by Clement as a pedagogical process. Much as in the case of Tertullian, my presentation of the concept of economy in Clement's thought is limited to its major contribution. Beside Richter, see Osborn 2005:31–55 on economy as a concept of history and Torrance 1967:223–38 on economy as divine providence.

30. At the beginning of his treatise *The Pedagogue* (I.1.1.4), he offers the following: "Let us then designate this Word appropriately by the one name pedagogue."

31. According to Clement, the origin of Greek philosophy is in Judaism, which he called "Barbaric philosophy." For a discussion and references to Clement, see Osborn 2005:92.

32. For a discussion of the concept of economy in the thought of Origen, see Benjamins 1994:138–221, which includes a comprehensive review of economy in the context of ecclesiastical writings; Anatolios 1999:165–71, on its role in God-world relations; and Trigg 2001: 27–52, on economy in the pedagogical context. For a more general review, see Richter 2005.

33. Whether the *Stromata* (Clement of Alexandria 2004b) is equivalent to the third stage or not was debated in the first half of the twentieth century. For the positions held by those who took part in the debate, see Wagner 1968:60–251; Osborn 2005:4–12.

34. "Time [in the *Timeaus*] so conceived is not the contrary of timeless eternity, but an approximation to it: its likeness (εἰκόνα 37b 6), its imitation (38a 8). Time is a finished product, the end result of a raw material which the Demiurge works over with the definite purpose of making it as much like eternity as he possibly can" (Vlastos 1965:388).

35. See also Arendt 1978:133–55. "What Pericles and the Philosophers had in common was the General Greek estimate that all mortals should strive for immortality, and this was possible because of the affinity between gods and men" (ibid., 134).

36. For a more nuanced discussion on the Cappadocian conception of time, see also Balas 1976:128–55; Limberis 1997:141–44; Plass 1980:180–92. On the way the three concepts are organized in Origen's conception of time, see Tzamalikos 2007:130–41.

37. See, for example: "This world is said to have seven ages, that is to say, from the creation of heaven and earth until the general consummation and resurrection of men. For, while there is a particular consummation, which is the death of each individual, there is also a general and final consummation which will come when the general resurrection of men takes place. The eighth age is that which is to come" (John of Damascus 1958:204).

38. These ages are sometimes called economies. See *AH* III:11.8

39. "After the resurrection, time will not be numbered by days and nights at all; rather, there will be one day without evening, with the Sun of Justice shining brightly upon the just and a deep and endless night reserved for the sinners" (John of Damascus 1958:204); see also Basil the Great 1963:II:8; Gregory of Nazianzus 1893, Oration XLI; for a comprehensive list of references, see Azkoul 1968a:67.

40. That is, cosmogony and cosmology.

41. Although Clement (2004b) used the term in a manner that can be understood as referring to Christianity. See Clement of Alexandria 2004b:I.13.

42. In most instances, economy means in Athanasius "the work of salvation by Christ qua homo." Economy usually means incarnation in his later writings. This meaning is contrasted with theology (which is found five times) as the accurate teaching about God or the Trinity itself (LaCugna 1993:38–39).

43. "We have completed our treaties on the doctrine of the holy trinity. . . . I therefore necessarily commence this work [on the inhumanation of the Lord], by connecting theology and oikonomia, and showing how greatly the creator looked after our kind" (Pásztori-Kupán 2006:138).

44. Who wrote a treatise entitled *Two Thousand Chapters on Theology and Economy*. According to Louth, "Maximus regards the distinction between apophatic and cataphatic theology as mirroring the patristic distinction between 'theology' and 'economy'-that is, the distinction between the doctrine of God as He is in Himself (in other words, the doctrine of the Trinity) and the doctrine of God's dealings with the world, especially in the Incarnation" (Louth 1996:54).

45. See John of Damascus 1958:162.

46. See Daley 2006a:43; Lossky 1985:15; LaCugna 1993:42–43; Winslow 1971:389–96; and Mondzain 2005:14.

47. Πρόνοια. For a discussion on its role in Stoicism, see Charlesworth 1936:107–32. For a detailed history of the concept and its reincarnation in Christianity, with special emphasis on Clement of Alexandria, see Ewing 2005. On the relation between economy and providence in Clement, see Torrance 1967:223–38.

48. Richter found evidence of the use of the economy alongside providence in Clement and argues that it is impossible to extrapolate a strict relation between the two. See Richter 2005.

49. The description given far from exhausts the complex relations between a single human and human community to the cosmos and between the economy incarnated and the cosmos. It seems as if the church father who wrote most extensively on the subject is Maximus the Confessor. For detailed and enlightening discussions, see Von Balthasar 2003; Thunberg 1985. For a more compact review, see Louth 1996:63–80.

2. Modeling the Economy

1. The term *hyperontological* would seem to better describe the conception of the Godhead as subsisting beyond the realm of being. For reasons of expedience, I shall henceforth in this chapter and in the remainder of the book use the simpler term *ontology* (therefore, Ontological Communion) and various conjugations of the verb *to be* (rather than the awkward but more accurate to *hyper-be*) to describe the constitution of this hyperontology and its events.

2. For a description of the function of models in contemporary economics see Yonay and Breslau 2006:345–86; McCloskey 2001:204–21. For a discussion of equilibrium in contemporary economic theory, see Weintraub 1985.

3. As for the contemporary economy, Michel Callon's description seems to capture this, saying: "Economics in the broad sense of the term performs, shapes and formats the economy, rather than observing how it functions. . . . Yes, homo economicus does exist, but is not an a-historical reality, it does not describe the hidden nature of the human being. It is the result of a process of configuration" (Callon 1998:2, 28).

4. For a discussion of ancient optics, accompanied by enlightening drawings, see Conford 1937:154–55.

5. Thomas Hopko presents the Cappadocian conception of the Trinity in the same manner. See Hopko 1986:271.

6. See Lienhard 2001:99–122; Studer 1993:142–44.

7. The Cappadocian Fathers used a variety of metaphors to explain how there could be one who is three; see, for example, Gregory of Nazianzus 1983, Oration 31:14, Basil the Great 2003b, Letter 38.5, 8.

8. For a review of the concept of persona in ecclesiastical texts until the fourth century and a thorough examination of the same concept in the writings of Gregory of Nyssa, see Lynch 1979:728–38.

9. *HC* 192–95. Arendt (1969a:102–4) explicitly connects the two (persona and self). However, the meaning of "being heard through" (Arendt 1969a:296, note 42) given by the eighteenth-century revolutionaries is the same meaning it acquired in Latin Christianity, along with the excess of theological connotations implied in the phrase. On persona in Arendt 1994:446–55, see Leshem 2014c.

10. There is a marked contradiction between the way Arendt presents the concept of the persona in the classical moment and the way in which Lossky and Zizioulas, who elaborates Lossky's conception, present it. See Zizioulas 1985:27–36 and 2006:178–205.

11. On this topic, see also Zizioulas 1995:44–60.

12. According to Zizioulas, "Basil does not particularly like this terminology [of substance], and prefers to use koinonia wherever reference is made to the oneness of divinity" (Zizioulas 2006:184). See, for example, Basil 2003b, Letter 38:4.

13. According to Hopko, Basil's Letter 38 and Gregory of Nyssa's *Not Three Gods* are the key texts on this theme in the Cappadocian corpus (Hopko 1986:267–68).

14. For a more concise formulation, see Basil the Great 2003b, Letter 236:6.

15. See Gregory of Nazianzus's (1893) orations 29:5–6, 30:10, 31:14, 39:11, 40:4; Basil the Great 2003b, Letter 38.

16. For a different position, see Clark 1982:3–28.

17. For a discussion of the meanings it acquired in Stoicism and in Christianity see Prestige 1964:282–300; Wolfson 1956:418–28; Harrison 1991:53–65; Egan 1993:21–28; Thunberg 1995:23–36; Vishnevskaya 2004:7–40, 202–51; and Lawler 1995:49–66.

18. For a discussion of contemporary "social Trinity" theories, see Horrell 2004:406.

19. For a discussion of the philosophical origins of the principle of transcription, see Parry 1996:20–64.

20. "Some of them daring to corrupt the mystery of the Lord's oikonomia for us and refusing [to use] the name Mother of God in reference to the Virgin. . . . And, on account of those who have taken in hand to corrupt the mystery of the oikonomia and who shamelessly pretend that he who was born of the holy Virgin Mary was a mere man . . . for it opposes those who would rend the mystery of the oikonomia into a Duad of Sons" (The Definition of Faith of the Council of Chalcedon 2005).

21. See Gregory of Nyssa 2000, Homily VI.

22. The notion that in the economy a mutual interpenetration of the divine and the human takes place, even if initiated by God, and that the depth of these penetrations is without comparison, is shared by Wolfson 1956; Harrison 1991; Thunberg 1995; and Vishnevskaya 2004. Against this conception, Prestige 1964 (who is joined with mild reservations by Von Balthasar 2003:246) argues that there is only a one-sided penetration by God.

23. The word perichoresis appears for the first time in relation to the economy and only later in reference to the Ontological Communion. Pseudo Cyril was the first to use it in reference to the latter, while John of Damascus was the first to explicitly state the ontological and conceptual primacy of perichoresis in the Ontological Communion, while conceiving of the economic perichoresis as its mimesis (Harrison 1991:61–62). That being said, the idea of mutual indwelling, even without it being formulated into a concept, can be traced back to Athanasius (Prestige 1964:284). See also Lawler 1995; Crisp 2005:119–40; and Parker 1980:176.

24. See also John of Damascus, *De Fide Contra Nestorianos*:36, quoted in Harrison 1991:61.

25. See also *G2G* 129.

26. I altered the translation from "operation" following Prestige's translation of the concept of *energia*; see Prestige 1964:256.

27. An imperative that one is tempted to call, in light of their habit of narrating their arguments with medical metaphors, the "Pauline oath," which economists since

Irenaeus up until contemporary practitioners swear to themselves in the secrecy of the chambers of their heart.

28. For a description of how the latter three are intertwined in the thought of Gregory of Nazianzus, see Winslow 1979:147–99.

29. Inspired by Cyril of Alexandria, the Council of Chalcedon condemned those

> persons undertaking to make void the preaching of the truth [who] have through their individual heresies given rise to empty babblings; some of them daring to corrupt the mystery of the Lord's oikonomia for us and refusing [to use] the name Mother of God (Θεοτόκος) in reference to the Virgin . . . on account of those who have taken in hand to corrupt the mystery of the oikonomia and who shamelessly pretend that he who was born of the holy Virgin Mary was a mere man, it receives the synodical letters of the Blessed Cyril, Pastor of the Church of Alexandria, addressed to Nestorius and the Easterns.
>
> (The Definition of Faith of the Council of Chalcedon 2005)

30. See also Harrison 1996:38–68, who treats the gender theory of the Cappadocian Fathers.

31. Translation from Gregory of Nyssa 2004f:II.

32. For a discussion illustrated by many supporting examples, see Harrison 1990:441–71; Harrison 1993:185–21 (also John of Damascus 1958, *The Orthodox Faith* III:12).

33. See Foucault 2005:316; and Arius Didymus's definition of economy as a practical and theoretical disposition, as discussed in Leshem 2013a.

34. On confessing to the human economist, see Foucault 2007:181–83. In view of the economic models presented in the foregoing discussion, we can see how this practice is in fact tantamount to confession to God, who appears in the mirror of the human economist.

35. Matthew 25:1–13.

36. "Eros and askesis are, I think, the two major forms in western spirituality for conceptualizing the modalities by which the subject must be transformed in order finally to become capable of truth" (Foucault 2005:16). "Being concerned about oneself implies that we look away from the outside. . . . I was going to say "inside" . . . looking from the outside . . . toward oneself" (Foucault 2005:11).

37. For a review of the classical origins of the concept of philanthropy and the uniqueness of the Christian interpretation of this concept, see Downey 1955:199–208 and Hatch 1897:141–43.

38. This concept is found for the first time in Ignatius 2002b, *Letter to the Ephesians* 6.1.

39. See Leshem 2013a.

40. See Basil the Great 1963:35.

3. Economy and Philosophy

1. Communal life appears shortly and in a non-Christian context in Foucault 2005:114–17.

2. Justin Martyr (2002b, *Second Apology* X.6), Minucius Felix (2006:*Octavius* 19), Athenagoras (2004, *Plea for the Christians*), Tertullian (2006a: *Apology* 46), Clement of Alexandria (2004b, *Stromata* 5.12); for later writers, see, for example, Gregory of Nazianzus, *Oration* 28:4.

3. See also Lilla 1971:43.

4. See Foucault 2005:65–80.

5. For a discussion, see Conford 1937:154–55.

6. A second-century Platonic philosopher and the author of *The True Logos* (fragments of it are reserved in Origen's book), an apology against Christianity.

7. See also *AC* 44.

8. For a slightly different view, see Davies 1898:737–62.

9. Proverbs—ethics, Ecclesiastes—physics, Song of Songs—insight (Origen). Lawson in Origen 1957:40; see Coakley 2002:136–37; and Louth 1981:52–75. On its Neoplatonic use, see Hadot 1995:137–38.

10. At times, this referred to greed. For a discussion, see Balot 2001:92–93.

11. See also Blowers 1992:152.

12. For a discussion of Origen's progressive circularity, see Rabinowitz 1984:319–29.

13. Gregory of Nysaa 2004e, *On the Making of Man* 23.

14. As Laird (1999:596) puts is: "The pattern is clear: (1) from the darkness of sin and error to light; (2) from the light of knowledge to the cloud (or shadow of the apple tree), (3) from the cloud to divine darkness (or divine night)."

15. To the aforementioned vices, Gregory adds licentiousness, greed, and other vices that are compared to despotic masters who rule man (*G2G* 89, 91).

16. For numerous examples and discussion, see Daniélou in *G2G* 48–51.

17. See Leshem 2013a.

18. ἀπάθεια was a central concept in Stoic ethics and was later adopted by Neoplatonists. See Foucault 2005, 2007:178–79, 205–7; Hadot 1995:126–44, 70–72, 136–40. For stoic influence on Gregory, see McCambley 1987:11.

19. Gregory of Nyssa 2009a.

20. Gregory is relying on the Stoic conception that the clarity of the appearance of the object see depend on reaching a state of apetheia (Culianu 1987:113).

21. For other references and discussion, see Balas 1976:128–55.

22. See also Gregory of Nysaa 2004b, Great Catechism 39.

23. See Gregory of Nazianzus 1893b, Oration 18:42.

24. For discussion, see Brown 1990:285–304 and Ludlow 2007:176.

25. According to Daniélou (1979:53), the above formulation is "the most important intuition in all of Gregory's mystical theology."

26. For a summary of the different interpretations of the concept of unlimited growth in Gregory's thought, see Ludlow 2007:125–34 and Blowers 1992:151–71. My presentation relies on Daniélou 1979.

27. Otis 1958:11. For a review, see Daniélou 1950:173. Ferguson 1973:59–78 finds its roots at Philo, Irenaeus, Clement of Alexandria, and Origen (as for Augustine, see

Meredith 1999:87). For growth in Irenaeus's thought, see *AH* 4:20.7 and discussion in Behr 2000:116–28.

28. See Leshem 2014b.

29. As Foucault (2005:33) puts it: "after *eros*, the *polis*."

30. On Christian life as philosophical life, see Hadot 1995 and Callahan 1967:xi, 80.

31. See also Gregory Nazianzus's eulogy of Basil (1893a, Oration 43:62) and Gregory of Nyssa 1967c:11.

32. For examples and discussion, see Daley 1999:431–61.

33. Gregory of Nyssa 2004e:XI:3–4.

34. See Foucault 2007:166–73.

35. Ibid., 123–91.

36. Philippians 3:20. "A *politeuma* was a recognized, formally constituted corporation of aliens enjoying the right of domicile in a foreign city and forming a separate, semi-autonomous civic body, a city within a city; it had its own constitution and administrated its internal affairs as an ethnic unit through officials distinct from and independent of those of the host city. *Politemata* were a regular feature of Hellenistic cities" (Smallwood 2001:225–26).

4. Economy and Politics

1. "Thus, shortly after his death, Socrates appears as a mythical figure. And it is exactly this myth of Socrates which has indelibly marked the whole history of philosophy" (Hadot 2004:24).

2. For a detailed discussion of the legal aspects of Church-empire relations, see Morrison 1964:3–55.

3. A theory that came to be known as caesaropapism.

4. See Setton 1967:78–79.

5. See Williams 1951a:5–6, 10; Azkoul 1971:455–56; and Setton 1967:78–108.

6. This meant the removal of the Christians from any educational position they held. For a translation of the edict and discussion, see Downey 1957: 97–103 and 1959:339–49.

7. See Williams 1951a:13.

8. Chrysostom wrote a short homily named Homily 21 on Empire, Power and Glory. see *PG* 63:695–702.

9. For other definitions see Kasher 1985:30, who compliments Smallwood's definition as "excellent."

10. "from where also we look for the Savior, the Lord Christ Christ."

11. According to Gilbert Dagron, this is "what is original about a Christian empire: its universality, at least in theory, and its role—as political structure, as society and as history—in an economy of salvation" (Dagron 2003:295).

12. According to Wilfrid Parsons, "Caesar stands in the sentence for all political power, and the name has become in all literature a synonym for government . . . Caesar

for all political authority as such, not merely the emperor who happened to sit at Rome at the moment (Parsons 1942: 220–21).

13. See *Against the Arians* III:5, II:79 (Athanasius 2004a).

14. See Setton 1967:15.

15. According to Setton, this passage shaped the patristic attitude toward the emperor in the fourth century; see ibid., 16.

16. "Submit yourselves for the Lord's sake to every human institution, whether to a king as the one in authority; or to governors as sent by him for the punishment of evildoers and the praise of those who do right" (1 Peter 2:13–14).

17. With the exceptions of Origen and Cyprian; see Parsons 1945:345–48.

18. Tertullian refers to 1 Peter 2:13–14.

19. Which, apparently, he did not compose and were written at a later date.

20. See also Ignatius 2002c, *Epistle to the Philadelphians* IV.

21. Ignatius 2002d:ix; see also Ignatius 2002c:IV.

22. Justin Martyr 2002a:1.

23. See also Athenagoras 2004:1, 37. According to Parsons, "the martyrs literally died defending a doctrine of the separation of the Church and state" (Parsons 1942:222).

24. See Cullmann in Schmemann 1953:8.

25. See Tertullian 2006b, Apology XXXIII.

26. See Blumenfeld 2003:95–119.

27. AC I:1.

28. See Origen 2002:224–25.

29. Ibid., 30.

30. Ibid.

31. Ibid., 225–26.

32. According to Dvornik, the idea appears in a crude form in the writings of Melito, Tertulian, and Irenaeus; see Dvornik 1966:604.

33. For references and discussion, see ibid., 725.

34. For discussion, see Taylor 1992 and Zimmerman 1996:451–76.

35. For a detailed discussion of this model, see Goodenough 1928:55–102.

36. Athanasius *History of the Arians*: 33; *De Synodes* I. see also Von Comphausen, quoted in Rahner 1992:63.

37. Putting it differently, "Caesaropapism is political Arianism" (Soloviev in Toumanoff 1946:218).

38. "The Bishop has the image of Christ, the king has the image of god." Ambrosiaster in Williams 1951a:7.

39. See also Athanasius 2004c:34, 52. The original letter of Hosius was lost.

40. The opinions about deity that hold pride of place are three in number: anarchy, polyarchy, and monarchy. With the first two the children of Greece amused themselves, and may they continue to do so. Anarchy, with its lack of a governing principle, involves disorder. Polyarchy, with a plurality of such principles, involves faction and hence the absence of a governing principle, and this involves disorder again. Both lead to an identical result—lack of

order, which in turn leads to disintegration, disorder being the prelude to disintegration. For us, however, monarchy is the most valuable, but not a monarchy defined by a single person, for unity establishing plurality is self-discordant but the single rule produced by equality of nature, harmony of will, identity of action, and the convergence toward their source of what springs from unity—none of which is possible in the case of created nature.

(Gregory of Nazianzus, Oration 29:2, translated in Geréby 2008:15–16)

As pointed out by Geréby, this is the main text used by Erik Petersen to refute Carl Schmitt's hypothesis that the Christian conception of God maintains an analogy between earthly monarchy and divine sovereignty (ibid., 15).

41. For a detailed discussion, see Parker 1980:84–165.

42. "To avoid the struggle, by embracing monarchy, you betray the Godhead" (Gregory of Nazianzus 1893b, Oration 31:5). Such a betrayal is first and foremost the erasure of the unbridgeable gap between theology and economy. This is done by applying the human condition, which does not allow the existence of full communion and monarchy at the same time, to the Godhead, which does not abide by this condition. I am relying on Geréby 2008:17.

43. For a comprehensive analysis of the way these relations are designed in the writings of Basil the Great, see Reilly 1945.

44. For a comprehensive analysis of the way these relations are designed in the writings of Basil the Great, see ibid. For a more general presentation of the patristic view of them, see Stratoudaki-White 2000.

45. Homily 26 on 1 Corinthians 2.

46. Women is equal to man in honor (homily in 1 Corinthians 26:2), essence (homily 34 on 1 Corinthians 34), form and kind (homily 1 on Genesis: 8), like him (homily 1 on Genesis 14), has the same properties, same respect, and the same essence, and is by no means less than him (Stratoudaki-White 2000:15); she an equal of the same nature (ibid., 17).

47. For a discussion on how Chrysostom constructs political rule as despotic in contrast to ecclesiastical free government, see Carter 1958: 367–70.

48. In her commentary Pagels (1985) "hypostatically unites" between two seemingly contradictory lines of thought that can be traced back to different texts of Chrysostom concerning Eve's subjection to Adam. The first one presents this subjection as given, while the second presents it as a punishment for her sin. For a detailed discussion of Chrysostom's treatment of feminine subjection that includes numerous references, see Clark 1977. According to Clark, the conception of Eve being subjected to Adam before she sinned gained dominance.

49. The distribution of the despotic rule from the rule of Adam over Eve to the earthly oikos, the earthly kingdom, and the empire is described by John Chrysostom in 2002b, homily 22:9, on Ephesians, Chrysostom 2002a, homily 23 on Romans; Chrysostom in Parsons 1940:356; Chrysostom 2004d, homily 34 on First Corinthians 7, in Parsons 1940:357; John Chrysostom 1986, homily on Genesis 4:2 and homily on Genesis 8, 17.

50. Resembling the matron of the classical oikos who, even when taking part in government, is always already governed; see Leshem 2014a:18–25.
51. See Clark 1982:2.
52. On the matron taking part in government, see homily 34:5–7 where the master of the oikos is compared to a king and the matron to a general and deputy, and the same distribution of the spheres of responsibilities in pre-Christian oikos literature. In his homilies on the book of Genesis, Eve's sin is her lack of knowledge of how to govern (John Chrysostom 1986:241). In these homilies Eve appears as an equal partner to Adam's dominion over the world before the fall. See, for example, ibid., 134. It is noteworthy that "those authors come to create a theory fluctuating between homo imago Dei and rex imago Dei. . . . The idea of man's inner kingship is found everywhere in early Christian literature" (Kantorowicz 1952:265). For a detailed discussion, see ibid., 253–77.
53. John of Damascus 1958, *The Orthodox Faith* III:12.
54. These are three of the names given to Mary.
55. Chrysostom's conception is also distinct from the spatial concept of freedom in Stoic thought, in which all spheres of life were considered as given to an economic government, while humans as governed creatures aimed at becoming at home in each of these spheres according to its distinctive qualities.
56. For a discussion of Gregory of Nyssa's and John Chrysostom's treatment of the question of marriage, see Brown 1990:305–22. For a presentation of Chrysostom as giving unparalleled preference to virgin life, see Clark 1982:15–21.
57. The double government of the social body shows similarity to the government of a human by himself. See also 2004d, homily 17 on First Corinthians, , 2004d, homily 35 on First Corinthians, 2002b, homily 20 on Ephesians 4.
58. See also Chrysostom 20004d, homily 15 on Second Corinthians 5.
59. See also: "No pious emperor ever chose to torture and punish an unbeliever so as to force him to withdraw from error" (John Chrysostom 1985:83n31).
60. The superiority of the ecclesial over political sovereignty is expressed most vividly in John Chrysostom 1983:69–76.
61. See also Chrysostom 2003, homily 5, 96–97.
62. For its origins in Greek political theory, see Nock 1947:102–16 and Goodenough 1928:61.
63. Parsons argues that its roots can be found in Athanasius (Parsons 1942:344).
64. "But you, when you hear, Render unto Caesar the things which are Caesar's, know that He is speaking only of those things, which are no detriment to godliness; since if it be any such thing as this, such a thing is no longer Caesar's tribute, but the devil's" (John Chrysostom 2004c, homily 70 on Mathew 2).
65. Chrysostom 2003, I, homily 4 on Isaiah 6.
66. See Kelly 1995:116. According to Setton 1967:108, this hierarchy appears in patristic thought toward the end of the fourth century. For a similar position, see Florovsky 1957:142; see also, for example, Gregory of Nazianzus 2003, Oration 17:8–9.

67. "And this he does to show that it was not for the subversion of the commonwealth that Christ introduced His laws, but for the better ordering of it" (Chrysostom 2002a:homily 23 on Romans)

68. Chrysostom 1986, homily on Genesis 4:2.

69. See also ibid.

70. For the conception of the economy appearing in the world many years before politics did, see Pseudo-Aristotle 1910:1343a.

71. Hippolitus of Rome (2004) forms an exception; see *Treatise on Christ and Antichrist* 25.

72. See also Tertullian 2006c, *On the Resurrection of the Flesh* 24, 2006b, *Apology* 32.

73. επίσκοπος των εκτός. See Eusebius 2002b, *Life of Constantine* IV:24. For discussion, see Dvornik 1951:12 and Setton 1967:131.

74. The participants of the Second Ecumenical Council restate the position when addressing Emperor Theoudisius I: "We begin our letter to your Piety with thanks to God, who has established the empire of your Piety for the common peace of the Churches and for the support of the true Faith." See also Momigliano 1987:156.

75. Parsons 1945:335–6. For the treatment of other writers, see Downey 1959:339–49; Dvornik 1951. Meyendorff 1968:49 interprets Justinian's approach in the same way. See also Stratoudaki-White 2000:443, 450.

76. For later examples, see *Epanagōgē* by Emperor Leo the Wise (translated in Barker 1957:92) and a passage attributed by the historian Leo the Deacon to Emperor John Tzimicas of the tenth century. According to Norman Baynes, these documents show that "the functions of patriarch and emperor are distinct, though complementary" (Baynes 1955:51).

77. According to George Florovsky, "There was but One and comprehensive Christian Society, which was at once a Church and a State. In this one society there were different orders or 'powers,' clearly distinguished but closely correlated—'spiritual' and 'temporal,' 'ecclesiastical' and 'political.' But the 'Society' itself was intrinsically One. . . . In the Christian Commonwealth 'Churchman-ship' and 'Citizenship' were not only 'co-extensive,' but simply identical" (Florovsky 1957:139).

78. See also Williams 1951b:3.

79. Somewhat similar description, including numerous examples, even if not explicit and analytically defined as in the case of Geanakopolos, can be found in Morrison 1964:3–55; Dagron 2003:282–312; and Meyendorff 1982:43–65.

80. On the emperors role in the ecumenical councils, see Dvornik (1951), who does not fail to mention that "not even Athanasius, the greatest opponent of Constantius's religious policy, denied the emperor the exclusive right to convoke an ecumenical councils" (ibid., 12).

81. For a detailed discussion, see Geanakoplos 1986:141–42.

82. See also Athanasius 2004, *Arian History* 33.

83. *Quoted in Lives of the Saints—January*, taken from the Chrysostom Press website: http://www.chrysostompress.org/lives_21_january.html (accessed September 21, 2015).

5. Economy and the Legal Framework

1. For a more detailed account of the theoretical, methodological, and historical differences between Foucault and Agamben, see Dean 2012. For an elaborated discussion on Agamben's engagement with Foucault's thought, see Bussolini 2010.
2. For a critical assessment of the differences between Agamben's theory of the signature and Foucault's genealogy, see Toscano 2011.
3. Tenth-century patriarch of Constantinople.
4. Nikodemos and Agapios 1957:774.
5. Although not canonized, the letters enjoy an authoritative status and are often quoted by later authors. In Cyril's letters we witness an expansion of the application of economy into inner-Orthodox cycles as part of doctrinal debates and struggle over dominance between Alexandria and Constantinople.
6. Corinthians 4:1.
7. Foucault 2007:174; Agamben 2011:19, 41, 64.
8. Agamben 1998:181.
9. A heterodox sect headed by Novatian.

6. From Ecclesiastical to Market Economy

1. See also Schabas 2005:4; Schabas and de Marchi 2003:3–4; Spary 1996:178–96.
2. See, for example, Rousseau 1997.
3. It appears with this meaning in Turqout de Mayerne's treatise of 1610. Foucault, following King 1949; uses this essay to demonstrate how the police state was organized during these centuries (Foucault 1999c:148–49, 2007).
4. Political economy carried two distinct meanings from its inception in antiquity: 1. a form of knowledge that is used to govern the political community and 2. a hybrid community that is of the same magnitude as a political community (if not larger), which is managed as if it were an oikos, i.e., as an absolute monarchy that lacks any public sphere. It is the latter meaning that appears first in seventeenth-century mercantilism. Toward the end of the eighteenth century this meaning is altered once again and reappears as a form of knowledge used to manage civil society. This later usage was abandoned toward the end of the nineteenth century when Alfred Marshall unleashed economy from its political chains, and economics—the term we use today—replaced political economy as the form of knowledge.
5. See also Arendt 1977:44–45.
6. Arendt states that the purpose of her historical analysis in *The Human Condition* is "to trace back modern world alienation" (*HC* 6).
7. The extent to which Arendt viewed the concept of society as central to Augustine's thought is attested by the fact that the chapter of her dissertation dealing with Augustine's notion of love is titled "Social Life" (Arendt 1996).
8. As Arendt puts it:

> The admission of labor to public stature . . . has, on the contrary, liberated this process from its circular, monotonous recurrence and transformed it into a swiftly progressing development whose results have in a few centuries totally changed the whole inhabited world. . . . It was as though the growth element inherent in all organic life had completely overcome and overgrown the processes of decay by which organic life is checked and balanced in nature's oikos. The social realm, where the life process has established its own public domain, has let loose an unnatural growth, so to speak, of the natural; and it is against this growth, not merely against society but against a constantly growing social realm, that the private and intimate, on the one hand, and the political (in the narrower sense of the word), on the other, have proved incapable of defending themselves. . . . The greatest single factor in this constant increase since its inception has been the organization of laboring, visible in the so-called division of labor, which preceded the industrial revolution.
>
> (Arendt 1958:47)

9. Foucault 2007:288–89, 296–97, 338–39.
10. Elsewhere in his lectures Foucault presents the idea of growth, or unlimited economic progress, as one of the three central ideas held by eighteenth-century political economists (Foucault 2008:61).
11. According to Arendt (HC:47), the growth element is "inherent to all organic life."
12. Introducing into Arendt's history the moment of the discovery of the human's unique capability for growth stands to shed new light on the crucial role she attributes to the Reformation in the advent of the society of believers in modern economy. The transformation that occurred may perhaps be described as a shift from concern for the world and indifference to the self to indifference to the world and concern for the self.
13. As reads the title of Adam Smith's 1776 masterpiece. Until the end of the 1820s, political economy was defined as the study of wealth, in most cases material wealth. This definition is associated with such classical economists as Smith, Thomas Malthus, who claims that political economy deals with material wealth (Malthus 1989); David Ricardo, whose focus is on the distribution of wealth; and Nassau Senior, who claims that political economy is "the science which states the laws regulating the production and distribution of wealth, so far as they depend on the action of the human mind" (Senior 1852:52). Even though classical economists (of the eighteenth and nineteenth centuries) held the view that selfish motives guide man in his pursuit of wealth and that the pursuit itself falls within the domain of their inquiries, these inquiries did not focus on the selfish aspect of human action, and they did not, according to Kirzner, assume that this is the only aspect of human action to partake in their object of research (Kirzner 1976:53). Here the historical trajectory of my analysis closely follows Kirzner's.
14. Mill is commonly treated by historians of modern economic thought as the first economist to conduct a serious and self-aware methodological discussion (Blaug

1980; Hausman 1992; Hands 2001) and as laying the foundation for the discussion concerning the "scientific" status of economic theory.

15. At approximately the same time, Whately (1832), claimed, in an apologetic speech, that economic theory is indifferent to the level of wealth humans gain in their pursuits. In so stating he tried to leave political economy (a title he opposed) at least theoretically within the scope of Aristotle's definition of the discipline. The apologetics that appeared in Mill's *Utilitarianism* stated that the happiness of society would grow if humans acted in a noble manner.

16. In one of the many premature eulogies for capitalism, the eminent economist and historian of economic thought Josef Schumpeter ascribed its ruin to this takeover of the pursuer of wealth by the second licentious type (see Schumpeter 1962).

17. This definition became commonplace and appears in most textbooks of economics (see Blaug 1980:87; Hands 2001): "significantly shaping the character of microeconomics as it would develop during the remainder of the century" (Kirzner 1976:17).

    One finds similar definitions in Samuelson and Nordhaus 1995:4; Friedman 1976:1; and Fischer, Dornbusch, and Schmalensee 1988:2. The last three authors emphasize society's ways of dealing with scarcity of means to attain its goals.

18. This loss of distinction between the different types of desires appears in the hypothesis of diminishing marginal rates of substitution (Hicks 1946). According to this hypothesis, when an individual's quantity of object X increases, he will be willing to trade it for a quantity of object Y that is smaller than the one he would have been willing to accept before his quantity of X increased. This stands in stark contradiction to Gregory of Nyssa's claim that the more a human experiences the desire for God, the less willing he becomes to trade it for earthly desires.

19. In the emerging subfield of economics of religion.

20. This came to be known as *nonsaturation*—a preference for more of the same or, as it is mathematically defined, a "monotonically increasing" preference.

21. The term *rationality* as it is now used implies that an individual's choices are "complete," "reflexive," "transitive," and "continuous."

22. This surplus is divided into "consumer surplus" and "producer surplus."

23. At the beginning of the *Politics*, Aristotle claims that "the natures of the statesman, the royal sovereign, the head of an estate and the master of a family are the same, [and they] are mistaken [if] they imagine that the difference between these various forms of authority is one of greater and smaller numbers, not a difference in the kind," and that it is "better [to] discern in relation to these different kinds of rulers what is the difference between them, and to find out whether it is possible to obtain any scientific precision in regard to the various statements made above" (*Pol.* 1252a).

24. With the exception of a few distinguished virtuous people who are not governed by the despotic rule of the politician and the Jews who do not subject themselves to the government of economists.

25. See Arendt 1977:46.

26. He did so in the context of discussing critical thought that is influenced by Marx, calling this type of critique socialist.
27. Moreover, Marx's devout followers reject altogether the possibility of political freedom that is based upon limiting the economy in order to generate an ungoverned sphere of action. Instead, the "novel form of government" developed by one of his Soviet interpreters, which is neither political nor economic, positioned "forced labor camps" as "more essential to the preservation of the regime's power as any of its other institutions" (Arendt 1994:456).
28. This is his proposed preliminary definition of critique; see Foucault 1996:384.
29. See Leshem 2014b.

Works Cited

Primary Sources

Anonymous. 1996. *Rhetorica ad Hernnium*, I:2.3. In M. H. Prosser, and T. W. Benson, eds., *Readings in Classical Rhetoric*, 163–71. Davis, CA: Hermagoras.

Anonymous. 2002. *Epistle to Diognetus*. In Philip Schaff, ed., *ANFO1. The Apostolic Fathers with Justin Martyr and Irenaeus*, 1:39–48. Grand Rapids: Christian Classics Ethereal Library.

Aristides. 2004. *Apology*. In Philip Schaff, ed., *ANF09. The Gospel of Peter, The Diatessaron of Tatian, The Apocalypse of Peter, The Vision of Paul, The Apocalypse of the Virgin and Sedrach, The Testament of Abraham, The Acts of Xanthippe and Polyxena, The Narrative of Zosimus, The Apology of Aristides, The Epistles of Clement (complete text), Origen's Commentary on John, Books 1–10, and Commentary on Matthew, Books 1, 2, and 10–14*, 9:425–33. Grand Rapids: Christian Classics Ethereal Library.

Aristotle. 1926. *Rhetoric*. In *Aristotle in Twenty-three Volumes*, vol. 22. Trans. J. H. Freese. Cambridge: Harvard University Press.

——. 1932. *Poetics*. In *Aristotle in Twenty-three Volumes*, vol. 23. Trans. W. H. Fyfe. Cambridge: Harvard University Press.

——. 1933–35. *Metaphysics*. Ed. Edward Walford, trans. Hugh Tredennick. In *Aristotle in Twenty-three Volumes*, vols. 17–18. Cambridge: Harvard University Press.

——. 1934. *The Nicomachean Ethics*. Trans. H. Rackham. In *Aristotle in Twenty-three Volumes*, vol. 19. Cambridge: Harvard University Press.

——. 1935. *The Eudemian Ethics*. In *The Athenian Constitution: The Eudemian Ethics; On Virtues and Vice*, 198–478. Cambridge: Harvard University Press.

——. 1944. *Politics*. In *Aristotle in Twenty-three Volumes*, vol. 21. Trans. H. Rackham. Cambridge: Harvard University Press.

Arius Didymus. 1999. *Epitome of Stoic Ethics*. Ed. Arthur J. Pomeroy. Atlanta: Society of Biblical Literature.

Athanasius. 2004a. *Against the Arians (Orationes Contra Arianos IV)*. In Philip Schaff, ed., *NPNF2-04. Athanasius: Select Works and Letters*, 666–929. Grand Rapids: Christian Classics Ethereal Library.

——. 2004b. *Against the Heathen (Contra Gentes)*. In Philip Schaff, ed., *NPNF2-04. Athanasius: Select Works and Letters*, 162–207. Grand Rapids: Christian Classics Ethereal Library.

——. 2004c. *Arian History (Historia Arianorum ad Monachos)*. In Philip Schaff, ed., *NPNF2-04. Athanasius: Select Works and Letters*, 598–662. Grand Rapids: Christian Classics Ethereal Library.

——. 2004d. "Letters of Athanasius with Two Ancient Chronicles of His Life." In Philip Schaff, ed., *NPNF2-04. Athanasius: Select Works and Letters*, 1014–179. Grand Rapids: Christian Classics Ethereal Library.

——. 2004e. *On the Councils of Ariminum and Seleucia (De Synodis)*. In Philip Schaff, ed., *NPNF2-04. Athanasius: Select Works and Letters*, 934–90. Grand Rapids: Christian Classics Ethereal Library.

Athenagoras. 2004. *Plea for the Christians*. In Philip Schaff, ed., *ANF02. Fathers of the Second Century: Hermas, Tatian, Athenagoras, Theophilus, and Clement of Alexandria (Entire)*, 200–36. Grand Rapids: Christian Classics Ethereal Library.

Barnabas. 2002. *The Epistle of Barnabas*. In Philip Schaff, ed., *ANF01. The Apostolic Fathers with Justin Martyr and Irenaeus*, 182–203. Grand Rapids: Christian Classics Ethereal Library.

Basil the Great. 1950. *The Long Rules*. In M. Monica Wagner, ed., *Ascetical Works*, 223–338, Washington: Catholic University of America Press.

——. 1963. *On the Hexaemeron*. In Agnes Clare Way, ed., *Exegetic Homilies*, 3–150. Washington, DC: Catholic University of America Press.

——. 2003a. *De Spiritu Sancto*. In Philip Schaff, ed., *NPNF2-08. Basil: Letters and Select Works*, 102–79. Grand Rapids: Christian Classics Ethereal Library.

——. 2003b. "Letters." In Philip Schaff, ed., *NPNF2-08. Basil: Letters and Select Works*, 260–614. Grand Rapids: Christian Classics Ethereal Library.

Becker, Gary. 1976. *The Economic Approach to Human Behavior*. Chicago: University of Chicago Press.

Clement of Alexandria. 2004a. *The Instructor*. In Philip Schaff, ed., *ANF02. Fathers of the Second Century: Hermas, Tatian, Athenagoras, Theophilus, and Clement of Alexandria (Entire)*, 328–483. Grand Rapids: Christian Classics Ethereal Library.

——. 2004b. *The Stromata, or Miscellanies*. In Philip Schaff, ed., *ANF02. Fathers of the Second Century: Hermas, Tatian, Athenagoras, Theophilus, and Clement of Alexandria (Entire)*, 484–951. Grand Rapids: Christian Classics Ethereal Library.

Bryson. 1928. In Martin Plessner, ed., *Der Oikonomikos des Neupythagoreers Bryson und sein Einfluss auf die islamische Wissenschaft*. Heidelberg: C. Winter.

Cyril of Alexandria. 1987. *St. Cyril of Alexandria: Letters 51–110*. Trans. John I. McEnerney. Washington, DC: Catholic University of America Press, 1987.

Diogenes Laertius. 1853. *The Lives and Opinions of Eminent Philosophers*. Trans. C. D. Younge London: George Bell.

Dionysius of Halicarnassus. 1975. *On Thucydides*. Trans. W. Kendrick Pritchett. Berkeley: University of California Press.

Edgeworth, Francis Y. 1881. *Mathematical Psychics.* London: Kegan Paul.

Eusebius. 2002a. *Church History.* In Philip Schaff, ed., *NPNF2-01. Eusebius Pamphilius: Church History, Life of Constantine, Oration in Praise of Constantine,* 96–812. Grand Rapids: Christian Classics Ethereal Library.

——. 2002b. *Life of Constantine.* In Philip Schaff, ed., *NPNF2-01. Eusebius Pamphilius: Church History, Life of Constantine, Oration in Praise of Constantine,* 96–812. Grand Rapids: Christian Classics Ethereal Library.

Gregory of Nazianzus. 1893a. "Select Orations of Saint Gregory Nazianzen." In Philip Schaff, ed., *NPNF2-07. Cyril of Jerusalem, Gregory Nazianzen by St. Cyril of Jerusalem,* 315–644. Grand Rapids: Christian Classics Ethereal Library.

——. 1893b. "Select Letters of Saint Gregory Nazianzen." In Philip Schaff, ed., *NPNF2-07. Cyril of Jerusalem, Gregory Nazianzen by St. Cyril of Jerusalem,* 645–709. Grand Rapids: Christian Classics Ethereal Library.

——. 2003. *Select Orations.* Trans. Martha Vinson. Washington, DC: Catholic University of America Press.

Gregory of Nyssa. 1967a. *The Life of Saint Macrina.* In Virginia Woods Callahan, ed., *Ascetical Works,* 161–94. Washington, DC: Catholic University of America Press.

——. 1967b. *On the Christian Mode of Life.* In Virginia Woods Callahan, ed., *Ascetical Works,* 125–60. Washington, DC: Catholic University of America Press.

——. 1967c. *On Virginity.* In Virginia Woods Callahan, ed., *Ascetical Works,* 6–78. Washington, DC: Catholic University of America Press.

——. 1978. *The Life of Moses.* Mahwah, NJ: Paulist.

——. 1979. *From Glory to Glory: Texts from Gregory of Nyssa's Mystical Writings.* Crestwood, NY: St Vladimir's Seminary Press.

——. 1987. *Commentary on the Song of Songs.* Brookline, MA: Hellenic College Press.

——. 2000. *Homilies on the Beatitudes.* In Hubertus R. Drobner and Albert Viciano, eds., *Gregory of Nyssa, Homilies on the Beatitudes: An English Version with Commentary and Supporting Studies. Proceedings of the Eighth International Colloquium on Gregory of Nyssa,* 21–90. Leiden: Brill.

——. 2004a. *Answer to Eunomius' Second Book.* In Philip Schaff, ed., *NPNF2-05. Gregory of Nyssa: Dogmatic Treatises, Etc.,* 398–496. Grand Rapids: Christian Classics Ethereal Library.

——. 2004b. *The Great Catechism.* In Philip Schaff, ed., *NPNF2-05. Gregory of Nyssa: Dogmatic Treatises, Etc.,* 746–808. Grand Rapids: Christian Classics Ethereal Library.

——. 2004c. *On Not Three Gods.* In Philip Schaff, ed., *NPNF2-05. Gregory of Nyssa: Dogmatic Treatises, Etc.,* 522–31. Grand Rapids: Christian Classics Ethereal Library.

——. 2004d. *On the Baptism of Christ.* In Philip Schaff, ed., *NPNF2-05. Gregory of Nyssa: Dogmatic Treatises, Etc.,* 817–28. Grand Rapids: Christian Classics Ethereal Library.

——. 2004e. *On the Making of Man.* In Philip Schaff, ed., *NPNF2-05. Gregory of Nyssa: Dogmatic Treatises, Etc.,* 606–73. Grand Rapids: Christian Classics Ethereal Library.

——. 2004f. *On Virginity.* In Philip Schaff, ed., *NPNF2-05. Gregory of Nyssa: Dogmatic Treatises, Etc.,* 497–576. Grand Rapids: Christian Classics Ethereal Library.

——. 2009a. *Concerning Those Who Have Died.* http://www.sage.edu/faculty/salomd/nyssa/mort.html#N_1_ (accessed January 8, 2015).

——. 2009b. *On the Sixth Psalm, Concerning the Octave.* http://www.sage.edu/faculty /salomd/nyssa/mort.html#N_1_ (accessed January 8, 2015).

——. 2009c. *Two Homilies Concerning Saint Stephen, Protomartyr.* http://www.sage.edu /faculty/salomd/nyssa/mort.html#N_1_ (accessed January 8, 2015).

Hypolitus of Rome. 2004. *Treatise on Christ and Antichrist,* in Philip Schaff, ed., *ANF05. Fathers of the Third Century: Hippolytus, Cyprian, Caius, Novatian, Appendix,* 364–91. Grand Rapids: Christian Classics Ethereal Library.

Ignatius. 2002a. *Epistle to the Antiochians.* In Philip Schaff, ed., *ANF01. The Apostolic Fathers with Justin Martyr and Irenaeus,* 151–56. Grand Rapids: Christian Classics Ethereal Library.

——. 2002b. *Epistle to the Ephesians: Shorter and Longer Versions.* In Philip Schaff, ed., *ANF01. The Apostolic Fathers with Justin Martyr and Irenaeus,* 71–85. Grand Rapids: Christian Classics Ethereal Library.

——. 2002c. *Epistle to the Philadelphians: Shorter and Longer Versions.* In Philip Schaff, ed., *ANF01. The Apostolic Fathers with Justin Martyr and Irenaeus,* 112–21. Grand Rapids: Christian Classics Ethereal Library.

——. 2002d. *Epistle to the Smyrnæans: Shorter and Longer Versions.* In Philip Schaff ed., *ANF01. The Apostolic Fathers with Justin Martyr and Irenaeus,* 122–30. Grand Rapids: Christian Classics Ethereal Library.

Irenaeus. 2002. *Against Heresies.* In Philip Schaff, ed., *ANF01. The Apostolic Fathers with Justin Martyr and Irenaeus,* 448–824. Grand Rapids: Christian Classics Ethereal Library.

Jevons, William Stanley. 1866. "Brief Account of a General Mathematical Theory of Political Economy." *Journal of the Royal Statistical Society* 29 (June 1866): 282–87. http://socserv2.socsci.mcmaster.ca/~econ/ugcm/3ll3/jevons/mathem.txt (accessed 1/5/2015).

——. 1888. *The Theory of Political Economy.* London: Macmillan.

John Chrysostom. 1963. *Baptismal Instructions.* Trans. Paul W. Harkins. New York: Newman.

——. 1983. *A Comparison Between a King and a Monk/Against the Opponents of the Monastic Life: Two Treatises by John Chrysostom.* Trans. David G. Hunter. Lewiston, NY: Edwin Mellen.

——. 1985. *Discourse on Blessed Babylas and Against the Greeks.* In Margaret A. Schatkin and Paul W. Harkins, eds., *Apologist,* 75–152. Washington, DC: Catholic University of America Press.

——. 1986. *Homilies on Genesis 1-17.* Trans. Robert C. Hill. Washington, DC: Catholic University of America Press.

——. 2002a. "The Homilies of St. John Chrysostom on Paul's Epistle to the Romans." In Philip Schaff, ed., *NPNF1-11. Saint Chrysostom: Homilies on the Acts of the Apostles and the Epistle to the Romans,* 542–884. Grand Rapids: Christian Classics Ethereal Library.

——. 2002b. *Homilies on Ephesians.* In Philip Schaff, ed., *NPNF1-13. Saint Chrysostom: Homilies on Galatians, Ephesians, Philippians, Colossians, Thessalonians, Timothy, Titus, and Philemon,* 85–283. Grand Rapids: Christian Classics Ethereal Library.

——. 2002c. *Homilies on Thessalonians.* In Philip Schaff, ed., *NPNF1-13. Saint Chrysostom: Homilies on Galatians, Ephesians, Philippians, Colossians, Thessalonians, Timothy, Titus, and Philemon,* 503–616. Grand Rapids: Christian Classics Ethereal Library.

——. 2003. *Six Homilies on Isaiah 6.* In Robert Charles Hill, ed., *St. John Chrysostom Old Testament Homilies II,* 46–113. Brookline, MA: Holy Cross Orthodox Press.

———. 2004a. *The Homilies on the Statues to the People of Antioch*. In Philip Schaff, ed., *NPNF1-09. St. Chrysostom: On the Priesthood; Ascetic Treatises; Select Homilies and Letters; Homilies on the Statutes*, 354–565. Grand Rapids: Christian Classics Ethereal Library.

———. 2004b. *On the Priesthood*. In Philip Schaff, ed., *NPNF1-09. St. Chrysostom: On the Priesthood; Ascetic Treatises; Select Homilies and Letters; Homilies on the Statutes*, 31–94. Grand Rapids: Christian Classics Ethereal Library.

———. 2004c. *NPNF1-10. St. Chrysostom: Homilies on the Gospel of Saint Matthew*. Ed. Philip Schaff. Grand Rapids: Christian Classics Ethereal Library.

———. 2004d. *NPNF1-12. Saint Chrysostom: Homilies on the Epistles of Paul to the Corinthians*. Ed. Philip Schaff. Grand Rapids: Christian Classics Ethereal Library.

John of Damascus. 1958. *The Orthodox Faith*. In Frederic H. Chase Chase, ed., *Saint John of Damascus: Writings*, 165–406. New York: Catholic University of America Press.

Justinian. 1932. *New Constitutions (Novels) Collections*. Ed. Samuel P Scott. Vols. 1–17. Cincinnati: Central Trust.

Justin Martyr. 2002a. *The First Apology*. In Philip Schaff ed. , *ANF01. The Apostolic Fathers with Justin Martyr and Irenaeus*, 212–53. Grand Rapids: Christian Classics Ethereal Library.

———. 2002b. *The Second Apology*. In Philip Schaff, ed., *ANF01. The Apostolic Fathers with Justin Martyr and Irenaeus*, 254–63. Grand Rapids: Christian Classics Ethereal Library.

———. 2002c. *Dialogue with Trypho* . In Philip Schaff, ed., *ANF01. The Apostolic Fathers with Justin Martyr and Irenaeus*, 263–384. Grand Rapids: Christian Classics Ethereal Library.

Malthus, T. R. 1989. *Principles of Political Economy for the Royal Economic Society, Includes Reprint of the 1820 ed. Published by J. Murray, London*. Cambridge: Cambridge University Press.

Marshall, Alfred. 1920. *Principles of Economics*. 8th ed. New York: Macmillan.

Mill, John Stuart. 1874. "On the Definition of Political Economy; and on the Method of Investigating Proper to It . . . " In *Essays on Some Unsettled Question of Political Economy*. 2d ed. London: Longmans, Green, Reader and Dyer.

Minucius Felix. 2006. *Octavius*. In Philip Schaff, ed., *ANF04. Fathers of the Third Century: Tertullian, Part Fourth; Minucius Felix; Commodian; Origen, Parts First and Second*, 324–67. Grand Rapids: Christian Classics Ethereal Library.

Nicholas Mystikos. 1973. *Letters/Nicholas I, Patriarch of Constantinople; Greek text and English Translation by R. J. H. Jenkins and L. G. Westerink*. Washington, DC: Dumbarton Oaks Center for Byzantine Studies.

Nikodemos and Agapios, eds. 1957. *The Pedalion*. Chicago: Orthodox Christian Educational Society.

Origen. 1957. *The Song of Songs: Commentary and Homilies*. Trans. R. P. Lawson. Westminster: Newman.

———. 1998. *Homilies on Jeremiah*. In John Clark Smith, ed., *Homilies on Jeremiah: Homily on 1 Kings 28*, 3–273. Washington, DC: Catholic University of America.

———. 2002. *Commentary on the Epistle to the Romans: Books 6-10*. Trans. Thomas P. Scheck Washington, DC: Catholic University of America Press.

———. 2006a. *Against Celsus*. In Philip Schaff, ed., *ANF04. Fathers of the Third Century: Tertullian, Part Fourth; Minucius Felix; Commodian; Origen, Parts First and Second*, 675–1187. Grand Rapids: Christian Classics Ethereal Library.

———. 2006b. De Principiis. In Philip Schaff, ed., ANF04. Fathers of the Third Century: Tertullian, Part Fourth; Minucius Felix; Commodian; Origen, Parts First and Second, 675–1187. Grand Rapids: Christian Classics Ethereal Library.

Photius. 2003. *Bibliothèque*, vol. 3. Ed. and trans. R Henry. Paris: Belles Lettres.

Plato. 1921. *The Statesman*. In *Plato in Twelve Volumes*, vol. 12. Trans. Harold N. Fowler. Cambridge: Harvard University Press.

———. 1925a. *Phaedrus*. In *Plato in Twelve Volumes*, vol. 9. Trans. Harold N. Fowler. Cambridge: Harvard University Press.

———. 1925b. *Sophist*. In *Plato in Twelve Volumes*, vol. 12. Trans. Harold N. Fowler. Cambridge: Harvard University Press.

———. 1925c. *Symposium*. In *Plato in Twelve Volumes*, vol. 9. Trans. Harold N. Fowler. Cambridge: Harvard University Press.

———. 1925d. *Timaeus*. In *Plato in Twelve Volumes*, vol. 9. Trans. W. R. M. Lamb. Cambridge: Harvard University Press.

———. 1955. *Alcibidias*. *Plato in Twelve Volumes*, vol. 8. Trans. W. R. M. Lamb. Cambridge: Harvard University Press.

———. 1966. *Apology*. In *Plato in Twelve Volumes*, vol. 1. Trans. Harold N. Fowler. Cambridge: Harvard University Press.

———. 1967. *Gorgias*. In *Plato in Twelve Volumes*, vol. 3. Trans. W. R. M. Lamb. Cambridge: Harvard University Press.

———. 1969. *Republic*. *Plato in Twelve Volumes*, vols. 5 and 6. Trans. Paul Shorey. Cambridge: Harvard University Press.

Polybius. 1889. *Histories*. Trans. Evelyn S. Shuckburgh. New York: Macmillan.

Polycarp. 2002. *Epistle to the Philippians*. In Philip Schaff, ed., ANF01. *The Apostolic Fathers with Justin Martyr and Irenaeus*, 91–105. Grand Rapids: Christian Classics Ethereal Library.

Pseudo-Aristotle. 1910. *Economics Book I*. In Edward Walford, ed., *The Politics and Economics of Aristotle*, 289–303. London: G. Bell.

Quintilian. 1920–1944. *The Institutio Oratoria/with an English Translation by H. E. Butler, in Four Volumes*. London: Heinemann.

Robbins, Lionel. 1935. *Essay on the Nature and Significance of Economic Science*. 3d ed. London: Macmillan.

Senior, Nassau W. 1852. *Four Introductory Lectures on Political Economy*. London: Longman, Brown, Green, and Longmans.

Stobaeus, Ioannis. 1884–1912. *Anthologium*, eds. Curtius Wachsmuth and Otto Hense. Berlin: Weidmann.

Tacitus, Cornelius. 2006. *Dialogue on Orators*. In Herbert W. Benario, ed. , *Agricola, Germany, and Dialogue on Orators*, 89–130. Indianapolis: Hackett.

Tatian. 1982. *Discourse to the Greeks*. Trans. Molly Whittaker. Oxford: Clarendon.

———. 2004. *Address to the Greeks*. In Philip Schaff, ed., ANF02. *Fathers of the Second Century: Hermas, Tatian, Athenagoras, Theophilus, and Clement of Alexandria (Entire)*, 98–129. Grand Rapids: Christian Classics Ethereal Library.

Tertullian. 2006a. *Against Praxeas*. In Philip Schaff, ed., ANF03. *Latin Christianity: Its Founder, Tertullian*, 1041–103. Grand Rapids: Christian Classics Ethereal Library.

——. 2006b. *Apology.* In Philip Schaff, ed., *ANF03. Latin Christianity: Its Founder,Tertullian,* 22–88. Grand Rapids: Christian Classics Ethereal Library.

——. 2006c. *On the Resurrection of the Flesh.* In Philip Schaff, ed., *ANF03. Latin Christianity: Its Founder, Tertullian,* 952–1041. Grand Rapids: Christian Classics Ethereal Library.

——. 2006d. *Scorpiace.* In Philip Schaff, ed., *ANF03. Latin Christianity: Its Founder, Tertullian,* 1103–30. Grand Rapids: Christian Classics Ethereal Library.

The Definition of Faith of the Council of Chalcedon. 2005. In Philip Schaff, ed., *NPNF2-14. The Seven Ecumenical Councils,* 386–91. Grand Rapids: Christian Classics Ethereal Library.

Theophilus of Antioch. 1970. *Theophilus of Antioch: Ad Autolycum.* Ed. and trans. Robert M. Grant. Oxford: Clarendon.

The Second Ecumenical Council: The First Council of Constantinople. 2005. *Letter of the Same Holy Synod to the Most Pious Emperor Theodosius the Great, to Which Are Appended the Canons Enacted by Them.* In Philip Schaff, ed., *NPNF2-14. The Seven Ecumenical Councils,* 267. Grand Rapids: Christian Classics Ethereal Library.

Tullock, Gordon and James M. Buchanan. 1962. *The Calculus of Consent: Logical Foundations of Constitutional Democracy.* Ann Arbor: University of Michigan Press.

Whately, Richard. 1832. *Introductory Lectures on Political Economy.* London: B. Fellowes.

Xenophon. 1994. *Oeconomicus: A Social and Historical Commentary.* Trans. Sarah B. Pomeroy. Oxford: Clarendon.

Secondary Literature

Agamben, Giorgio. 1998. *Homo Sacer: Sovereign Power and Bare Life.* Trans. Daniel Heller-Roazen. Stanford: Stanford University Press.

——. 2005. *State of Exception.* Chicago: University of Chicago Press.

——. 2011. *The Kingdom and the Glory: For a Theological Genealogy of Economy and Government (Homo Sacer II, 2).* Stanford: Stanford University Press.

Alexander, Paul J. 1958. *The Patriarch Nicephorus of Constantinople: Ecclesiastical Policy and Image Worship in the Byzantine Empire.* Oxford: Clarendon.

Alivisatos, Hamilcar S. 1944. "Economy from the Orthodox Point of View." In *Dispensation in Practice and Theory: With Special Reference to the Anglican Orders,* 27–44. London: Society for Promoting Christian Knowledge.

Anatolios, Khaled. 1999. "Theology and Economy in Origen and Athanasius." In W. A. Bienert and U. Kuhneweg, eds., *Origeniana Septima: Origenes in den Auseinandersetzungen des 4. Jahrhunderts,* 165–71. Leuven: Leuven University Press.

Arendt, Hannah. 1958. *The Human Condition.* Chicago: University of Chicago Press.

——. 1969a. *On Revolution* New York: Viking.

——. 1969b. *On Violence.* San Diego: Harcourt.

——. 1977. *Between Past and Future: Eight Exercises in Political Thought.* New York: Penguin.

——. 1978. *The Life of the Mind.* New York: Harcourt Brace.

——. 1994. *The Origins of Totalitarianism.* San Diego: Harcourt.

——. 1996. *Love and Saint Augustine.* Ed. Joanna Vecchiarelli Scott and Judith Chelius Stark. Chicago: University of Chicago Press.

——. 2003. *Responsibility and Judgment.* New York: Schocken.

——. 2004. "Philosophy and Politics." *Social Research* 71 (3): 427–54.

——. 2005. *The Promise of Politics.* New York: Schocken.

Arendt, Hannah and Karl Jaspers. 1992. *Correspondence, 1926–1969.* Trans. Robert and Rita Kimber. San Diego: Harcourt Brace.

Azkoul, Michael. 1968a. "On Time and Eternity: The Nature of History According to the Greek Fathers." *St Vladimir's Theological Quarterly* 12 (2), 56–77.

——. 1968b. "Peri Oikonomia Theou: The Meaning of History According to the Greek Fathers." PhD diss., Michigan State University.

——. 1971. "Sacredotium et Imperium: The Constantinian Renovatio According to the Greek Fathers." *Theological Studies* 32:431–64.

——. 1995. *St. Gregory of Nyssa and the Tradition of the Fathers.* Lewiston, NY: Edwin Mellen.

Balas, David L. 1976. "Eternity and Time in Gregory of Nyssa's Contra Eunomium." In Heinrich Dörrie, Margarete Altenburger, and Uta Schramm, eds., *Gregor von Nyssa und die Philosophie: Zweites internationales Kolloquium über Gregor von Nyssa, Freckenhorst bei Münster 18–23 September 1972,* 128–55. Leiden: Brill.

Balot, Ryan Krieger. 2001. *Greed and Injustice in Classical Athens.* Princeton: Princeton University Press.

Barker, Ernest. 1957. *Social and Political Thought in Byzantium: From Justinian I to the Last Palaeologus: Passages from Byzantine Writers and Document.* Oxford: Clarendon.

Baynes, Norman H. 1955. *Byzantine Studies and Other Essays.* London: University of London Press.

Behr, John. 2000. *Asceticism and Anthropology in Irenaeus and Clement.* New York: Oxford University Press.

Benjamins, Hendrik S. 1994. *Eingeordnete Freiheit: Freiheit und Vorsehung bei Origenes.* Leiden: Brill.

Bennett, Beth S. 2005. "Hermagoras of Temnos." In Michael G. Moran and Michelle Ballif, eds., *Classical Rhetorics and Rhetoricians: Critical Studies and Sources,* 187–93. Westport: Praeger.

Blaug, Mark. 1980. *The Methodology of Economics: Or How Economists Explain.* Cambridge: Cambridge University Press.

Blowers, Paul M. 1992. "Maximus the Confessor, Gregory of Nyssa, and the Concept of 'Perpetual Progress.'" *Vigiliae Christianae* 46 (2): 151–71.

Blumenfeld, Bruno. 2003. *The Political Paul: Justice, Democracy, and Kingship in a Hellenistic Framework.* London: T&T Clark.

Boff, L. 1988. *Trinity and Society.* Maryknoll, NY: Orbis.

Botte, Bernard. 1980. "Oikonomia in L'histoire du Salut dans la Liturgie." In *Triacca Achille Maria,* 59–72. Rome: CLV-Edizioni Liturgiche.

Brown, Peter. 1990. *The Body and Society: Men, Women, and Sexual Renunciation in Early Christianity.* New York: Columbia University Press.

Burns, J. Patout. 1976. "The Economy of Salvation: Two Patristic Traditions." *Theological Studies* 37 (4): 598–619.

Bussolini, Jeffrey. 2010. "Critical Encounter Between Giorgio Agamben and Michel Foucault: Review of Recent Works of Agamben." *Foucault Studies* 10:108–43.

Callahan, Virginia Woods. 1967. *Saint Gregory of Nyssa: Ascetical Works*. Washington, DC: Catholic University of America Press.

Callon, Michel. 1998. "Introduction: The Embeddedness of Economic Markets in Economics." In Michel Callon, ed., *The Laws of the Market*, 1–57. Oxford: Blackwell.

Carter, Robert. 1958. "Saint John Chrysostom's Rhetorical Use of the Socratic Distinction Between Kingship and Tyranny." *Traditio* 14:367–71.

Chadwick, Henry. 1966. *Early Christian Thought and the Classical Tradition: Studies in Justin, Clement, and Origen*. Oxford: Clarendon.

Chadwick, Henry and Origen. 1980. *Contra Celsum*. Cambridge: Cambridge University Press.

Charlesworth, Martin Percival. 1936. "Providentia and Aeternitas." *Harvard Theological Review* 29 (2): 107–32.

Clark, Elizabeth A. 1977. "Sexual Politics in the Writings of John Chrysostom." *Anglican Theological Review* 59:3–20.

——. 1982. *Jerome, Chrysostom, and Friends: Essays and Translations*. Lewiston, NY: Edwin Mellen.

Clifford, Richard and Khaled Anatolios. 2005. "Christian Salvation: Biblical and Theological Perspectives." *Theological Studies* 66:739–69.

Coakley, Sarah. 2002. Powers and Submissions: Spirituality, Philosophy, and Gender. Oxford: Blackwell.

Conford, Francis MacDonald. 1937. *Plato's Cosmology: The Timaeus of Plato*. London: Kegan Paul Trübner.

Cooper, Adam G. 2005. *The Body in St. Maximus the Confessor: Holy Flesh, Wholly Deified*. New York: Oxford University Press.

Crisp, Oliver D. 2005. "Problems with Perichoresis." *Tyndale Bulletin* 56 (1): 119–40.

Culianu, Ioan P. 1987. *Eros and Magic in the Renaissance*. Chicago: University of Chicago Press.

Cullmann, Oscar. 1964. *Christ and Time: The Primitive Christian Conception of Time and History*. Philadelphia: Westminster.

Dagron, Gilbert. 2003. *Emperor and Priest: The Imperial Office in Byzantium*. Cambridge: Cambridge University Press.

D'ales, Adhemar. 1919. "Le mot «Oikonomia» dans la langue théologique de S. Irênée." *Revue des Études Grecques* 32:1–9.

Daley, Brian E. 1999. "1998 NAPS Presidential Address. Building a New City: The Cappadocian Fathers and the Rhetoric of Philanthropy." *Journal of Early Christian Studies* 7 (3): 431–61.

——. 2006a. *Gregory of Nazianzus*. London: Routledge.

——.2006b. "'One Thing and Another': The Persons in God and the Person of Christ in Patristic Theology." *Pro Ecclesia* 15 (1): 17–46.

Daniélou, Jean. 1950. "The Conception of History in the Christian Tradition." *Journal of Religion* 30 (3): 171–79.

——. 1956. *The Bible and the Liturgy*. Notre Dame: University of Notre Dame Press.

——. 1979. *From Glory to Flory: Texts from Gregory of Nyssa's Mystical Writings*. Crestwood, NY: St Vladimir's Seminary Press.

Davies, Henry H. 1898. "Origen's Theory of Knowledge." *American Journal of Theology* 2 (4): 737–62.

Dean, Mitchell. 2012. "Governmentality Meets Theology: 'The King Reigns, but He Does Not Govern.'" Theory, Culture, and Society 29 (3): 145–58.

Downey, Glanville. 1955. "Philanthropia in Religion and Statecraft in the Fourth Century After Christ." *Historia: Zeitschrift fur Alte Geschichte* 4:199–208.

——. 1957. "Education in the Christian Roman Empire: Christian and Pagan Theories Under Constantine and His Successors." *Speculum: A Journal of Mediaeval Studies* 32:148–61.

——. 1959. "Julian and Justinian and the Unity of Faith and Culture." *Church History* 28: 339–49.

——. 1964. "From the Pagan City to the Christian City." *Greek Orthodox Theological Review* 10 (1): 121–39.

Dvornik, Francis. 1951. "Emperors, Popes, and General Councils." *Dumbarton Oaks Papers* 6:1–23.

——. 1956. "Byzantine Political Ideas in Kievan Russia." *Dumbarton Oaks Papers* 9:73–121.

——. 1966. *Early Christian and Byzantine Political Philosophy II*. Washington, DC: Dumabrton Oaks Center for Byzaantine Studies.

Edwards, Mark J. 2005. "Father B. Systematic and Historical Theology." In Jean-Yves Lacoste ed., *Encyclopedia of Christian Theology*, 1:568–71. New York: Routledge.

Egan, John. 1993. "Primal Cause and Trinitarian Perichoresis in Gregory Nazianzen's Oration 31.14." *Studia Patristica* 27:21–28.

Ewing, Jon D. 2005. "The Christianization of Pronoia: Clement of Alexandria's Conception of Providence." PhD diss., Graduate Theological Union.

Ferguson, Everett. 1973. "God's Infinity and Man's Mutability: Perpetual Progress According to Gregory of Nyssa." *Greek Orthodox Theological Review* 18:59–78.

Fischer, Stanley, Rudiger Dornbusch, and Richard Schmalensee. 1988. *Economics*. 2d ed. New York: McGraw-Hill.

Florovsky, George. 1933. "The Limits of the Church." *Church Quarterly Review* 117:117–31.

——. 1957. "Empire and Desert: Antinomies of Christian Histories." *Greek Orthodox Theological Review* 3 (2): 133–59.

——. 1950. "The Doctrine of the Church and the Ecumenical Problem." *Ecumenical Review* 2(2): 152–61.

Foucault, Michel. 1973. *The Order of Things: An Archeology of the Human Sciences*. New York: Vintage.

——. 1988a. "Politics and Reason." In Lawrence D. Kritzman, ed., *Politics, Philosophy, Culture: Interviews and Other Writings, 1977–1984*, 57–85. New York: Routledge.

——. 1988b. *The History of Sexuality*, vol. 3: *The Care of the Self*. New York: Vintage.

——. 1988c. *Technologies of the Self: A Seminar with Michel Foucault*. Amherst: University of Massachussetts Press.

——. 1990. *The History of Sexuality*, vol. 2: *The Use of Pleasure*. New York: Vintage.

——. 1996. "What Is a Critique?" In James Schmidt, ed., *What Is Enlightenment?: Eighteenth-Century Answers and Twentieth-Century Questions.* 382–98. Berkeley: University of Califronia Press.

——. 1999a. "About the Beginning of the Hermeneutics of the Self." In Jeremy R. Carrette, ed., *Religion and Culture,* 158–81. New York: Routledge.

——. 1999b. "On the Government of the Living." In Jeremy R. Carrette, ed., *Religion and Culture,* 154–57. New York: Routledge.

——. 1999c. "Pastoral Power and Political Reason." In Jeremy R. Carrette, ed., *Religion and Culture,* 135–52. New York: Routledge.

——. 2005. *The Hermeneutics of the Subject: Lectures at the Collège de France, 1981–1982.* Trans. Graham Burchell. New York: Picador.

——. 2007. *Security, Territory, Population: Lectures at the Collège de France, 1977–1978.* Trans. Graham Burchell. New York: Palgrave Macmillan.

——. 2008. *The Birth of Biopolitics: Lectures at the Collège de France, 1978–1979.* Trans. Graham Bruchell. New York: Palgrave Macmillan.

——. 2014a. *On the Government of the Living: Lectures at the Collège de France, 1979–1980.* Trans. Graham Burchell. New York: Palgrave Macmillan

——. 2014b. *Wrong-Doing, Truth-Telling: The Function of Avowal in Justice.* Trans. Stephen W. Sawyer. Chicago: University of Chicago Press.

Friedman, Milton. 1976. *Price Theory.* Chicago: Aldine.

Geanakoplos, Deno J. 1965. "Church and State in the Byzantine Empire: A Reconsideration of the Problem of Caesaropapism." *Church History* 34 (4): 381–403.

——. 1986. *Byzantium: Church, Society, and Civilization Seen Through Contemporary Eyes.* Chicago: University of Chicago Press.

Geréby, György. 2008. "Political Theology Versus Theological Politics: Erik Peterson and Carl Schmitt." *New German Critique* 35 (3): 7–33.

Goodenough, Erwin R. 1928. *The Political Philosophy of Hellenistic Kingship.* New Haven: Yale University Press.

Grant, Robert M. 1958. "Studies in the Apologists." *Harvard Theological Review* 51 (3): 123–34.

——. 1997. *Irenaeus of Lyons.* London: Routledge.

Hadot, Pierre. 1995. *Philosophy as a Way of Life.* Oxford: Blackwell.

——. 2004. *What Is Ancient Philosophy?* Cambridge: Belknap.

Halleux, Andre de. 1987. "Oikonomia in the First Canon of Saint Basil." *Patristic and Byzantine Review* 6 (1): 53–64.

Hands, Wade D. 2001. *Reflection Without Rules: Economic Theory and Contemporary Science Theory.* Cambridge: Cambridge University Press.

Harrison, Verna. 1990. "Male and Female in Cappadocian Theology." *Journal of Theological Studies* 41 (2): 441–71.

——. 1991. "Perichoresis in the Greek Fathers." *St Vladimir's Theological Quarterly* 35:53–65.

——. 1993. "The Fatherhood of God in Orthodox Theology." *St Vladimir's Theological Quarterly* 37:185–212.

——. 1996. "Gender, Generation, and Virginity in Cappadocian Theology." *Journal of Theological Studies* 47 (1): 38–68.

Hatch, Edwin. 1897. *The Influence of Greek Ideas on Christianity.* London: Williams and Norgate.

Hausman, Daniel M. 1992. *The Inexact Science and Separate Science of Economics.* Cambridge: Cambridge University Press.

Hicks, John R. 1946. *Value and Capital: An Inquiry Into Some Fundamental Principles of Economic Theory.* New York: Oxford University Press.

Hopko, Thomas. 1986. "The Trinity in the Cappadocians." In Bernard McGinn, John Meyendorff, and Jean Leclercq, eds., *Christian Spirituality: Origins to the Twelfth Century,* 260–76. New York: Crossroad.

Horrell, J. Scott. 2004. "Toward a Biblical Model of the Social Trinity: Avoiding Equivocation of Nature and Order." *Journal of the Evangelical Theological Society* 47:399–421.

Jastrow, M. 1926. *Dictionary to the Targumim, the Talmud Babli and Yerushalmi, and the Midrashic Literature.* Berlin: Choreb.

Kantorowicz, Ernst H. 1952. "Deus per Naturam, Deus per Gratiam: A Note on Medieval Political Theology." *Harvard Theological Review* 45 (4): 253–77.

Kasher, Arie. 1985. *The Jews in Hellenistic and Roman Egypt: The Struggle for Equal Rights.* Tübingen: Mohr.

Kelly, John N. D. 1995. *Golden Mouth: The Story of John Chrysostom—Ascetic, Preacher, Bishop.* London: Duckworth.

Kennedy, George Alexander. 1994. *A New History of Classical Rhetoric.* Princeton: Princeton University Press.

——. 1995. "Attitudes Toward Authority in the Teaching of Rhetoric Before 1050." In Michael C. Leff Winifred Bryan Horner, ed., *Rhetoric and Pedagogy: Its History, Philosophy, and Practice,* 65–71. Mahwah, NJ: Erlbaum.

——. 1999. *Classical Rhetoric and Its Christian and Secular Tradition from Ancient to Modern Times.* Chapel Hill: University of North Carolina Press.

King, James E. 1949. *Science and Rationalism in the Government of Louis XIV, 1661–1683.* Baltimore: Johns Hopkins University Press.

Kirzner, Israel. 1976. *The Economic Point of View.* Kansas City: Sheed and Ward.

——. 2000. "Human Nature and the Character of Economic Science." *Harvard Review of Philosophy* 8:14–23.

Kovacs, Judith L. 2001. "Divine Pedagogy and the Gnostic Teacher According to Clement of Alexandria." *Journal of Early Christian Studies* 9 (1): 1–24.

Kustas, George L. 1981. "Saint Basil and the Rhetorical Tradition." In Paul Jonathan Fedwick, ed., *Basil of Caesarea: Christian, Humanist, Ascetic—Part One,* 221–79. Toronto: Pontifical Institute of Mediaeval Studies.

LaCugna, Catherine Mowry. 1993. *God for Us: The Trinity and Christian Life.* San Francisco: HarperCollins.

Laird, Martin. 1999. "Gregory of Nyssa and the Mysticism of Darkness: A Reconsideration." *Journal of Religion* 79 (4): 592–616.

Lawler, Michael G. 1995. "Perichoresis: New Theological Wine in an Old Theological Wineskin." *Horizons* 22 (1): 49–66.

Lenz, John R. 2007. "Deification of the Philosopher in Classical Greece." In Michael J. Christensen and Jeffery A. Wittung, eds., *Partakers of the Divine Nature: The History and*

Development of Deification in the Christian Traditions, 47–67. Cranbury, NJ: Fairleigh Dickinson University Press.

Leshem, Dotan. 2013a. "Oikonomia Redefined." *Journal of the History of Economic Thought* 35 (1): 43–61.

———. 2013b. "Oikonomia in the Age of Empires." *History of the Human Sciences* 26 (1): 29–51.

———. 2013c. "Aristotle Economizes the Market." *Boundary 2* 40 (3): 39–57.

———. 2014a. "The Ancient Art of Economics." *European Journal for the History of Economic Thought* 21(2): 201–29.

———. 2014b. "The Distinction Between Economy and Market in Aristotle's Thought and the Rise of the Social." *Constellations*. http://onlinelibrary.wiley.com/doi/10.1111/1467-8675.12128/full (accessed September 16, 2015).

———. 2014c. "The Martyr as the Vanishing Point for a New Political Philosophy." *Radical Orthodoxy: Theology, Philosophy, Politics* 2 (3): 379–99.

———. 2015. "Embedding Agamben's Critique of Foucault: The Pastoral and Theological Origins of Governmentally." *Theory, Culture, and Society* 32 (3): 93–113.

Lienhard, Joseph T. 2001. "Ousia and Hypostasis: The Cappadocian Settlement and the Theology of 'One Hypostasis.'" In Daniel Kendall, Stephen T. Davis, Gerald O'Collins, eds., *The Trinity: An Interdisciplinary Symposium on the Trinity*, 99–122. New York: Oxford University Press.

Lilla, Salvatore R. C. 1971. *Clement of Alexandria: A Study in Christian Platonism and Gnosticism.* London: Oxford University Press.

Limberis, Vasiliki. 1997. "καιρος and χρονος in Gregory of Nyssa." *Studia Patristica* 32:141–44.

Lossky, Vladimir. 1976. *The Mystical Theology of the Eastern Church.* Crestwood, NY: St Vladimir's Seminary Press.

———. 1978. *Orthodox Theology: An Introduction.* Crestwood, NY: St Vladimir's Seminary Press.

———. 1985. *In the Image and Likeness of God.* Crestwood, NY: St Vladimir's Seminary Press.

Louth, Andrew. 1981. *The Origins of the Christian Mystical Tradition: From Plato to Denys.* Oxford: Clarendon.

———1996. *Maximus the Confessor.* New York: Routledge.

Ludlow, Morwenna. 2000. *Universal Salvation: Eschatology in the Thought of Gregory of Nyssa and Karl Rahner.* New York: Oxford University Press.

———. 2007. *Gregory of Nyssa: Ancient and (Post) Modern.* New York: Oxford University Press.

Lynch, John J. 1979. "Prosopon in Gregory of Nyssa: A Theological Word in Transition," *Theological Studies* 40 (4): 728–38.

Maifreda, Germano. 2012. *From Oikonomia to Political Economy: Constructing Economic Knowledge from the Renaissance to the Scientific Revolution.* Farnham: Ashgate.

Maloney, George A. 1971. "Oeconomia: A Corrective to Law." *Catholic Lawyer* 17 (2): 90–109.

Markus, R. A. 1954. "Pleroma and Fulfillment: The Significance of History in St. Irenaeus' Opposition to Gnosticism." *Vigiliae Christianae* 8 (4): 193–224.

———. 1958. "Trinitarian Theology and the Economy." *Journal of Theological Studies* 9:89–102.

McCambley, Casimir. 1987. "Preface." In Casimir McCambley, ed., *Commentary on the Song of Songs/Gregory of Nyssa*, 1–30. Brookline, MA: Hellenic College Press.

McCloskey, D. N. 2001. "Storytelling in Economics." In S. T. Ziliakm, ed., *Measurement and Meaning in Economics: The Essential Deirdre McCloskey*, 204–21. Northampton: Edward Elgar.

McCruden, Kevin B. 2002. "Monarchy and Economy in Tertullian's Adversus Praxeam." *Scottish Journal of Theology* 55 (3): 325–37.

Meijering, Roos. 1989. *Literary and Rhetorical Theories in Greek Scholia*. Groningen: Egbert Forsten.

Meredith, Anthony. 1995. *The Cappadocians*. London: Geoffrey Chapman.

——. 1999. *Gregory of Nyssa*. London: Routledge.

Meyendorff, John. 1968. "Justinian, the Empire and the Church." *Dumbarton Oaks Papers* 22:43–60.

——. 1979. "The Christian Gospel and Social Responsibility." In George Huntston Williams, F. Forrester Church, and Timothy George, eds., *Continuity and Discontinuity in Church History: Essays Presented to George Huntston Williams on the Occasion of His Sixty-fifth Birthday*, 118–30. Leiden: Brill.

——. 1982. *The Byzantine Legacy in the Orthodox Church*. Crestwood, NY: St Vladimir's Seminary Press.

Minear, Paul S. 1944. "Time and the Kingdom." *Journal of Religion* 24 (2): 77–88.

Minns, Denis. 1994. *Irenaeus*. London: Geoffrey Chapman.

Moltmann, Jürgen. 1981. *The Trinity and the Kingdom of God: The Doctrine of God*. Trans. M. Kohl. London: SCM.

Momigliano, Arnaldo. 1987. *On Pagans, Jews, and Christians*. Middletown: Wesleyan University Press.

Mondzain, Marie-Jose. 2005. *Image, Icon, Economy: The Byzantine Origins of the Contemporary Imaginary*. Stanford: Stanford University Press.

Morrison, Karl F. 1964. *Rome and the City of God—an Essay on the Constitutional Relationship of Empire and Church in the Forth Century*, 3–55. Philadelphia: American Philosophical Society.

Murphy, Francis X. 1967. *Politics and the Early Christian*. New York: Desclée.

Murphy, James J. 2003. "Hermagoras of Temnos." In James J. Murphy, ed., *A Synoptic History of Classical Rhetoric*, 131–32. Mahwah, NJ: Erlbaum.

Nock, Arthur D. 1947. "The Emperor's Divine Comes." *Journal of Roman Studies* 37 (1–2): 102–16.

Osborn, Eric. 2000. "Love of Enemies and Recapitulation." *Vigiliae Christianae* 54 (1): 12–31.

——. 2001. *Irenaeus of Lyons*. Cambridge: Cambridge University Press.

——. 2003. *Tertullian, First Theologian of the West*. Cambridge: Cambridge University Press.

——. 2005. *Clement of Alexandria*. Cambridge: Cambridge University Press.

Ostrogorski, Georgije. 1969. *History of the Byzantine State*. New Brunswick, NJ: Rutgers University Press.

Otis, Brooks. 1958. "Cappadocian Thought as a Coherent System." *Dumbarton Oaks Papers* 12:97–124.

Pagels, Elaine H. 1972. "The Valentinian Claim to Esoteric Exegesis of Romans as Basis for Anthropological Theory." *Vigiliae Christianae* 26 (4): 241–58.

——. 1974. "Conflicting Versions of Valentinian Eschatology: Irenaeus' Treatise vs. the Excerpts from Theodotus." *Harvard Theological Review* 67 (1): 35–53.

——. 1985. "The Politics of Paradise: Augustine's Exegesis of Genesis 1–3 Versus That of John Chrysostom." *Harvard Theological Review* 78 (1): 67–99.

Parker, Thomas D. 1980. "The Political Meaning of the Doctrine of the Trinity: Some Theses." *Journal of Religion* 60 (2): 165–84.

Parry, Kenneth. 1996. *Depicting the Word: Byzantine Iconophile Thought of the Eighth and Ninth Centuries*. Leiden: Brill.

Parsons, Wilfrid. 1940. "The Influence of Romans XIII on Pre-Augustinian Christian Political Thought." *Theological Studies* 1 (4): 337–64.

——. 1942. "The Political Theory of the New Testament." *Catholic Biblical Quarterly* 4:218–29.

——. 1945. "Lest Men, Like Fishes." *Traditio* 3:380–88.

Pásztori-Kupán, István. 2006. *Theodoret of Cyrus*. New York: Routledge.

Plass, Paul. 1980. "Transcendent Time and Eternity in Gregory of Nyssa." *Vigiliae Christianae* 34 (2): 180–92.

Prestige, George Léonard. 1964. *God in Patristic Thought*. London: SPCK.

Quinn, Jerome D. and William C. Wacker. 2000. *The First and Second Letters to Timothy: A New Translation with Notes and Commentary*. Grand Rapids: Eerdmans.

Rabinowitz, Celia E. 1984. "Personal and Cosmic Salvation in Origen." *Vigiliae Christianae* 38 (4): 319–29.

Rahner, Hogu. 1992. *Church and State in Early Christianity*. San Francisco: Ignatius.

Rai, Pier. 1973. "L'économie dans le Droit Canonique Byzantin des Origines jusqu'au XI Siècle: Recherches Historiques et Canoniques." *Istina* 3:260–326.

Reid, Robert S. 1997. "Hermagoras' Theory of Prose Oikonomia in Dionysius of Halicarnassus." *Advances in the History of Rhetoric: Disputed and Neglected Texts in the History of Rhetoric* 1:9–24.

Reilly, Gerald F. 1945. *Imperium and Sacerdotium According to St. Basil the Great*. Washington, DC: Catholic University of America.

Reumann, John. 1957. "The Use of Oikonomia and Related Terms in Greek Sources to About AD 100 as a Background for Patristic Applications." PhD diss., University of Pennsylvania.

—— 1967. "OIKONOMIA—Terms in Paul in Comparison with Lucan Heilsgeschichte." *New Testament Studies* 13 (2): 147–67.

——. 1992. *Stewardship and the Economy of God*. Grand Rapids and Indiapopolis: Eerdmans and the Ecumenical Center for Stewardship Studies.

Richter, Gerhard. 2005. *Oikonomia: Der Gebrauch des Wortes Oikonomia im Neuen Testament, bei den Kirchenvatern und in der Theologischen Literatur bis ins 20. Jahrhundert*. Berlin: de Gruyter.

Rousseau, Jean-Jacques. 1997. "A Discourse on Political Economy." In Victor Gourevitch, ed., *The Social Contract and Other Later Political Writings*, 3–38. Cambridge: Cambridge University Press.

Sagovsky, Nicholas. 2000. *Ecumenism, Christian Origins, and the Practice of Communion*. Cambridge: Cambridge University Press.

Samuelson, Paul and William D. Nordhaus. 1995. *Economics*, 15th ed. New York: McGraw-Hill.

Schabas, Margaret. 2005. *The Natural Origins of Economics*. Chicago: University of Chicago Press.

Schabas, Margaret and Neil de Marchi. 2003. "Introduction to Oeconomies in the Age of Newton." *History of Political Economy* 35 (annual supplement): 1–13.

Schmemann, Alexander. 1953. "Byzantine Theocracy and the Orthodox Church." *St Vladimir's Seminary Quarterly* 1 (2): 5–22.

Schumpeter, Joseph Alois. 1962. *Capitalism, Socialism, and Democracy*. New York: Harper and Row.

Setton, Keneth M. 1967. *Christian Attitude Towards the Emperor in the Fourth Century, Especially as Shown in Addresses to the Emperor*. New York: AMS.

Shaw, Brent D. 1985. "The Divine Economy: Stoicism as Ideology." *Latomus* 44 (1): 16–54.

Singh, Devin. 2015. "Anarchy, Void, Signature: Agamben's Trinity Among Orthodoxy's Remains." *Political Theology*. http://www.maneyonline.com/doi/abs/10.1179/146231 7X14Z.000000000133?af=R (accessed September 16, 2015).

Smallwood, E. Mary. 2001. *The Jews Under Roman Rule: From Pompey to Diocletian, a Study in Political Relations*. Leiden: Brill.

Smith, Adam. 1904. *An Inquiry Into the Nature and Causes of the Wealth of Nations*. London: Methuen.

Sorabji, Richard. 1983. *Time, Creation, and the Continuum: Theories in Antiquity and the Early Middle Ages*. London: Duckworth.

Spary, Emma. 1996. "Political, Natural, and Bodily Economies." In James A. Secord Nicholas Jardine and Emma C. Spary, ed., *Cultures of Natural History*, 178–96. Cambridge: Cambridge University Press.

Stratoudaki-White, Despina. 2000. "The Dual Doctrine of the Relations of Church and State in Ninth Century Byzantium." *Greek Orthodox Theological Review* 45 (1): 443–52.

Strikis, Steven G. 1981. "The Theology and Ecclesiology of Eulogius, Patriarch of Alexandria: A Study and Translation." Master's thesis, St. Vladimir's Orthodox Theological Seminary.

Studer, Basil. 1993. *Trinity and Incarnation: The Faith of the Early Church*. Collegeville: Liturgical.

Swanson, Judith Ann. 1992. *The Public and the Private in Aristotle's Political Philosophy*. Ithaca: Cornell University Press.

Tacitus, Cornelius. 2006. *Dialogue on Orators*. In Herbert W. Benario, ed., *Agricola, Germany, and Dialogue on Orators*, 89–130. Indianapolis: Hackett.

Tarn, William Woodthorpe. 1952. *Hellenistic Civilization*. London: E. Arnold.

Taylor, Nicholas. 1992. *Paul, Antioch, and Jerusalem: A Study in Relationships and Authority in Earliest Christianity*. Sheffield: JSOT.

Thunberg, Lars. 1985. *Man and the Cosmos: The Vision of St. Maximus the Confessor* Crestwood, NY: St Vladimir's Seminary Press.

——. 1995. *Microcosm and Mediator: The Theological Anthropology of Maximus the Confessor*. Chicago: Open Court.

Tooley, W. 1966. "Stewards of God." *Scottish Journal of Theology* 19:74–86.

Torrance, Thomas F. 1967. "The Implications of Oikonomia for Knowledge and Speech of God in Early Christian Theology." In Felix Crist, ed., *Oikonomia heilsgeschichte als thema der Theologie*, 223–38. Hamburg: H. Reich.

Toscano, Alberto. 2011. "Divine Management: Critical Remarks on Giorgio Agamben's *The Kingdom and the Glory*." Angelaki 16 (3): 127–29.

Toumanoff, Cyril. 1946. "Caesaropapism in Byzantium and Russia." *Theological Studies* 7:213–43.

Trigg, Joseph W. 1998. *Origen*. New York: Routledge.

———. 2001. "God's Marvelous Oikonomia: Reflections of Origen's Understanding of Divine and Human Pedagogy in the Address Ascribed to Gregory Thaumaturgus." *Journal of Early Christian Studies* 9 (1): 27–52.

Tsirpanlis, Constantine N. 1987. "Doctrinal Oikonomia and Sacramental Koinonoa in Greek Patristic Theology and Contemporary Orthodox Ecumenism." *Patristic and Byzantine Review* 6 (1): 30–43.

Tsouna, Voula. 2007. *The Ethics of Philodemus*. Cambridge: Cambridge University Press.

Tzamalikos, Panagiotes. 2007. *Origen: Philosophy of History and Eschatology*. Leiden: Brill.

Vishnevskaya, Elena. 2004. "Perichoresis in the Context of Divinization: Maximus the Confessor's Vision of a 'Blessed and Most Holy Embrace.'" PhD diss., Drew University.

Vlastos, Gregory. 1965. "The Disorderly Motion in the *Timaeus*." In Reginald E. Allen, ed., *Studies in Plato's Metaphysics*, 379–99. London: Routledge and Kegan Paul.

Von Balthasar, Hans Urs. 2003. *Cosmic Liturgy: The Universe According to Maximus the Confessor*. San Francisco: Ignatius.

Wagner, Walter. 1968. "Another Look at the Literary Problem in Clement of Alexandria's Major Writings." *Church History* 37 (3): 251–60.

Waithe, Mary Ellen, ed. 1987. *Ancient Women Philosophers, 600 B.C.–500 A.D.* Dordrecht: Kluwer Academic.

Ware, Kallistos. 1979. *The Orthodox Way*. Crestwood, NY: St Vladimir's Seminary Press.

Weil, Constant van de. 1991. *History of Canon Law*. Leuven: Peeters.

Weintraub, E. Roy. 1985. *General Equilibrium Analysis—Studies in Appraisal*. Cambridge: Cambridge University Press.

Williams, George Huntston. 1951a. "Christology and Church-State Relations in the Fourth Century." *Church History* 20 (3): 3–33.

———. 1951b. "Christology and Church-State Relations in the Fourth Century." *Church History* 20 (4): 3–26.

Wilson-Kastner, Patricia. 1983. *Faith, Feminism, and the Christ*. Philadelphia: Fortress.

Winslow, Donald F. 1971. "Christology and Exegesis in the Cappadocians." *Church History* 40 (4): 389–96.

———. 1979. *The Dynamics of Salvation: A Study in Gregory of Nazianzus* Cambridge: Philadelphia Patristic Foundation.

Wolfson, Harry Austryn. 1956. *The Philosophy of the Church Fathers*. Cambridge: Harvard University Press.

Yonay, Yuval and Daniel Breslau. 2006. "Marketing Models: The Culture of Mathematical Economics." *Sociological Forum* 21(3): 345–86.

Zimmermann, Reinhard. 1996. *The Law of Obligations: Roman Foundations of the Civilian Tradition.* Oxford: Oxford University Press.

Zizioulas, John. 1985. *Being as Communion: Studies in Personhood and the Church.* Crestwood, NY: St Vladimir's Seminary Press.

———. 1995. "The Trinity and Personhood." In Christoph Schwöbel, ed., *Trinitarian Theology Today,* 44–60. Edinburgh: T&T Clark.

———. 2006. "Pneumatology and the Importance of the Person." In *Communion and Otherness,* 178–205. New York: Continuum.

Index

CPSIA information can be obtained
at www.ICGtesting.com
Printed in the USA
LVOW08s0838260617

539387LV00001B/4/P